Researching the
World of Work

D0869134

Researching the World of Work

Strategies and Methods in Studying Industrial Relations

Edited by Keith Whitfield
and George Strauss

ILR Press
an imprint of
Cornell University Press
Ithaca and London

Copyright © 1998 by Cornell University

All rights reserved. Except for brief quotations in a review, this book, or parts thereof, must not be reproduced in any form without permission in writing from the publisher. For information, address Cornell University Press, Sage House, 512 East State Street, Ithaca, New York 14850.

First published 1998 by Cornell University Press

Printed in the United States of America

Library of Congress Cataloging-in-Publication Data

Researching the world of work : strategies and methods in studying
    industrial relations / Keith Whitfield and George Strauss, editors.
        p.   cm.
    Articles by contributors recruited by the Research Methods Study
Group of the International Industrial Relations Association (IITA).
    Includes bibliographical references and index.
    ISBN 0-8014-3290-1 (alk. paper). — ISBN 0-8014-8549-5
(pbk. : alk. paper)
    1. Industrial relations—Methodology.   I. Whitfield, Keith.
II. Strauss, George, b. 1923.
HD6961.R37   1998
331'.07'2—dc21   97-48339

Cornell University Press strives to use environmentally responsible suppli-
ers and materials to the fullest extent possible in the publishing of its
books. Such materials include vegetable-based, low-VOC inks and acid-free
papers that are recycled, totally chlorine-free, or partly composed of non-
wood fibers.

Cloth printing   10 9 8 7 6 5 4 3 2 1

Paperback printing   10 9 8 7 6 5 4 3 2 1

*Dedicated
to the memory of
Jan Bruins*

Contents

Preface

The motivation to produce this volume came from the Research Methods Study Group of the International Industrial Relations Association (IIRA). Members of this group noted that although there have been numerous texts on research methods in the social sciences, few deal with industrial relations per se, and there has been little discussion of the relative usefulness of alternative research strategies and techniques in addressing industrial relations issues. Further, this relative neglect has occurred in an area of study that has a strong tradition of empirical research. A contrast can be made with the number of books concerned with other aspects of industrial relations, such as whether it is a discipline or a field and whether there is an industrial relations theoretical framework.

This volume addresses the practical and critical issues that researchers must face when studying industrial relations phenomena. The focus is on how different methods have been used, their limitations, and some of the problems that may arise in undertaking industrial relations research. An explicit effort has been made to go beyond "how-to-do" contributions. This area is already well covered, and, moreover, such exercises typically fail to address the pivotal questions confronting researchers.

The primary objective of this volume is to acquaint the reader with the range of techniques available and to suggest when each may be employed appropriately. It is not intended to be a comprehensive handbook. Some major strategies and methods are either barely mentioned or not mentioned at all. For example, the distinctive approaches of sociologists, historians, and lawyers are discussed in separate chapters but not those of economists or psychologists, in the belief that these latter approaches are well covered (albeit tangentially) in other chapters.

The contributors have been chosen for their ability to say something that is both well grounded and interesting about their subjects. Some are known to have views that are distinctly different from the mainstream; others are leading lights in the mainstream. All have been encouraged to write personal accounts of their topics. Bland overviews have been ruled off-limits.

This volume is the product of the work of a large number of people. The contributors have all worked hard to produce stimulating chapters in response to our original briefs and have generally responded positively to our requests for revision. To those who feel that we overstepped the mark of good editors, we can only apologize, express our thanks, and hope that they feel as positive about the end product as we do.

We are also extremely grateful to Tom Kochan for his early support for the project and hope that he sees it as another positive outcome of his extremely productive time as president of the International Industrial Relations Association. Thanks are also due Fran Benson of Cornell University Press for her constructive and supportive advice.

We would like to express special thanks to Ron Callus for his assistance in planning and developing the project, despite considerable demands on his time from elsewhere. Not only was he the inaugural convenor of the Research Methods Study Group and one of the instigators of this project, but he also stepped in at the eleventh hour when one of the original contributors failed to deliver. Further, he provided valuable advice and criticism at every stage of the project.

Sadly we report that Jan Bruins, one of the contributors, passed away shortly before this book went to press. Death brought a premature close to a promising career. We anticipate our readers will find his chapter ample evidence of his analytic and expositional skills.

KEITH WHITFIELD *and* GEORGE STRAUSS

Cardiff, Wales, and Berkeley, California

Researching the
World of Work

Part I

Some Basic Issues

Some Basic Issues

*T*he aim of Part I is to place the various contributions in this volume in an overall context. Each field or discipline has its own mix of strategies and methods and industrial relations is no exception. It is notable, however, that industrial relations has an extremely broad mix, drawing on a range of cognate fields and disciplines. Moreover, the dominant strategies and methods tend to vary markedly across countries.

The debate on strategies and methods in industrial relations is closely intertwined with that on its status and future as an analytical field. If it is going to prosper despite the incursion of a number of cognate fields and disciplines into its research territory, it must have something unique and valuable to contribute to the research process. This raises the question of whether industrial relations has anything in the area of research methods and strategies that could be deemed distinctive.

CHAPTER ONE

Research Methods in Industrial Relations

George Strauss and Keith Whitfield

R esearch in industrial relations is in a state of flux. Its subject matter has changed markedly, its conceptual framework is under intense scrutiny, the boundaries between it and related fields of study are increasingly blurred, and new research techniques are continuously being adopted.

These changes are broadly linked to a sea change in the ways in which employment and the employment relationship are perceived. There is now a much broader recognition of the importance of what some call "labor" (and others "human resources" or "human capital") to the prosperity of modern economies and the development of a "good society." Of particular note is the recognition that the organization of employment is pivotal in attaining competitive advantage in ever-more-complex product markets.

Until recently academic industrial relations in most countries focused primarily (though not exclusively) on union-management relations, including their causes, functioning, and impact, in single countries. But over the last few years the scope has broadened to include the entire world of work—issues such as "high-performance" work practices, occupational health and safety, employment discrimination, employee satisfaction, job security, and comparative international industrial relations.

This broadening of scope has resulted in greater interchange between industrial relations researchers and scholars from other fields, such as economics, sociology, law, organizational behavior, and political science. This is not completely new, but compared with the past, industrial relations scholars are interacting more frequently with those whose backgrounds are distinctly different. This interaction calls into question many well-established wisdoms. Moreover, the potential exists for the development of a host of new ways of seeing and doing.

Concomitantly, there has been a broadening of research strategies and methods. Until recently industrial relations research was largely confined to institutional descriptions, historical narrative, case studies, and simple descriptive statistics. In contrast, the contemporary researcher needs considerably more technical skills. As this volume illustrates, these include ethnography, laboratory experimentation, legal analysis, and the sophisticated statistical analysis of massive data sets.

What Is Industrial Relations?

There is considerable disagreement as to what the field of industrial relations comprises. Some define it narrowly, to include just union-management relations. Others adopt a broader definition that covers all aspects of the employment relationship. Operationally defined by the interests of those who call their field industrial relations, it has varied greatly but has tended to broaden through time.

The definition adopted in this volume is, in line with much current practice, extremely broad. Indeed, several of our authors would describe their primary area of research as something other than industrial relations (e.g., sociology or psychology), though all would agree they deal with the world of work and therefore they cover issues that industrial relations researchers explore.

Industrial relations in English-speaking countries has traditionally been problem centered, normative, historically oriented, multidisciplinary, and multimethod. The field developed in English-speaking countries largely from the work of institutional labor economics, although it has been influenced to some degree by other fields, particularly industrial sociology and occupational psychology. The relationship between industrial relations and the other social sciences has never been clear, however. This uncertainty has led to continuous debate as to the nature of the field and where it is going.

The boundaries between industrial relations and other disciplines or fields vary across countries as well as time. In the United States, the Industrial Relations Research Association claims jurisdiction over "all aspects of labor, employment, and the workplace." In practice, however, most of what has been called industrial relations research has focused on union-management relations and their impact. Admittedly, during the 1950s personnel (later renamed human resource management) was treated as a low-status subfield within the broader industrial relations framework, but the main interest at the time was in collective bargaining. During the same period, industrial relations and labor economics were viewed as a single field; in recent years they have grown increasingly apart.

American industrial relations researchers have often taken a narrower definition of the field than have researchers in other countries in the Anglo-Saxon tradition, such as the United Kingdom, Australia, and Canada. In these countries the dominant definition has focused on the rules governing employment—both formal and informal. As Paul Edwards (1995) notes, this does not restrict the subject simply to collective relations between unions and management but potentially allows the whole world of work to be included. On the European continent a separate field of industrial relations did not exist until recently (Hyman 1995). Instead, depending on the country, academic research on industrial relations topics was subsumed under other fields, especially law and sociology.

Industrial relations researchers worldwide seem to be becoming more eclectic in both the topics they study and the methods they use to study them. Newer studies examine management and managerial strategies with the same intensity that earlier studies investigated unions and union strategy. Almost everywhere there is greater interest in workplace relations and in how work is organized. More attention is also being given to comparative international analysis. Taking the world as a whole, there is less interest in unions or national systems of industrial relations.

Industrial Relations and Human Resource Management

In recent years there has been severe questioning of the long-term viability of industrial relations as a distinct academic subject. The main threat has come from the growth of human resource management as an area of study. Courses, university departments, and job titles have all undergone name changes, from industrial relations to human resource management or organizational behavior, and there have been associated changes of focus in both research and teaching. Symptomatic of this trend, most emerging journals focus on human resource management, and existing journals are publishing an increasing number of articles with "human resource management" (or similar phrases) in their titles.

One consequence of this shift in focus has been a heated debate on whether the field is appropriately named. On one side are those who view the term "industrial relations" as outdated, more suited to the days of the steam engine than the computer, and relevant to only a declining number of factory workers. On the other side are many researchers who are prepared to fight hard to retain the old name, on the grounds that it conveys a subject matter and approach to analysis that is generally recognized and widely respected. Opponents of the name change are in many cases strong union supporters who identify industrial relations with unions and suspect that those who want to abandon the old name would like to abandon unions as well. As a compromise, some institutions have adopted the more neutral term "employment relations."

Associated with the question of the name of the discipline is that of the relationship between industrial relations and human resource management. Are they two parts of a single whole and, if so, which is dominant? At the moment, university administrators and journal publishers seem to be giving human resource management priority. This pecking order mirrors important changes in the world of work, especially the decline of unions and the growing interest in worker commitment and involvement. Indeed, in some countries the question must be raised "Can there be industrial relations without unions?"

Is Industrial Relations a Discipline or an Applied Field?

Much verbiage has been spent on whether industrial relations is a separate basic discipline equivalent to, say, economics or psychology or whether it is more akin to marketing and medicine, an applied field that draws on the basic disciplines.

In an effort to claim the status of a discipline, numerous attempts have been made to develop a separate industrial relations theory. Perhaps the most successful has been Dunlop's (1958) *Industrial Relations Systems,* although whether this is a theory or only a typology is a matter of debate. Whether the debate is of any significance is more doubtful. There are, for example, well-established disciplines (for instance, sociology) that lack integrated, generally accepted theories. In the final analysis, however, it has to be said that industrial relations does not have a well-established theoretical base. True, there are many academic courses entitled "Industrial Relations Theory," but most of the theories offered are rather incomplete.

A related question is whether industrial relations has a separate paradigm. As Kochan puts it in the next chapter, "What Is Distinctive about Industrial Relations Research?" "For a paradigm to be accepted in the social sciences, it must demonstrate that it is able to conceptualize, explain, or solve some set of questions or problems better than alternative approaches." Although industrial relations deals with a distinct (and important) set of problems, and traditionally its inductive approach distinguished it from such disciplines as psychology and economics, it has increasingly come to resemble its more deductive counterparts.

There are some practical issues of academic politics here. If industrial relations is a separate discipline, its case for being treated as a separate academic department is strengthened. Further, there is less reason for its students to take courses outside their core department. In this regard students in the United States typically have broader training in economics and organizational behavior than do their counterparts in Australia or Great Britain, reflecting the greater acceptance in the latter countries of the view that industrial relations is a basic discipline in its own right.

Strategies and Methods

All research projects are guided by a strategy for how their main objectives can best be achieved. Three issues are of particular concern: (1) the overall methodological approach, (2) the purpose of the research, and (3) various forms of validity.

Inductive and Deductive Approaches

The two main approaches to research strategy are the deductive and the inductive. Inductive researchers tend to immerse themselves in the facts of specific cases. From these facts, theories or rules are suggested that are then used to draw inferences about behavior generally (Cappelli 1985: 91).

Inductive research has generally (but not exclusively) been based on qualitative research methods, such as the case study. The main aim has been to understand and explain how and why specific institutions develop the forms they do. Institutions are examined "holistically," that is, in their context (both socioeconomic and historical) and in detail. Inferences drawn from such an approach have proved especially useful in developing policy advice and middle-range theory. To understand institutions often requires an examination over time, that is, longitudinal research. At the least their history (thus, the term "historicism") needs to be examined. On the one hand, knowledge is developed by combining insights from the understanding developed in a number of distinct settings. On the other hand, most case-based research involves only a few cases, often too few to make safe generalizations (see our discussion of external validity).

The deductive approach is distinctly different. It seeks general laws that apply in every situation to some extent, even though they may explain only a part of any given situation. The search for such laws starts from hypotheses (for this reason it is sometimes called the "hypothetical-deductive" approach). In industrial relations these hypotheses have traditionally been drawn from economics but increasingly come from psychology or one of the other social sciences as well. Hypotheses developed logically from such assumptions are tested against empirical facts, as rigorously as possible. This process typically involves the use of quantitative methods, which are invoked to hold constant factors other than those not directly related to the relationship being tested.

In short, inductive research is conducted from the bottom (field) up, while deductive research moves from the top (theory) down. Inductive research is generally better suited to generating theory, deductive to testing theory.

A third academic approach can be discerned in some parts of the broad industrial relations literature. This involves the construction and analysis of purely theoretical models of human behavior and has been most common in legal and economic analysis. It is, of course, of little relevance for this volume because no research methods are used, although scholarly activity of this sort is not uncommon.

Industrial relations research makes use of all three approaches. In contrast to related disciplines that seem to have settled on one dominant approach, the issue in industrial relations is still open for debate. Some research uses a mixture of strategies. The inductive strategy has dominated the field, however, until recently and outside the United States. There are signs that this may be changing, particularly because of the strong influence of labor economics and organizational behavior.

Induction and Deduction in Different Countries

The inductive approach was developed in Germany by the "historical" school of economists. It was transmitted to the United States by American professors who received their doctoral training in Germany. Adapted to its new setting and subject matter, it became known as the institutional or Wisconsin school. This strategy had its greatest impact on the nascent field of industrial relations through the influence of Commons.

Early institutional researchers sought to understand how specific institutions work, especially unions, collective bargaining, and labor markets. Although they did not reject theories in total, they insisted that they had little value unless they closely approximated the real world. Their main concern, however, was not with developing theories but with influencing public policy.

British research has also been heavily influenced by the inductive, institutional approach, though not as clearly by German historicism. The Webbs were archetypal inductivists in their pioneering research, and others, such as Clay and Cole, followed the same strategy. For them the purpose of industrial relations was to reform as much as to understand. The Oxford school, mainly associated with Flanders, Fox, and Clegg, preached a "pound of facts, an ounce of theory," and this strategy was exported to the University of Warwick when the Social Science Research Council established the Industrial Relations Research Unit there. To this day much British industrial relations research is inductive.

Australian and to a lesser extent Canadian research has been heavily influenced by the British example. Many of the key industrial relations departments in Australia and Canada contain staff who completed postgraduate degrees at either Warwick or Oxford. Associated with indigenous traditions that were highly skeptical of deductivism (typically as practiced in economics), these scholars helped develop distinctive inductive approaches that put great emphasis on the particular institutions found in their countries. This is especially true of Australia, with its comprehensive conciliation and arbitration structure.

Until recently research on the European continent has been difficult to slot as either inductive or deductive. Much European research has been dominated by wide-ranging theories such as Marxism. During the last few years, however, increasing interest has emerged in conducting studies similar to those in Britain that are inductive and institutional, particularly case studies. Some of this research has been influenced by labor process theory and the attempt to explain why the structures associated with the employment relationship vary so much in different settings.

The deductive strategy has been most fully developed by neoclassical labor economists. This approach first achieved prominence in the United States in the 1960s and was associated with human capital theory and later with efficiency wage models. The main motivating force behind this development was the desire of some labor economists to align their methodology more closely with that of mainstream economics, while simultaneously making (minor) allowance for the fact that the labor market is more replete with distinctive institutions than are other economic markets (Zappala 1993).

The deductive strategy is not confined to economics. In recent years it has been used increasingly to test noneconomic hypotheses, many deriving from organizational behavior. Typical studies of this sort seek to predict, for instance, the circumstances under which participative work schemes lead to increased productivity and when specific union strategies lead to organizing success.

British research has also experienced the development of a more deductive tradition associated with neoclassical labor economics. This research has been particularly strong in the area of wage bargaining. To some extent this research has followed the American lead, though it has made significant contributions of its own. It has been supported by the increasing availability of large employer-based data sets, such as the Workplace Industrial Relations Series.

At the moment inductive, institutional research still prevails in Britain, in Australia, and on the European continent, while the vast majority of U.S. studies test theories in the deductive tradition.[1]

Purpose of the Research

Hakim (1987) has suggested that the nature of the end use of a research project has a major effect on the strategy adopted. She makes a distinction between theoretical and policy-based research. Theoretical research is concerned mainly with identifying causal relationships and explaining real-world phenomena. The long-term aim is to develop knowledge and understanding. Policy research, by contrast, is aimed more at changing the world. It differs from theoretical research in that it deals with policy makers' concerns rather than with those of academics.

Among the main differences that can be observed between these approaches is that policy-oriented research is more likely (1) to be multidisciplinary, (2) to be conducted at a number of different levels, (3) to be based on representative samples rather than those that cannot be generalized, (4) to involve respondents who are role holders rather than private individuals, and (5) to involve complex causal processes.

Industrial relations research has always been closely connected with policy formulation. It has therefore been more akin to the policy-based model than research in such cognate disciplines as economics and psychology. This seems to be changing, however, as industrial relations research becomes increasingly focused on hypothesis testing. This trend might weaken the link between research and policy and make research less useful for policy, as suggested in chapter 16, "Industrial Relations Research and the American Policy-Making Process."

Simultaneous with this growing separation between research and policy in the industrial relations mainstream, there has been growth of a new strand of research aimed explicitly at influencing policy. Called, among other things, participatory action research, it aims to incorporate re-

---

1. In organizational behavior, a field closely related to industrial relations, the emphasis until rather recently was heavily deductive. After a twenty-year hiatus, inductive work is returning, particularly in the *Administrative Science Quarterly*.

searchers into the policy-making process by merging the research and implementation stages (see chapter 8, "Participatory Action Research). This form of research is even closer to the policy-making process than the archetypal policy-based research suggested by Hakim and comes very close to consultancy, thereby raising a number of attendant ethical issues.

Maximizing Validity

One of the key differences between the various strategies for empirical research is the attention given to the validation of constructs, models, and findings. A distinction is often made between *construct, internal,* and *external* validity. Construct validity concerns the degree to which the proxy variables accurately reflect the factors composing the underlying model, for example, the degree to which IQ accurately measures natural ability. Internal validity relates to the causal model itself and concerns the degree to which the empirical model estimated is consistent on its own terms. For instance, if a study was estimating the effect of natural ability on earnings, high internal validity would indicate that the correct causal mechanisms had been specified. External validity concerns the degree to which the results can be generalized to the populations to which they relate. Studies based on random samples that are drawn from the general population have high external validity, whereas those based on particular samples or even extreme groups (outliers) have low external validity.

The attainment of high degrees of all three forms of validity by any given project is rare. Typically, they are traded off against each other and against more practical considerations such as cost and time. The nature of the trade-off reflects the resources available to the researcher, the rationale for the study, and the research tradition within which the work is being undertaken. Construct validity is particularly important for researchers in psychology but less so for economists and is more significant for policy-based than for theoretical researchers. Internal validity has been a particularly important concept for economists, and it is notable that much econometric research is concerned with ensuring that a statistical model has internal consistency.[2] External validity is especially important for policy-based researchers, given that their work is likely to influence policies that will affect general populations. By contrast, much theoretical research explicitly fo-

---

2. As described in chapter 4, "Quantitative Methods," internal validity is concerned with (1) whether the *statistical* model that is estimated is compatible with the underlying *theoretical* model, (2) whether the estimation technique is appropriate for the dependent variable, and (3) whether the independent variables are intercorrelated or not.

cuses on extreme or atypical cases to test whether theoretical ideas are widely applicable.

Research methods vary markedly in the degree to which they maximize the differing types of validity. Laboratory experiments, for example, are strong on internal validity but weak on external validity, whereas field experiments typically are the reverse (see chapter 5, "Experimental Methods"). Case studies are generally strong on construct and internal validity but weak on external validity, whereas secondary statistical analyses of large data sets typically possess the opposite characteristics. In general, qualitative analyses and inductively oriented projects have high construct validity, whereas quantitative and deductively oriented projects have high external validity, although there are many variations on this theme.

Qualitative versus Quantitative Methods

Just as the inductive and deductive approaches are the two main *strategies* employed in industrial relations, so the *methods* used to conduct research may be divided into the qualitative and the quantitative. The main qualitative methods are discussed in chapters 6, "The Role and Challenge of the Case Study Design in Industrial Relations," 7, "In the Eye of the Beholder: Ethnography in the Study of Work," 8, "Participatory Action Research," and 13, "Digging Up the Past: Historical Methods in Industrial Relations," although all four may include some quantitative analysis. The other methods discussed make heavy use of quantitative analysis.

Most inductive research is qualitative and most deductive research is quantitative, but this isn't always the case. Sometimes quantitative researchers will analyze a set of available data with no hypotheses in mind, hoping for a pattern of interest to emerge. Only then is an attempt made to explain this pattern logically. Though sometimes sneeringly called the "kitchen sink" approach ("magic computer on the wall, what's the meaning of this all?"), quantitative inductive research occasionally yields unexpected results, just as random testing of drugs sometimes provides unexpected cures.

By contrast, qualitative methods may be employed in a deductive fashion when, having completed one case study, the researcher undertakes another with the intent of determining whether the same relationships hold in both cases. Often they do not, and this may lead the researcher to look for explanations of the difference. This is a common approach in comparative international studies (see chapter 11, "Comparative International Industrial Relations"). Often this approach involves what Everett Hughes calls a "process" sample. In getting such a sample, "One cares less about quantities of each kind so long as he gets the full variety and contrast that will allow him to tell the particular from the general" (1952: 424).

Among the advantages of the quantitative approach is *transparency:* how the research is conducted is generally clear, others may replicate the study, and often the data on which the conclusions are based are made generally public. By contrast, the reported results of qualitative research may be affected by the researcher's biases and expectations. In this regard, chapter 9, "Large-Scale National Surveys for Mapping, Monitoring, and Theory Development," argues that surveys are less likely to be seen as biased than are qualitative forms of research, such as case studies.

Another advantage of the quantitative approach is its *generalizability.* Conclusions based on qualitative research in a limited number of situations may have limited external validity. While qualitative research may suggest hypotheses, quantitative research assists in determining how widely these hold and the strength of the relationship.

Compared with the quantitative approach, qualitative research typically considers a broader range of variables and issues, many of which are difficult to quantify. This approach helps the researcher understand the dynamics of a relationship—how it actually operates (what some call "getting into the little black box"). Although quantitative research may indicate factors A and B are correlated, unless the data are longitudinal it may be hard to determine the direction of causation, thereby yielding low internal validity. Qualitative research can often tell us something about causation. Further, it typically yields a richer picture of actual behavior than quantitative research and so may be more useful in policy making.

Influences on Strategies and Methods

The subjects that industrial relations scholars study and the methods they use to study them are influenced implicitly or explicitly by a variety of factors. Research on the world of work has always been problem oriented and thus problems in the real world influence both the questions researchers ask and how they ask them. Further, there is a clear link between the academic discipline in which a researcher is trained and the strategies and methods he or she most commonly deploys. Other factors influencing research methodology are the researcher's personal ideology and the availability of computers and data.

Nature of Social and Economic Problems

One of the distinctive characteristics of industrial relations is its focus on socially defined problems. For example, before 1940 industrial relations research in the United States concentrated on the legitimation of unions and the institution of social insurance. During the immediate postwar period, there was much industrial unrest and the research focus turned to strikes and inflation. During the 1960s it was race relations. More recently the dominant themes have been the decline of unions and the impact of participation schemes, such as work teams. As social priorities have changed, so has the nature of research.

Early British industrial relations research focused on unions and union-management relations during the 1960s, on shop-floor labor-management relations during the 1970s, and, more recently, on the role of management and how work is organized. The decentralization of bargaining in contemporary Australia has been accompanied by a greater research emphasis on workplace issues. Earlier it was concerned chiefly with union histories and the conciliation and arbitration system. The heightened interest in human resource management has contributed to a burst of British scholarship in that area.

The perceived nature of problems also affects the funding that is available, and this in turn greatly influences the research that is done. Circa 1970 there was liberal government financing of poverty and training studies in the United States. More recently, Sloan Foundation funding has paved the way for extensive research on "high-commitment" workplaces. Perceived social problems led to the establishment of the Donovan Commission in Britain, the Hancock Committee in Australia, and the Dunlop Commission in the United States. Each sponsored important research and also inspired a host of related but nonsponsored studies. The Donovan Commission was particularly influential in orienting industrial relations research in Britain.

Disciplinary, Theoretical, and National Backgrounds

Industrial relations, broadly defined, involves contributions from a variety of cognate disciplines and fields. Not only do researchers from different disciplinary backgrounds look at different questions, but they use different methods. And these methods, in turn, influence the nature of the findings.

Methods change over time. The big change has been the increasing use of quantitative methods. Early industrial sociologists specialized in ethnography and case studies; now they often use quantitative methods. Psychologists were among the first to quantify, then economists, and, more recently, institutional industrial relations people and labor historians. Today scholars in most areas studying work engage in calculations.

Even among quantitative studies there are differences among fields. Economists generally favor regressions, while psychologists are more likely to use techniques that identify patterns in data sets, such as factor analysis. Psychologists emphasize the need to validate proxy measures; economists typically do not see this as a problem. Younger U.S. industrial relations scholars, who have been broadly trained in both economics and organizational behavior, feel comfortable with both econometric and psychometric techniques. Consequently, linear regression analysis, which was for a while the almost standard technique used in quantitative research, is being increasingly supplemented by factor, path, cluster, maximum likelihood, and meta-analysis.

There are national differences, too. American sociologists make greater use of quantitative techniques than do those in either Britain or Australia, while many continental European sociologists shun them altogether, arguing that these techniques merely deal with superficial aspects of underlying problems.

Beyond this there are schools of thought (even conflicting ideologies) within most formal disciplines. Their influences also vary significantly across national boundaries. Examples include labor process theory in the United Kingdom, human capital and efficiency wage theory in the United States, and Marxism and postmodernism, two related analytical approaches common on the European continent.

Some industrial relations researchers reject quantitative analysis as suggesting spurious and misleading exactitude. A related approach argues that valid research should involve "subjects" who participate in gathering and evaluating the data (see chapter 8).

This diversity complicates scholarly communication. The problem is no longer one of national languages (major academic reports are now published in English, regardless of the author's nationality) but of differences in frames of reference and theoretical paradigms. Though seemingly translated into English, much German sociology is virtually unintelligible to U.S. readers, even to U.S. sociologists. Many of the technical terms that constitute the common discourse of postmodernists are meaningless to quantitative labor economists. The reverse is also true: most postmodernists are mathematically illiterate (and proud of it). Yet both deal with the world of work. They might learn from each other.

Beyond this, disciplinary parochialism may promote a narrow focus for research—a form of intellectual tunnel vision. Every researcher should be aware that a presumed relationship between variables A and B may be moderated by other variables, C, D, and E, for which data (at least quantitative data) are not available or that the investigator's disciplinary background has not prepared him or her to recognize or analyze.

Values and Personal Interests

Industrial relations is a normative, value-oriented field. Many industrial relations scholars have at least moderately left-wing leanings and identity with unions. Consequently, until recently unions received more attention than management. By contrast, those who receive part of their income as management consultants are likely to deal with managerial problems and from a managerial perspective.

One of the personal advantages of more traditional forms of face-to-face research, such as ethnography and interviewing, was that it provided the researcher with a sense of psychological involvement that may be largely lacking in the computerized study of data sets. The passion and excitement that once characterized industrial relations may be lost, and those who crave personal involvement may pick other fields of study.

Journal Preferences

In academia it is increasingly the case, particularly for younger researchers, that they publish or perish. The preferences of journal editors carry great weight, at least in the English-speaking world. Recent changes in British research funding arrangements, for instance, have increased the kudos for publishing in a small number of "front-rank" journals.

This editorial system generally encourages safe, narrow articles that can pass the scrutiny of often-hostile reviewers. Most journals today seem to prefer highly empirical studies, heavily buttressed with statistics, to think pieces with unorthodox new ideas. Particularly in the United States, few articles without numerical data get published. Editors also want to publish "new" research; mere replication of previous studies rarely gets into print. Consequently, favored articles are based on small "advances" on previous studies which are heavily supported by statistics. The net effect is to discourage inductive research.

Technology

Computers have revolutionized the social sciences. They have made it possible to store and analyze large amounts of data cheaply, as long as these data can be reduced to symbolic (largely numerical) form. In recent years there has been not only a phenomenal growth in the capacity of computer hardware but also an increase in supporting software and particularly in statistical programs that allow a wider range of data to be analyzed. Calculations that previously might have taken hundreds of hours can now be done almost instantaneously. Given the availability of computers and the growing number of databases, quantitative research can be converted into article form without ever leaving the office.

Another result of computerization is the growing sophistication in the statistical methods employed, from merely adding up numbers, to simple regressions, and, more recently, to such techniques as maximum likelihood estimation and path analysis (see chapter 4, "Quantitative Methods"). But to make use of all these techniques requires that researchers themselves become statistically more sophisticated and has thereby helped change doctoral training programs.

Availability of Data

Data availability has a strong impact on the nature of industrial relations research and on the methods researchers use. National workplace surveys in Australia and the United Kingdom (see chapter 9), as well as a series of somewhat similar U.S. studies, have created a bonanza for scholars. These data have facilitated a growing interest in both workplace studies and the use of quantitative techniques.

The availability of statistics (on tape) showing votes in National Labor Relations Board (NLRB) elections contributed to a plethora of U.S. research on voting behavior. Later, the decision to stop collecting data on all but large U.S. strikes has inhibited studies of strike incidence. Similarly, the availability of surveys of the population generally (such as the Panel Study of Income Dynamics in the United States and the Socio-Economic Panel in Germany) has encouraged studies that can utilize these data and has discouraged other kinds of research. In other words, the availability of potential answers has encouraged questions.

A lack of appropriate data often hinders or distorts research. A lamentable tendency among some researchers when good data are not available is to test a hypothesis by selecting the best alternative (technically "proxy") around. Often this best alternative is pretty bad. This is like the drunk looking for lost keys under the street lamp because this is where the light is. For example, in a study in which union uncertainty was an important variable but no direct measure of this variable was easily available, the author decided instead to use "measures of investor uncertainty over the firm's future unprofitability as a proxy for the union's uncertainty" (Tracy 1987: 150).

As often is the case in studies of this sort, the author made no attempt to determine whether union uncertainty and investor uncertainty were equivalents.

An unfortunate consequence of the greater availability of survey data (as well as of computers to analyze them) is that industrial relations researchers are now less likely to go out into the field to talk to real workers and real managers. (As the old saw put it, "An economist is someone who heard people described but never actually saw one." Someday the same comments may be made regarding industrial relations.) One danger, particularly for a problem-oriented field, is that important insights are lost and overly simple conclusions accepted. A second danger is we will lose the colorful, even arresting, descriptions that once were common in the industrial relations literature.

Level of Analysis

The level of analysis one is studying is an important research question (see especially Klein, Dansereau, and Hall 1994). On what level is the research focused: the individual worker; the workplace; the enterprise, firm, industry, or country; or the entire world? Traditionally, the primary focus of industrial relations has been on unions, management, and especially their collective bargaining relationship. A second stream of research has dealt with unions and companies, as aggregates, and the state. In both cases, the emphasis was generally institutional and inductive.

By the mid-1970s in the United States, as Cappelli (1985) points out, the individual level began to assume greater importance, as did deductive analysis. Studies of high-priority issues, such as discrimination, equal employment, training, and poverty, focused on individual behavior and experience (this despite the fact that institutional factors played an important role in all these areas). At times the behavior of institutions was viewed as little more than the summed total of the behaviors of its members. A good example is the median voter theory, which seeks to explain union behavior in terms of the median member's preferences (and so ignores the complexities of union government and politics).

A major reason for this shift, Cappelli argues, was the availability of individual-level data and of generally accepted social science propositions from which specific hypotheses could be logically deduced and quantitatively tested. In addition, most of the other social sciences were becoming more rigorous (quantitatively and theoretically) and, for reasons of institutional survival, industrial relations researchers felt it necessary to do likewise.

Although union-management relations in the United States had stabilized by the mid-1950s (and stayed so until the 1980s), the same was not true in Britain. Consequently, union-management relations presented a more urgent social problem and union–management research in Britain was heavily funded, at least until the advent of Margaret Thatcher. More recently, in most countries the major focus has shifted to workplaces, the role of managers, and human resource management. Consequently, surveys of workplace practices have become increasingly common (see chapter 9).

The different disciplines within industrial relations focus on different levels: economics and psychology on individuals, sociology on groups and larger aggregations, and political science on countries. It should not be surprising, therefore, that the recent spurt in interest in comparative international relations has contributed to the fact that some of the most interesting industrial relations work in the United States today is being done by younger scholars, such as Lowell Turner and Richard Locke, who have backgrounds in political science.

Naturally, different techniques are relatively more appropriate for research at each level. Further, different insights emerge, depending on the level on which one focuses. Thus, if one is concerned with strikes at the individual level, one looks at phenomena such as needs, attitudes, and frustrations. At the workplace level, the behavior of specific members of management, the social structure of the group, and perhaps the nature of technology may be most germane. To study these issues, ethnography may be appropriate. At the plant level, fine-grained ethnographic studies may be too difficult; hence, plant-level research may take the character of case studies. At higher levels, quantitative analyses of economic data (profits, changes in the cost of living, and the like) may be more relevant. And still other variables must be considered in comparing strike rates among countries.

Care must be exercised in drawing conclusions as to behavior at one level based on research done on another. We have already cautioned against drawing conclusions as to the behavior of an entire union based on the preferences of its median member as expressed in an attitude poll. In general, a theory focusing at one level should be based on data collected at that level. If, for example, an essential part of a theory is that large firms behave differently than small firms, the data testing that theory should be collected at the firm not the industry level. Unfortunately, studies of accidents, turnover, and wages often use industry-level data with the implicit assumption that all enterprises and workers in a given industry are the same (or at least that the differences are not relevant).

Interdisciplinary Research

Industrial relations claims to be interdisciplinary. There are obvious advantages to utilizing several disciplines, in that each discipline can provide its own insights and so reduce the likelihood of narrow, single-dimensional perspectives on complex, multidimensional problems. Unfortunately, these advantages are rarely garnered in practice. Indeed, there are many examples of failure, despite highly laudable attempts to break down disciplinary barriers.

There are two main types of interdisciplinary research. The first involves a single researcher (or a research team from a common discipline) drawing on a variety of disciplines. The second involves several researchers, each from a different discipline. To date, neither type has been common, though this may be changing. Generally, the first type has been more fruitful. Researchers from different backgrounds may have trouble communicating and could therefore produce what some have called "the cross-sterilization of the social sciences."

There are relatively few examples of research that extends beyond discipline-specific boundaries. Among these is a study by Getman, Goldberg, and Herman (1976), two lawyers and a psychologist, who employed an attitude survey to test legal propositions (see chapter 14, "Legal Methods"). Similarly, some economists, such as Freeman and Medoff (1984) and Farber and Krueger (1993), have introduced attitudinal variables in their equations. Studies of the individual propensity to vote for union representation in U.S. elections often make use of both attitudinal and economic variables.

In some cases industrial relations scholars have borrowed from other fields. For example, the concept of "union commitment," which has been fairly commonly used as a variable in attitude studies, is derived from an analogous concept, "organizational commitment," which is widely employed in organizational behavior. Somewhat similarly, Walton and McKersie ([1965] 1991) drew on game theory and psychology but applied its conceptual apparatus directly to collective bargaining.

On the whole, however, industrial relations researchers have been rather parochial. Some may be uncomfortable with any conceptualization that treats industrial relations as only one form of a broader category rather than as something unique. A good example is the reluctance of researchers to follow up on Walton and McKersie's study, thus permitting the new academic field of negotiations and conflict resolution to develop with little industrial relations participation. Similarly, industrial relations has made little use so far of the highly relevant concepts of transaction cost economics or collective action (in sociology).

The advent of workplace industrial relations surveys (see chapter 9) was expected to encourage interdisciplinary analysis. Representative sample surveys, it was hoped, would build on the experience of many nongeneralizable case studies. Yet the British experience is that little interdisciplinarity has occurred. Much of the analysis of survey data has been conducted by economists using a narrow range of quantitative methods, and very little has been undertaken by industrial relations specialists (Millward 1993). Indeed, many of the latter have been highly critical of survey data, stating that it fails to capture the true complexity and dynamic character of British industrial relations (McCarthy 1994). The Australian experience has been similar, though not so stark.

A common problem is that researchers from different disciplines may deal with the same phenomena but fail to communicate with each other because they use different languages and read different journals. Psychologists and economists, for example, study labor turnover, sometimes using equivalent data, yet they rarely cite each other. "Organizational justice," especially "procedural justice," is one of the most popular subjects in microorganizational behavior today (Greenberg 1990). Much of the research has involved industrial relations issues, such as compensation, promotion, and discipline; Jack Barbash called "justice" the key industrial relations question. Yet, despite its obvious relevance, little research in the procedural justice tradition has appeared in industrial relations publications or has been cited by those who call their field industrial relations.

One of the major factors inhibiting interdisciplinary research is that it takes research from the comfort of the shared assumptions and ways of seeing and doing that exists within disciplinary boundaries. In particular, the criteria used to judge a "good" piece of research differ between disciplines, and few studies satisfy all of them. For example, Getman, Goldberg, and Herman's highly policy-relevant study was criticized by economists on methodological grounds (Dickens 1983) and for lacking in realism (see chapter 16). Psychologists would no doubt regard the attitudinal variables in Freeman and Medoff's and Farber and Krueger's work as rather primitive.

But there is some room for hope. There is, for example, a largely new approach to compensation and careers that links psychology, sociology, and economics, making use of such concepts as procedural justice; agency, tournament, expectancy, and equity theories; organizational ecology; and commitment (see, for example, the June 1992 special issue of the *Administrative Science Quarterly* "Process and Outcomes: Perspectives on the Distribution of Rewards in Organizations"). Few of the scholars contributing to this development identify their field as industrial relations, however.

In short, despite much talk about industrial relations being distinctive because of its interdisciplinarity, it is hard to point to many studies, either theoretical or empirical, that achieve this aim. In most cases in which disciplinary boundaries are presumably transcended, the studies concerned are either nondisciplinary or dominated by a single discipline.

Multimethod Research

Methods should not be confused with disciplines. Sociological studies of employment relations (see chapter 15, "Sociological Approaches to Employment Research") make use of many methods and so certainly does "mainstream" industrial relations. The use of more than one method in a research project has numerous advantages. First, through "triangulation," it helps validate findings. If two methods lead to the same conclusion, the findings are more robust than if one method is used alone. If they disagree, more research may be necessary. The findings of the International Motor Vehicle Project were based largely on managers' responses to detailed questionnaires (MacDuffie and Pil 1995). But to ensure that the questions were understood and answered accurately, the researchers personally visited most of the plants around the world. Similarly, in an effort to determine the validity of the experimental approach for studying arbitrators' decisions, Olson, Dell'Ormo, and Jarley (1992) compared how arbitrators dealt with interest arbitration issues in an experimental situation with how the same arbitrators decided real cases (see chapter 5).

Second, if several methods are employed, each may provide different nuances or insights. Consequently, the ultimate findings are richer. And if the results differ, totally new questions may be raised. In research on local union participation, Strauss observed the meetings of a union local for a period of a year, taking careful note of who attended (easy to do because attendance was low). In addition, a questionnaire was administered to the entire local membership that asked each member how often he had attended union meetings over the last year. Most respondents exaggerated their attendance. More significantly, reported and observed attendance were poorly correlated. Based on this discrepancy, interviews, and a year of ethnographic observation, Strauss concluded that, at least in this local, reported attendance was related to union loyalty, while actual (observed) attendance was based on political and social needs (it was something to do in the evening).

Third, one method can be used to improve another. Focus groups, for example, can be used to help design survey questions. Case studies can help improve causal models used in quantitative studies. Experimental methods can be used to evaluate different econometric models (see chapter 4).

Fourth, and finally, one method can lead to another when the techniques are used in sequence, one after another, rather than simultaneously. Thus, one study may be "nested" within another. Case studies may be used at first to suggest relationships, and, afterward, surveys or other quantitative measures can be employed to determine how extensive these relationships are—that is, the extent to which they can be "generalized."

Alternatively, if a survey finds that X is correlated with Y, case studies can be used to get into "the black box" and analyze the dynamics of this relationship. Case studies may be run on typical examples, as revealed by surveys, or on deviant ones (Lipset, Trow, and Coleman 1956). Another approach is to administer surveys of workplace practices to key union and management leaders in a large sample of organizations and then survey the attitudes of all the workers in a small sample of firms taken from the larger sample. In this way, the larger study can determine the extent of a practice, while the smaller ones looks at its impacts.

Further, the multimethod approach permits researchers to alternate strategies, from inductive to deductive and back again to inductive. Studies of this sort have become increasingly common as the training of industrial relations scholars has broadened.

Sources of Data

Scholars dealing with the world of work are likely to gather their data from a variety of sources. Those who are interested in bargaining behavior may set up laboratory experiments or perhaps observe real union-management bargaining sessions (in the ethnographic tradition). Those whose research focuses on workers' attitudes favor attitude surveys. Institutional researchers examining union-management behavior traditionally engage in case studies (but more recently may also use workplace surveys). In doing research of this type, researchers typically gather their own data (although some research involves meta-analysis that makes use of quantitative techniques to draw generalizations from studies previously done by others).

Economists, by contrast, typically base their research on data collected by others, usually a government agency. However, a few U.S. economists have conducted carefully controlled field experiments designed to measure the impact of various forms of training and income supplements on the employment history of disadvantaged workers. And there is a field of experimental economics that utilizes laboratory experiments to study economic behavior, such as risk taking.

On the one hand, a major advantage of gathering one's own data is that the nature of the data collected and the data-collecting technique can be tailored to fit the questions being asked (in other words, there may be high construct and internal validity). On the other hand, it is generally cheaper to use data collected by others. Further, there is the advantage of transparency: if generally available data are used, other researchers can repeat and check on the original researcher's findings. Researchers who collect their own data may bias the questions they ask so as to get the answers they want. In addition, what ethnographers and case study collectors "see" may be heavily influenced by their own expectations and values.

Ethics and Public Policy

It may seem cynical to link these two topics, but both are concerned with researchers' relationships with the people and organizations they study, the institutions for which they work, the agencies that fund them, their fellow researchers, and the larger society. All these relationships involve tricky moral-ethical and practical-political issues. (For further discussion of the dilemmas in this area, see chapters 6 and 17).

As a policy-oriented field in a highly controversial area, industrial relations can involve particularly sensitive diplomatic relations. The relations between labor and management are typically adversarial and often quite hostile. In this charged environment, professed neutrals are often suspect. Indeed, some practitioners are suspicious of academics as a class. And so the researcher who claims to be neutral (an in-between) may be attacked by both sides.

The problem is often more complex because many industrial relations researchers are committed to one side, or may have worked for one of the parties as a consultant or instructor. Funding agencies themselves may be seen as biased. Government-financed studies may be suspected of being in-

fluenced by the views of the party in power. At one time, private foundations, such as the Rockefeller Foundation, were viewed as sharing the values of the wealthy tycoons who established them. Even the most
dispassionate researchers who want to get their projects refunded may pull
their punches, depending on the funder's perceived interests (see chapter
17). Under these circumstances, both actual and perceived objectivity may
be difficult. Some commentators argue that neutrality is never possible, that
all research is influenced by the researcher's perceptions and biases.

Beyond this, nonacademics frequently misunderstand the nature of academic freedom. Academic researchers typically work for an industrial relations institute or department that claims to be neutral. When a researcher
takes a controversial position, however, nonacademics often assume that
this position represents that of the organization for which he or she works.
In this way, the entire institution may become identified with a single person's research conclusions, regardless of how carefully they are buttressed.
The institution may be particularly blamed if these findings are injudicious
or plain wrong. For this reason, many institutions insist on the right to review and even approve their employees' reports before they are published.
Industrial relations scholars may therefore have less academic freedom than
scholars in less controversial fields (at least they must behave more cau-
tiously). In short, not only should the industrial relations scholar be objective but he or she should seem to be objective as well. No easy task!

Diplomatic problems arise at many stages in the research process. Frequently researchers must obtain the permission of "gatekeepers" (often key
union and management officials) before beginning research. There is often
an explicit or implicit "understanding" as to how the study is to be conducted and how the research findings are to be employed. To gain access to
the research situation, the researcher may (sometimes unwittingly) fail to
disclose the use to which the research findings will be used, thus leading
to hard feelings and even a sense of betrayal.

Let us illustrate the issue. Is it ethical for a pro-union researcher to make
use of a university letterhead to survey workers' reactions to unions without divulging that this research has been financed by a union and that its results will be used in an organizing drive? Most people would say it is not.
But suppose the same researcher conducts the same survey but this time it is
without union funding; the findings will be generally available, but the researcher still hopes that they will be of use in organizing. Or suppose the researcher hopes that they will be useful to employers in resisting unions.
Does it make a difference whether the particular research site is identified?
What are the critical issues here: Who funds the research? The researcher's

intentions? The use to be made of the findings? Failure to reveal any of the foregoing?

Gatekeepers may often ask for the right to review or even approve research before it is published. Such understandings may create expectations on the part of "subjects" that only favorable findings will be published, regardless of the truth. To violate such an agreement may be unethical, but to allow gatekeeper censorship may bias the final conclusions. Some material is made available to researchers only in confidence. Violating confidences is unethical; to be seen as doing so is poor public relations.

Further, most researchers would agree that no one should be "harmed" by their research, but interpreting or enforcing this obligation may be difficult. Suppose the research uncovers serious crimes or social evils. Publication of the findings would "harm" the transgressors. Is this a valid reason to withhold publication? (Some fields, such as psychology, anthropology, and management, have codes of ethics. Industrial relations does not.)

Researchers also have obligations to those who may come after them. If people who have been studied feel they have been treated unfairly, they will be less likely to allow other researchers to engage in similar studies in the future. Stated crudely, researchers may foul their collective nests.

Few researchers are willing to let their findings speak for themselves. Although there is a continuum of research, from that designed to develop or test theories to that specifically designed to evaluate policy alternatives, most researchers hope that their efforts will influence policy. This raises yet another question—namely, how research can be conducted so that the findings are accepted by practitioners (see chapter 8).

Put another way, the questions industrial relataions researchers study are rarely of purely academic interest. Typically, they have ethical components in that policy changes based on research findings may affect people's well-being. While medical scientists often take such issues into account when they pick research methods, few social scientists worry about them. Yet misused social research may also cause great harm.

Industrial relations scholars have an obligation to ensure that their policy recommendations are not based on insufficient or inappropriate data (see chapter 16). Policy-oriented research has the potential to alter the behavior of policy makers and consequently the lives of countless individuals. Badly undertaken research can yield unnecessary suffering and expense for all concerned.

Scope of This Volume

This volume deals with many difficult questions that confront researchers in industrial relations. The answers to these questions will have a major impact on the development of the field. None of the questions is unique to industrial relations, but they take particular forms when researching workplace issues.

Part I, which includes this chapter and the next, examines the nature of industrial relations as a field of study. Part II addresses the main research strategies and methods deployed and is followed, in Part III, by a consideration of comparative research. Next, the volume focuses on the contributions of three major disciplines sometimes viewed as peripheral to industrial relations: history, law, and sociology. Part V deals with the relationship between research and policy. Finally, a brief conclusion attempts to connect the various contributions and suggest avenues for future development.

CHAPTER TWO

What Is Distinctive about Industrial Relations Research?

Thomas A. Kochan

A number of years ago I described industrial relations as "a broad, interdisciplinary field of study and practice that encompasses all aspects of the employment relationship" (Kochan 1980: 1). Despite this broad definition, in practice researchers in this field have focused most of their attention on the role of unions, collective bargaining, and related institutions and policies. I will stay within these narrower bounds in this chapter but will note at the end the need for our field to live up to its claim to having a broader focus and definition if we are to be significant contributors to the study of the world of work in the future.

Industrial relations has a rich intellectual tradition dating back in the United States to the works of Commons and his associates and in Britain to the works of Sidney and Beatrice Webb. Since much of the work in this field has revolved around the role, structure, and effect of unions and other forms of collective representation and action, and given the decline in unions in many industrialized countries and the rise of neoliberal thought in social science and public policy-making circles, it is not surprising that the field of industrial relations is in a state of profound crisis. Thus, it is an opportune time to both look back and ahead, to identify the essence of industrial relations as a field of study and to outline a strategy for the future.

In this chapter I attempt to do a little of both. I review what I believe to

The material in the section "Enduring Features" draws heavily on my essay in Adams and Meltz 1993. The material in the section "International Perspective" is drawn from my presidential speech to the Tenth World Congress of the International Industrial Relations Association. For the full text, see Kochan 1996.

have been the key features that have distinguished industrial relations research to date and then suggest how it needs to change if it is to survive and prosper in the future.

Enduring Features

Industrial relations competes with many other disciplines and approaches to the study of labor and employment issues. The disciplines of economics, law, the behavioral sciences, history, and political science all share an interest in and offer alternative perspectives on these issues. Kuhn (1970) argues that for a paradigm to be accepted in the social sciences, it must demonstrate that it is able to conceptualize, explain, or solve some set of questions or problems better than alternative approaches. I believe there are a number of features of industrial relations research that differentiate it from the approaches found in other disciplines or paradigms. Among these, one stands out as what I believe is the primary feature that distinguishes industrial relations from other social sciences, namely, its normative foundations. Together, these features help industrial relations meet Kuhn's test.

Problem-Centered Orientation

One of the most enduring features of industrial relations research has been its problem-centered orientation. Moreover, the "problems" are generally framed with a societal or public interest point of view in mind. Indeed, Kaufman (1993) traces the origin of the term "industrial relations" and the emergence of the field as an area of scholarly inquiry and teaching in the United States to the "labor problem" of the early part of this century. The most critical labor problems of the time were the poor wages and working conditions and the lack of public policies governing labor markets or union representation. These concerns gained national attention with the bombing of the *Los Angeles Times office,* which in turn led to the creation of the 1911–13 Commission on Industrial Relations. Commons, the father of U.S. industrial relations research, was a member of that commission, and Kaufman lists as research assistants to the commission a veritable "Who's Who" of early industrial relations scholarship: Perlman, Leiserson, Slichter, Wolman, McCabe, and Witte (1993). Thus, the problem focus and involvement in public policy research and analysis featured prominently even in the early stages of the field's development in the United States.

The exposure of these early scholars to the firsthand issues of the day left an indelible imprint on the field. It established the scholar-practitioner, or, as Commons called it, a researcher capable of producing practical theory, as the model for future researchers in industrial relations.

This tradition carried over to the next generation as well. A similar list of "Who's Who" in post–World War II industrial relations research could be assembled from those involved in one way or another in the War Labor Board (e.g., Taylor, Kerr, Dunlop, Livernash, Ross, Lester, Finsinger, Myers, Brown, Derber). The emergence of labor problems in the public sector in the 1960s and 1970s saw a repeat performance with governors and state legislatures from states such as New York, Pennsylvania, Illinois, Michigan, Wisconsin, and California turning to the ideas and experience of industrial relations researchers in designing and administering their public-sector collective bargaining statutes.

Although industrial relations as an academic discipline developed later in Canada, Canadian academics have also played active roles in policy debates and the government. In the 1960s the *Report of the Task Force on Labour Relations,* written by four leading academics—Woods, Dion, Carrothers, and Crispo (1968) —and supported with background papers from many other Canadian academics, structured debates over the role of collective bargaining in policies seeking both to stimulate economic growth and to control inflation. Craig's expansion of Dunlop's (1958) industrial relations system framework provided the organizing analytical framework for the task force report (Craig 1990). Although it had less impact on policy, a similar exercise in the 1980s, the MacDonald Commission, also drew heavily on industrial relations and labor economics researchers in producing a four-volume analysis of labor relations and labor market policies.

Several Canadians also moved between academic and policy roles. For example, Carter and Weiler served as chairs of the Ontario and British Columbia Labour Relations Boards, respectively. Weiler's book *Reconcilable Differences* (1980) also played an important role in shaping the debates over labor policy in British Columbia and other parts of Canada.

Industrial relations in Britain and Australia evolved in similar ways. In Britain, from the time of the Webbs to the Donovan Commission to the current debates over the role of statutory rights and procedures for representation, industrial relations research and policy debates have been closely interrelated (see McCarthy 1994 for a thorough review). As Brown and Wright (1994) note, the deeply ingrained empirical tradition in British industrial relations produced lively policy debates from the 1950s onward among scholars such as Flanders, Clegg, Phelps Brown, McCarthy, Roberts, and their various students at the key industrial relations centers, such as the

University of Warwick and the London School of Economics. The sociological perspectives of Fox and Batstone further grounded the analysis of workplace issues and laid the foundation for the contemporary focus on workplace research that is thriving in Britain.

In Australia, the central role of the Federal Commission (now the Australian Industrial Relations Commission) and more recent debates over the process of decentralizing industrial relations and the changes in the labor movement and enterprise-level employment practices have been the focal points of industrial relations scholarship. Australian academics have played key roles in national and state-level policy formulation from at least the time of the Hancock Committee in the 1980s to the present. Indeed, Dabscheck (1989: 69–76) critiques the Hancock Committee for failing to make enough use of contemporary industrial relations theory and research in the committee's deliberations or final report. Niland (1989), however, did draw heavily from recent Australian and international research in preparing a "green paper" that served as a blueprint for the initial movement toward decentralization in the state of New South Wales and later the federal system. Thus, a focus on public policy–related problems and a willingness to move from research to policy advocacy appear to be both long-standing and rather universal characteristics of industrial relations in English-speaking countries.

Multidisciplinary, Holistic Approach

A second feature of industrial relations research is that it draws on multiple disciplines in an effort to conceptualize the problem under study in a holistic fashion. Because of the problem focus, industrial relations researchers do not have the luxury of pursuing a narrow piece of a labor or employment problem. This leads industrial relations theorists and researchers to be more holistic in their definitions of research questions and multidisciplinary in perspective.

Unlike colleagues who define their primary intellectual mission as the deepening of a discipline, there is little opportunity for those taking a multidisciplinary approach to explore in depth what a single discipline such as economics has to offer to the understanding of a complex phenomenon. A disciplinary perspective can offer sharp, deep, and rich insights into a problem but seldom can provide a complete or practical solution or approach to solving the problem. This does not, however, imply that industrial relations researchers should not be well grounded in some established discipline. Recall that most of the leading scholars in our field came from a strong disciplinary training either in economics (Commons, Sidney Webb, Flanders,

Dunlop, Kerr, and others), history (Perlman, Brody, Gutman, Taft), or one of the behavioral sciences (McGregor, Whyte, Fox, Woodward). Yet these scholars tended to go beyond the boundaries of their disciplines to examine the broader contours of the problems of interest to them and borrowed insights from other disciplines and from their own experiences. Thus, the value of the multidisciplinary perspective found in the best industrial relations research is not that it *denies* or minimizes the contributions and insights of the various disciplines that also speak to the issue but that it builds on and integrates prior and current work from these fields and does so at a sufficient depth to gain the respect of those working on the same issues within the discipline. This is a tall order, especially for graduate students in our field, but one that is the price of admission.

One implication of this multidisciplinary perspective is that the best industrial relations teaching and research programs involve scholars each trained in a different discipline. In this way the diverse theories and insights from the disciplines are brought to bear on research problems, teaching, and intellectual debates. Of course this diversity often leads to vigorous (one hopes healthy) debates over how best to study an issue. But what should bind this diversity together is not a single effort to homogenize individual research interests or perspectives but a shared interest in employment problems and an interest in enriching their own theoretical perspectives from interaction and debate with colleagues with other approaches. The best industrial relations seminars and conferences reflect this mixture and tolerance for different approaches.

Attention to History

A third feature of industrial relations research is its reverence for and appreciation of history. As Jacoby (1990) has noted, this approach derives from the nineteenth-century German school of economics, which placed a high value on history and inductive approaches to economic analysis in contrast to the more deductive and mathematically oriented Austrian school. Commons and the Webbs, not to mention Karl Marx, all demonstrated through their work the importance of putting any contemporary problem or theoretical insight in its proper historical perspective. Indeed, perhaps Commons's most enduring theoretical work—the paper in which he develops his proposition about the effects of the expansion of the market on employment conditions—is his essay on the history of the shoemakers (Commons 1909). Moreover, the multivolume history of labor that Commons and his students and colleagues produced between 1918 and 1935 is a lasting tribute to the importance attached to the study of history for its insight into the problems of the day. The British equivalent, the Webbs' *History of Trade Unionism* (1895), established this same deep commitment to embedding analysis of labor issues in their appropriate historical context in British academic industrial relations traditions. Thus, it is not accidental that Flanders and Clegg's classic study of British industrial relations, *The System of Industrial Relations* (1954), uses as its subtitle *Its History, Law, and Institutions*.

History provides another important lesson to industrial relations researchers. It suggests that the problems we study are enduring and not simply transitory features of either an early stage of industrial development or something so new that there is nothing to learn from a look at prior experience. I believe this is especially important at this juncture in our field's history, a point I will return to later in this chapter.

Multimethods Approach

A fourth feature of industrial relations theory follows from its development by scholars trained in multiple disciplines—it must be multimethod as well. This has not always been the case, however. Those of us trained in the late 1960s were expected to become competent in social science theory, quantitative methods, and experimental designs. The emphasis on methodology was designed to bring home two central points: (1) it was time (indeed overdue) for industrial relations researchers to enter the realm of the quantitative social sciences, and (2) neither econometricians nor psychometricians had a monopoly on the best way to design and conduct quantitative analysis.

Industrial relations researchers were slow to take up quantitative analysis. For this reason, the field lost ground to other disciplines that had added quantitative analysis to their tool kit at an earlier date. Indeed, it became quite obvious that one could not reasonably study many of the most interesting and important issues of the day, such as the effects of unions on wages, the determinants of inequality at the workplace and in society, or the impacts of alternative employment and training policies and institutions on labor market outcomes, without a sound preparation in research design and quantitative methods.

Yet, while recognizing the value of quantitative analysis, respect for the insights of institutions, history, and case study research was never and should never be lost on industrial relations. (Some might argue, with some justification, that this multimethod perspective was nearly lost in the rush toward quantitative methods in the 1970s.) Industrial relations researchers are encouraged to combine the use of these tools with the institutional research traditions of earlier generations so as to interpret how individual-level data are influenced by the context in which these data are collected. This perspective flows directly from the core proposition of institutional theory—namely, individual attitudes, interests, and behavior are mediated and, over time, shaped by the institutional structures and processes in which they are situated. The institutional perspective was the original motivation behind the development of institutional economics—a recognition that the laws of supply and demand do not operate in a deterministic fashion.

An institutional perspective is especially important in labor economics and employment relations because critical transactions affecting personnel policies involve not just individuals acting alone or in isolation but also agents and collective bodies (firms, industry associations, unions, government regulatory agencies, and so forth) and take place within organizational and institutional settings. Industrial relations researchers, therefore, remain properly skeptical of the use of models that rely on individual-level data to predict labor market behavior or employment outcomes that ignore the influence of broader institutional influences. Nor is this a new insight. Brown and Wright (1994) note that the Webbs brought home this point in their *Methods of Social Science,* published in 1932. This need to maintain an institutional perspective places a greater methodological burden on students of industrial relations than it does on their colleagues in disciplines such as economics and psychology, but perhaps this is the price of admission to the field.

Normative Assumptions about Conflict

Although the above are all important and distinctive features of industrial relations research, I believe the primary feature that distinguishes the field from its counterparts lies in the normative assumptions and perspectives that underlie our conceptualization of the employment relationship. Industrial relations theory starts from an assumption that an enduring conflict of interests exists between workers and employers in employment relationships. Different schools of thought within the field vary, however, in their assumptions about the sources of these conflicts, their scope (full or partial), and how they should be handled. What has come to be known as the pluralist school of thought (Barbash 1984; Walton and McKersie ([1965] 1991); Clegg 1975) views the sources of conflict as embedded in the structure of authority relations and the separation of economic interests of workers and employers. Furthermore, pluralists view the employment relationship as mixed motive in nature (Walton and McKersie [1965]

1991); that is, they view the conflict as partial in nature. Thus, the parties to the employment relationship are viewed as tied together in an enduring web of partially conflicting and partially common interests or objectives. From this perspective, the key task of industrial relations theory and research is to contribute to an understanding of how conflicting interests can be resolved periodically and how the parties can expand the frontier of joint problem solving (Cutcher-Gershenfeld 1991). Since this perspective accepts the legitimacy of both the efficiency interests of employers and the personal interests of employees, a key task of industrial relations theory and research is to identify ways of achieving *efficiency with equity* at the workplace and in society (Meltz 1993).

In contrast, a Marxist or neo-Marxist perspective views the source of conflict as embedded in the separation of workers from the ownership of the means of production, a defining feature of capitalism. Conflict is viewed as more all-encompassing than partial, and the task of industrial relations theory and research is to understand the labor process—that is, the struggle for control that occurs in the interactions of workers and those who represent employers at the workplace (Hyman 1975).

These normative assumptions have several important implications for industrial relations research. First, they set the definitions of industrial relations problems and predictions apart from pure neoclassical economic models and from much of organizational behavior and human resource management research. Neoclassical economics starts from a normative perspective that assumes pure competition in labor (and product) markets produces optimal economic and social outcomes. Although various bilateral monopoly models (Edgeworth 1881) have recognized a potential value for unions when employers hold monopsony power, to classical and neoclassical economists, perfectly competitive markets remain the first and best setting for economic transactions, including transactions in the labor market. Thus, at their core, classical and neoclassical economics envision no useful role for unions or any other collective institutions that seek to regulate labor markets or change the balance of power in employment relationships. In contrast, industrial relations researchers build on the views first clearly expressed by the Webbs and Commons that individual workers are generally at a bargaining power disadvantage vis-à-vis employers. If left solely to the "higgling of the market," wages and working conditions will be driven down to socially unacceptable levels. Much organizational theory sees organizations as essentially cooperative systems or takes a top-down managerial perspective in framing research problems. One consequence of this perspective is that it also denies or at best ignores the legitimacy of institution-alized or collective challenges to managerial authority.

Second, these assumptions set up a rich debate within the field between pluralists and neo-Marxists over the approach to research, the definitions of problems of interest, and the types of data viewed as valid. Marxist re-searchers distrust or discount any evidence collected from worker inter-views or surveys (even those that recognize the importance of institutional contexts) since these methods cannot get beyond individual false conscious-ness shaped by the authority and control structures under which people work. Instead, preference is given to in-depth studies of the labor process (Burawoy 1979) that document the ongoing struggle for control over power and resources in employment relationships. Pluralists may share some of the skepticism of relying too much on attitude surveys of individu-als; however, they tend to take a more eclectic approach to the range of data deemed valid and the range of issues and processes deemed important to understand. Labor-management cooperation, for example, is viewed in a more positive light and therefore serves as a worthy and fruitful topic for research and policy advice.

These differences in normative assumptions produce an unresolvable de-bate among adherents to the different perspectives. This applies equally to the normative debates that separate industrial relations from other social sciences as well as to debates between the Marxist and pluralist perspectives within the field. There is no common ground between these different para-digms that can be resolved through empirical research or theory (see, for example, the exchange in *Industrial Relations* in 1982). Thus, the choice of a normative perspective on the employment relationship is something every student of industrial relations must come to grips with for him or herself. It is not surprising, therefore, that these debates feature prominently in the teaching of industrial relations theory and the training of graduate students (Kochan 1993; Godard 1993). Unfortunately, as students are quick to point out, sensitivity to the norms implicit in one's research often gets ignored or suppressed in published empirical studies.

Future Challenges

The features of industrial relations described above have served our field well for many years. But they need to be applied in new ways and to a rapidly changing set of issues to be relevant to today's labor markets, insti-tutions, and employment practices. Specifically, the increased diversity in the labor force, the intensification of competitive pressures, the rapid changes in technologies producing shifts in labor demand and skill requirements, the increased mobility of capital, and the increased speed of communication have challenged many of the institutions and principles that have governed employment relations over the past fifty years. Indeed, some would suggest that the term "industrial relations" or even "employment relations" does not adequately capture the nature of economic relations among individual contractors in contemporary labor markets. An increasing number of researchers have argued that taken together these forces are producing fundamental transformations in employment relationships (Piore and Sabel 1984; Kochan, Katz, and McKersie [1986] 1994).

The experimentation with new approaches to organizing work and involving employees in problem solving spurred by these developments led to a considerable increase in workplace-based research designed to describe and assess the effects of the changes in employment practices on economic performance (see Ichniowski et al. 1996 for a review). Currently, the restructuring and downsizing of many of these same firms are sparking a new wave of studies aimed at assessing the consequences of these developments for both firm performance and worker welfare. These studies may serve as the contemporary equivalent of the early contributions of the Webbs and Commons in documenting both the problems and the promising features of the practices they observed at workplaces.

Yet a major task remains, namely, updating the institutions needed to sustain and reinforce the most promising of these new developments and limiting the negative effects of those undesirable consequences. Stated most starkly, the institutions with which the old industrial relations systems are most closely identified, that is, unions and collective bargaining, have lost their power and appeal in many settings. This is especially the case in the United States, where union membership has fallen to levels not observed since the Great Depression, the law governing collective bargaining no longer works as promised (Commission on the Future of Worker Management Relations 1994a, 1994b), and a long-standing political stalemate continues to render it unlikely that significant public policy reforms will be achieved in the foreseeable future. Although the situation in the United States is perhaps more stark than in other countries, I believe it may only be a more extreme example of the challenges facing researchers in other parts of the world.

Nor is this phenomenon limited to the highly industrialized economies. The traditional approaches used to promote the values that underlie industrial relations have not fared well in newly industrializing and newly democratizing economies either. Those economies that have grown the fastest—such as the Asian small tigers of Hong Kong, South Korea, Taiwan, and Singapore—have done so in the absence of democratic labor market institutions or policies. The emerging democracies of Eastern Europe have implemented legal systems that support free trade unions and collective bargaining or works councils, but to date the performance of these institutions appears to be rather poor (e.g., Weinstein 1995b). Thus, I believe we are in an era in which academics in our field face a major challenge of updating, modernizing, and in some cases inventing new institutional structures and processes to promote "efficiency with equity" in our workplaces and societies. The question is how should we go about meeting this challenge.

Although the answer to this question will vary considerably depending on one's national setting, I believe a number of general points can be made.

International Perspective

Although industrial relations has a long history of international and comparative research, an international perspective and approach are especially needed now if we are to make significant advances in industrial relations theory. Over the past decade a large number of researchers have begun rethinking traditional concepts and models on the basis of changes occurring in our respective countries. While an important first step, this approach has now reached its natural limit. Each national system carries with it certain historical patterns of development and features that restrict the range of variation on critical variables such as culture, ideology, and institutional structures that affect how individual actors respond to similar changes in their external environments. Taking an international perspective broadens the range of comparisons available on these and other variables and increases the chances of discovering the systematic variations needed to produce new theoretical insights and explanations. The challenge we face is *how* to modernize both our methods and models to take full advantage of this rich international laboratory.

For too long comparative industrial relations was dominated by two research typologies. First, the lack of an analytical model for comparison meant that research remained largely descriptive of historical developments or current practices. Second, when analytical comparisons were invoked, they tended to be at the level of national systems or broad typologies. The U.S. industrial relations system was typically described as decentralized, while Sweden served as the model of a highly centralized and integrated labor market and collective bargaining system. The Japanese industrial relations system was characterized by its "four pillars" (enterprise unionism, seniority wage structures, the spring wage offensive, and lifetime employment). The problem with these typologies is that they both glossed over variations in practices within national systems and failed to produce a parsimonious set of "system types" that could explain variations in employment outcomes. The closest efforts to do so have come from economists who have attempted to predict inflation and unemployment performance by the degree of centralization of bargaining (Cameron 1984; Calmfors and Drifill 1988). Even here disagreements over how to classify certain systems have led to confusion over results (Bruno and Sachs 1985). Thus, this work, while rich in institutional detail, failed to produce an analytical framework suitable for the hypothesis testing needed to move analysis forward.

The current trend in international research is to take a more micro and comparative approach by drawing on common and varying practices and trends within and across national systems. In a series of projects involving networks of research teams from different countries (Locke, Kochan, and Piore 1995; Verma, Kochan, and Lansbury 1995), we are using changes in four sets of practices—work organization, compensation structures, staffing and employment security, and skill formation and training—as windows on developments within and across national systems. These specific comparisons are embedded in an analysis of the relationship between these practices and overall national industrial relations systems, institutional contexts, and organizational governance arrangements, recognizing, as Locke and Thelen (1995) have suggested, that each practice plays a somewhat different role within its particular system. Thus, we need to be particularly sensitive to these different contexts in making cross-national comparisons.

Rogers and Streeck (1995) and Freeman (1994) have taken a similar approach in their recent studies of works councils and labor markets in various countries. The advantage of this approach is that it allows one to combine the well-structured comparisons needed for hypothesis testing with the deep institutional understanding necessary to draw conclusions about the applicability of the four sets of practices in different settings.

In some areas we can go a step farther and carry out quantitative comparisons where cross-national data exist or can be collected, as in the Cranfield human resource management project (Brewster and Hegewisch 1994), the earlier Industrial Democracy in Europe (IDE) study (IDE 1981), or the various cross-national studies of union density (Visser 1994; Blanchflower and Freeman 1992) and strike activity (Hibbs 1976; Shalev 1983). Cross-national comparisons using micro-level data are always difficult given differences in institutions (see chapter 12, "Using Workplace Surveys for Comparative Research," in this volume). Ultimately, however, a combination of careful contextualized comparisons, deep institutional analysis, and large-scale quantitative comparisons will be needed to reinvigorate the study of international and comparative industrial relations. For this reason, it is important to foster a dialogue among the researchers engaged in these different approaches.

Inventing New Alternatives and Institutions

If we are to be true to our traditions, we must be proactive in using our research to inform debates over public policies and developments in private practice in our respective national and local settings. But in doing so, at this particular stage in our history, I believe we have a particular obligation to be proactive in using our research to produce new ideas and bring new alternatives to bear in policy debates. The reason is that in many situations incremental adjustments of existing policies or practices are not sufficient to meet the challenges of the day.

A personal example may help make this point. In the United States we recently attempted to reach a compromise between business and labor over ways to modernize American labor and employment law. The Commission on the Future of Worker Management Relations, led by former secretary of labor John Dunlop, labored for nearly two years as it tried to develop recommendations of ways to update our laws to support employee participation, reduce conflicts over workers' rights to join a union, and encourage private resolution of workplace disputes.[1] The result, at least to date, is, unfortunately, a continuation of the stalemate that has characterized policy in this area for more than two decades. Neither the organized interests of business nor labor were able or willing to negotiate compromises that would modernize the existing system. Nor was business or labor willing to consider seriously any fundamentally new approaches or ideas for structuring worker-management relations.

As a result, the commission's recommendations stopped short of proposing any alternatives to the current U.S. institutions, such as works councils, board representation, employee stock ownership, labor courts, or various forms of individual or nonexclusive union representation. Basic issues of corporate governance and the weak role of human resources in American corporations were not addressed since this would have opened a debate

---

1. I was a member of this commission.

about the very nature and objectives of American corporations and their role in society. The structure, governance, and leadership of the labor movement were not critically analyzed, even though some of these features may also limit the diffusion of innovations. Nor did the commission vigorously critique how labor policy is situated in economic policy making or in the political process, even though some of us on the commission have criticized U.S. labor policy in our individual writings for being marginalized as "interest group politics" rather than treated as an integral aspect of the nation's economic policy and strategy (Kochan 1994).

The point of this example is simple. Unless the research community is willing to address these more fundamental questions and bring them into the debates over policy and practice, new ideas will not enter into public policy debates. Policy making instead will be limited to debates over incremental adjustments of existing practices and traditions or, worse, will remain stalemated until an economic or political crisis forces more fundamental change. Then the changes that will be imposed may not be those that we would prefer. Perhaps we in the United States are living through such an experience at the moment.

This brings us full circle back to the early years of industrial relations inquiry. The Webbs produced a volume entitled *Industrial Democracy* in 1897 in which they coined the term "collective bargaining." That volume both described what trade unions and their predecessor organizations were doing at the time and argued for an evolutionary strategy they believed would produce a more efficient and equitable relationship among workers, employers, and the larger society. Similarly, much of the work of Commons and his associates from the early part of the century through the 1920s involved a mixture of historical documentation and case studies of emerging union-management relationships and dispute resolution procedures, the promotion of state-level experimentation with new labor market institutions such as an industrial commission responsible for regulating workplace safety and workers' compensation, and an unemployment compensation and administration system. Taken together, these studies laid the intellectual foundation for much of the New Deal labor and social security legislation enacted in the United States in the 1930s.

If, as it appears, the New Deal labor relations system and its associated legal doctrines are no longer working, we in the United States face a task similar to that of Commons and his colleagues. Stated succinctly, the most critical task for contemporary industrial relations researchers in the United States is to produce the ideas and the experiments needed to test the viability of institutional structures and legal principles better suited to the needs of today's workforce and economy. Inevitably this means that we must think beyond the bounds of current institutions and broaden our focus beyond unions and collective bargaining as practiced today. Discovering and designing viable institutions for the workforce and economy of the future requires us to apply the enduring features of industrial relations outlined above to all aspects of the world of work.

Whether the U.S. situation is unique or comparable to the situations in other countries now or will be at some time in the future is best left for others to judge. But whenever and wherever these conditions prevail, industrial relations researchers must be willing to step beyond the constraints of interest group battles by calling for fundamental changes in industrial relations policies, institutions, and workplace practices. If, as I believe, now is such a time, as it was at the time of Marx, the Webbs, and Commons, our generation, like those before us, will be judged by whether we carry on their legacy with equal imagination, clarity, and consequence.

Part II

Strategies and Methods

Strategies and Methods

Our primary aim here is to outline the main strategies and methods used by industrial relations researchers. The first two chapters provide a broad look at the two main research methods: qualitative and quantitative analysis. Qualitative analysis is generally associated with the inductive approach and quantitative with the deductive. Inductive research can be quantitative, however, and deductive research can be qualitative. Indeed, it is becoming increasingly common for qualitative and quantitative research to be used in conjunction and for research projects to involve both deductive and inductive elements.

Case studies, ethnography, and participative action research projects are generally qualitative, although sometimes they involve the collection of data that can be quantified. By contrast, data collected through experiments and surveys are generally quantified.

Qualitative researchers typically put greater emphasis than do quantitative researchers on the need for construct validity and are less concerned with obtaining external validity. Both groups place great weight on the need for internal validity, though how this is achieved varies. Qualitative researchers typically focus on getting behind the facade of formal structures to uncover the "true" causal mechanisms. Quantitative researchers, by contrast, concentrate on ensuring that the causal processes in their statistical models mirror those "in the real world."

Increasingly, researchers recognize that good research design requires the use of both qualitative and quantitative methods. The former is seen as essential in the search for realistic models of causal relationships and the latter for testing competing explanations of key relationships. We note, however, that the use of both methods is not as common as might be desirable.

CHAPTER THREE

Qualitative Methods: Technique or Size?

Richard Whipp

Q ualitative methods continue to have a profound impact on research on the employment relationship. Case studies, interviews, and ethnographic techniques are commonly used in research into such diverse topics as workplace culture and new technology. The nature of this research has changed parallel with that of the subjects these methods are used to address. Likewise, many of the techniques have been strengthened by their links with new theoretical orientations. The techniques and their adherents are at an important juncture, and, arguably, the term "qualitative methods" could evolve to embrace a more extensive set of methods, including, for example, software applications for the analysis of textual data. The aim of this chapter is to present an overview of the current state of qualitative research methods and to suggest how these techniques might be used in the future.

The employment relationship involves a rich set of researchable issues (Salaman 1992: 29) centered on the processes by which employers and the employed adjust to each other's needs and wants (Rollinson 1993: 4). Such complex processes are especially suited to the range of techniques encompassed by the umbrella term "qualitative" (Van Maanen 1979: 520).

This chapter begins by comparing quantitative and qualitative methods. It then summarizes the main methods used by qualitative researchers. Next, the advantages and limitations of these methods are discussed. Building on this general appreciation of the technical possibilities and drawbacks of a qualitative orientation, examples are offered of ways in which this ap-

The author is grateful for the comments and suggestions of Ed Heery.

proach has been used to study three aspects of the employment relationship. The conclusion looks to the future.

Qualitative versus the Quantitative Approach

In the social sciences a line is frequently drawn between qualitative and quantitative methods. Some argue (Bogdan and Taylor 1975: 1) that the division is deep and relates to theoretical and epistemological issues. Qualitative and quantitative approaches are appropriate for examining different types of problems, but these approaches are not antithetical; indeed, they are often used together. The answer to the question posed in the subtitle of this chapter—"Technique or Size?"—is therefore both, so far as the study of work is concerned. The following points illustrate the separate strengths of the two traditions as well as important areas of overlap.

Much quantitative research arises from a positivist paradigm that is centered on the search for objective truth, the use of scientific methods, and the systematic measurement of phenomena (see chapter 4, "Quantitative Methods"). The emphasis is on discovering statistical relationships that allow generalizations to be made or that point to specific links between elements of a problem. Qualitative researchers, by contrast, are generally part of a phenomenological tradition that does not recognize the existence of unambiguous objectivity; the way individuals construct the meanings of phenomena is paramount. Quantitative scholars place great faith in the rational basis of their data and analytical techniques; qualitative specialists (especially postmodernists) are more likely to acknowledge multiple interpretations.

These differing orientations have given rise to contrasting approaches to theory building, the questions asked by researchers, and the kinds of data that are collected. The positivist/quantitative perspective relies on testing existing theory through the use of data. Theoretical explanations are "deduced" from these data, previous theory, and *a priori* reasoning and are ordered according to statistical protocols. New theories are created to explain the relationships suggested by testing. By contrast, qualitative research typically develops theories inductively. In this case scholars construct explanatory frameworks by examining evidence that they relate to personal experience through interviews or observations. Theory emerges from the data and is said to be "grounded" in the empirical detail.

Although the distinctions between the qualitative and quantitative traditions are well established, researchers are, in practice, pragmatic; the two methods can be used together. Many argue that since some phenomena are more measurable than others, to study different research issues may require alternative research techniques (Bryman 1988). It is feasible, therefore, to link qualitative and quantitative approaches within the same study or at different stages of a research program (Jick 1989). Bringing the results together is often instructive, not least since new questions are generated. The qualitative method may suggest hypotheses to test quantitatively. Conversely, the qualitative approach can be used to investigate why quantitative relationships exist. Quantitative techniques can be used to identify outliers that might be studied in order to validate or falsify hypotheses advanced on the basis of quantitative analysis. Marginson et al. (1988), using a survey conducted in the United Kingdom, identified the formal human resource management policies senior executives had apparently adopted. Subsequently, Morris and Wood (1991) investigated practices at the firm level and concluded that managers in the earlier sample operated in ignorance of such policies (Hartley 1994: 215).

Main Methods

Qualitative analysis, when used by those concerned with the relations between employers and employed, has involved a profusion of techniques. The common denominator has been an emphasis on the meaning of the employment relationship as seen by those involved. The aim has been to describe, decode, translate, and come to terms with such meanings (Van Maanen 1983: 9). The three methods most commonly employed by qualitative researchers are interviews, ethnography, and the case study (which itself typically involves both interviews and ethnography).

In addition, specialized techniques may be used, such as the critical incident technique, the repertory grid, cognitive mapping, and projective methods (Easterby-Smith, Thorpe, and Lowe 1991: chap. 5). The critical incident technique concentrates (via interview or questionnaire) on specific events in the past in an effort to reveal actions and motives relevant to broader problems and processes. A repertory grid is a matrix used to represent a person's view of the world by linking the people/ideas central to his or her existence with the qualities the person uses to describe those people/ideas. Cognitive mapping is a process in which individuals, sometimes groups, are encouraged to explore all facets of a problem. During the process the researcher stores each contribution (on paper or computer), thereby building up a representation of the respondents' perceptions of the issue. The map is immediately available for reflection and adjustment. Projective techniques aim to uncover unconscious thoughts by making people react to stimuli, especially drawings or photographs.

Interviews

The interview is the primary means of accessing the experiences and subjective views of actors. Detailed, vivid, and inclusive accounts of events and processes may be generated. The flexibility of the interview enables the researcher to open up new dimensions of a problem or to discover clues that connect its different elements. Interviews enable individuals to reveal the personal framework of their beliefs and the rationales that inform their actions.

Interview formats vary. At one extreme is the highly structured type in which questions are pretested and asked in a fixed form and sequence. The aim is to produce quantifiable results from set samples that may provide generalizable findings. The systematic collection of interview data from a large number of people is the basis of a survey (see chapter 10, "Employee Attitude Surveys").

At the other end of the scale is the open or nondirected interview; it is particularly useful if the subject matter is sensitive and especially when the respondents do not want their identities to be revealed. The objective here is to provide the greatest opportunity for the views and values of the respondents to become known. Interviews of this kind are based on lists of themes or key issues rather than set questions. The researcher has to become adept at shaping questions in response to the interviewees' replies and ensuring that the discussion remains relevant. A balance has to be struck between open questions and more specific prompts.

Experienced interviewers employ a combination of questioning techniques. These include repeating key questions to check responses, asking for clarification of statements, leaving silent spaces in the dialogue for the interviewee to fill as he or she reflects on given questions and their implications, and playing back comments as a way of inviting respondents to amplify or reconsider their responses.

The social skills required by interviewers are demanding. Establishing personal credibility with members of organizations who may be wary of academics and yet retaining independence of judgment is a major challenge. Maintaining trust, avoiding the projection of assumptions on to respondents, and handling the social interaction (including nonverbal signals) that interviewing involves are all part of the interviewer's craft. Interview techniques are as important to contemporary studies of new forms of employment in Australia (Patrickson, Bamber, and Bamber 1995) as they were to earlier accounts of union operations in the United Kingdom (Batstone, Boraston, and Frenkel 1978) or the United States (Gutman 1977).

Ethnography

Ethnography is widely used in employment research, although its exact form may vary (see chapter 7, "In the Eye of the Beholder"). The benefits are broadly similar to those of interviewing; accessing the rules that govern individual or collective behavior is the priority. Interviews generate separate pieces of evidence and testimony. Ethnography is more inclusive: it involves direct observation of respondents in context, and it enables the researcher to interact with both respondents and the setting and to link values, behavior, and circumstance. Ethnographers witness patterns of human behavior in their natural settings.

The demands on the researcher are more acute when doing ethnography than when interviewing. In addition to having to maintain all the skills of the interviewer, there is a major need to preserve the goals of the research, even when there is a strong pull to "go native."

Ethnographic techniques have underpinned some of the most illuminating appreciations of shop-floor work and manufacturing (Roy 1954; Burawoy 1985). Roy, for example, was able to reveal how workers in a machine shop controlled the pace of work processes by work-group action. By living and working with the workers, he was able to witness the practices as well as comprehend the workers' logic. Fixed-format questionnaires would lack the flexibility to uncover such informal work-group behavior.

Case Studies

The case study is often regarded as the emblem of qualitative research (see chapter 6, "Case Studies"). Case studies involve the detailed investigation of a single or small number of research objects (such as groups, organizations, or industries) in their often complex contexts or settings. Case researchers address this complexity in a number of ways. The case study typically uses a combination of specific techniques: interviews, observations, questionnaires, and documentary sources. In studying how strategic decisions were made in a union during a major steel strike, Hartley (1994: 212) and colleagues combined interviews, ethnography, and documentary sources. In their theoretical orientation, most case studies move inductively from detailed findings to more general explanations (210).

A case study may also be used as a falsification test (Yin 1989). In this case an extreme or apparently unusual example of the phenomenon in question (often called an outlier) is studied with a view to challenging the conclusions reached by other researchers. For example, earlier research may have developed a view on the distinctive management practices of the large organizations in a given industry. Studying one of the industry's few small companies would test if those practices are found only in the larger counterparts. If they appear in the small outfit, the project's interim conclusions are shown to be false. The researchers must think again.

Advantages of Qualitative Research

The main advantages of qualitative methods stem from their sensitivity to context and that they enable problems to be investigated in their natural settings. This orientation has produced three main advantages—namely, exploration can take place, hidden features can be revealed, and processes can be examined in depth.

Exploration Possible

The techniques just outlined are ideal for opening up new topics. When there is no clear theoretical framework from which to derive hypotheses, the exploratory character of qualitative research is an ideal starting point. The relative openness of qualitative methods should mean that data and interpretations that fall outside conventional thinking are more readily developed. By the same token, methods that allow data and tentative frameworks to influence one another during the research process (notably case studies) are well suited to hypothesis generation and concept building (Eisenhardt 1989).

Hidden Features Revealed

Qualitative techniques are also an advantage when trying to uncover the many hidden features of the employment relationship. Informal or even illicit behavior can be examined as a result of the trust that may develop in association with interviewing or the use of ethnographic methods. Shopfloor organization, for example, has been shown to be sophisticated yet entirely informal within workplaces where union membership is absent (Burawoy 1985).

In-Depth Examination Possible

Finally, the open-ended and iterative character of qualitative research enables full appreciation of processes in depth. Survey and related questionnaires may determine associations between variables, but it is the battery of techniques deployed in some case studies (see chapter 6, "Case Studies") that enable researchers to identify, track, and interpret the processes that connect such variables (for a full overview, see Pettigrew 1990). Surveys are necessarily fixed in time and provide cross-sectional views of a phenomenon. By contrast, qualitative studies enable researchers to pursue processes in an unbroken way through time.

Limitations of Qualitative Research

The limitations of qualitative research depend partly on the standpoint of the researcher. To many, these constraints are bound up with its inherent strengths. Careful evaluation of the use of such methods is required according to the purpose or context of the research. The three main problems, which go by the technical terms of generalization, induction, and transparency, will illustrate the point.

Generalization

Qualitative studies are often criticized for their concern with the particular at the expense of the general. In one sense the point is a fair one: it is impossible to reap the benefits of a case study and match the coverage of a nationally representative survey. Yet the issue is not clear-cut. Both qualitative and quantitative techniques have limitations in providing a totally reliable base from which to generalize. Some measurements of association are so tightly qualified for technical reasons that the conclusions produced are, of necessity, highly specific. Heterogeneous populations often defy statistical capture. It should also be remembered that some case studies are conducted on a broad scale, sometimes covering whole sectors (Räsänen and Whipp 1992).

Induction

The positivist tradition produces theory by testing hypotheses that confirm or deny existing orthodoxies (i.e., through a deductive process). With much qualitative research, in contrast, theory emerges from the evidence collected; data collection should allow grounded propositions to result. And here lies the problem: the propositions and theories that emerge from this induction are sometimes the result of "creative leaps" (Eisenhardt 1989: 533). These leaps are not always fully reported, or they arise from a process of constant iteration between theory, data, and relevant literatures that is not written up in publications. Such research is also more difficult for other authors to replicate.

Transparency

It is the problem of transparency that most bedevils qualitative research. Given that many qualitative techniques rely on in-depth examinations of research issues, the process of immersion by the researcher can be dangerous. How data were collected, catalogued, and analyzed is often explained only briefly in final reports. The result is that an aura of mystery surrounds some interview- and observation-based findings. The conclusions may be challenging and innovative, but other academics are left to speculate on how the results were reached.

Readers of qualitative research findings are advised to show a healthy skepticism toward studies that fail to declare the intellectual or practical starting point of the research, the source of the funding, or the relationship between the researcher and those being researched. Given that most qualitative techniques rely on close contact with respondents and their organizations, the nature of any prior ties or obligations should be made clear. The academic using qualitative techniques is wise, therefore, to treat the entire research process in a reflexive way. This means recording all the key choices and assumptions made throughout the process of framing the questions, data collection, and the generation of organizing ideas or frameworks. Projects are illuminated by researchers' ability to reflect on their own role and their interactions with the people and circumstances being studied (Hammersley and Atkinson 1983:14–16).

Uses of Qualitative Research

Qualitative methods are particularly appropriate for studies of culture, power, and change, as the following examples illustrate.

Culture

Arguably, the qualitative approach to studying the employment relationship has been at its most useful in the area of culture. One of the imperatives informing this research has been the desire to uncover aspects of work that have conventionally been hidden from study. The benefits are striking.

The work of Kunda (1992) is a case in point. His study of a high-tech corporation (Digital) offers painstaking details of not only the experience of work but the way culture is codified in contemporary organizations, the centrality of rituals, and, not least, the nuances of language and the reproduction of ideology. The qualitative approach impels Kunda through a wealth of sources, including company videos, newsletters, and memoranda, as well as interviewing and observing the roles of staff, consultants, union officers, and others from across the computer industry. In one of the strongest recent ethnographic studies of an organization, he painstakingly observes the details of daily (and nightly) work routines and contrasts them with the practices outlined in the company's "operating manuals." Reporting on the role of conversations in men's and ladies' rooms as part of the wider discourse is one example of the author's coverage.

The outcome of such scholarship is impressive and matches the insights of earlier studies of shop-floor culture by Roy (1954), for example. Many employment analysts bemoan the apparent dominance of managerial cultures under neoliberal thinking. Kunda provides a contrary view. In his findings, attempts at managing or controlling culture by corporations are shown to be riddled with contradictions. At the individual or group level, ambivalence is the keynote. Morality and cynicism coexist. Commitment is tinged with ironic detachment. Kunda would never have discovered this rich, contradictory picture had he and his colleagues used survey instruments. Questionnaires would have confirmed much of the compliant behavior but missed the resistance found in everyday humor and alternative practices. By sharing the lives of the employees, not only did Kunda produce a subtle and penetrating account of work but he also challenged the accepted image of Digital that had been built up over decades.

Power

The objective of exploring the meanings that people generate around work has been a constant within qualitative research. Nowhere is this better illustrated than in studies of power. Some organization specialists draw attention to the ability of social actors to influence behavior and alter premises of action and to the way interest groups form around issues and compete for resources (Pfeffer 1992). Others concentrate more on the way power is mobilized. The means to establishing legitimacy is often derived from shaping language and constructing supporting symbols. Bargaining is one formal arena of power, but it is in the interstices of such structures of negotiation where legitimization processes operate. The use of subtle means to uncovering these unofficial relationships through interviews, observation, and oral history has led to a strong seam of industrial relations research in its own right (see, for example, the account of the politics of new technology in Wilkinson 1983).

The work of Knights and Morgan (1991) in the United Kingdom is instructive. Their study centered on the restructuring of the financial services sector as banks and insurance companies merged in the early 1990s. The particular emphasis of the research was on power and discourse. Close attention was paid not only to written documents but to observing, recording, and analyzing verbal exchanges between all levels of staff. By concentrating on the use of the word "strategy," for example, the researchers were able to demonstrate how staff were identified according to their participation in this official company discourse as defined by the company. Those who used the new tools of market analysis and employed the correct terminology prospered; they enjoyed the credentials of expertise (251–53). Informed by linguistic theory, the authors demonstrated how the language, symbols, and exchanges around the strategy concept have important political outcomes. Although other authors have applied quantitative techniques to textual analysis, the political context of the discourses around such key topics in organizations can be fully appreciated only by blending a mixture of qualitative sources and techniques.

Change Processes

The dominant subject among many students of work provides yet another example. During the current decade there has been rare fusion between process experts from the strategy and employment fields. These seemingly different approaches have converged around the overwhelming significance of the way contemporary organizations seek to manage change. As this research illustrates, the process of strategic change cannot be explained by the technical logics of planning or marketing. Instead, the shape, pace, and outcomes of the process are the product of an amalgam of forces. Above all, the uneven, often irrational course of strategic changes has multiple consequences for all those involved (for an overview, see Whipp 1996).

One of the more reflective examinations of change is offered by Johnson in his book *Strategic Change and the Management Process* (1987), which includes an extensive account of the rationale and experiences associated with his method. His aim was to understand why a major fashion retail chain displayed a sharp downturn in performance in the 1980s after an extended period of relatively uninterrupted profitable growth. Before Johnson's study, the strategic change literature had been dominated by a positivist tradition. Quantitative approaches had been used to assess the rational fit between company strategies and market structures. Johnson was an example of a new breed of scholars who adopted a phenomenological stance and relied on qualitative techniques. The problems of the company were shown to arise from the breakdown of its existing commercial and cultural paradigm, the disjunction between senior executives and other groups in the company, and the consequent problem of strategic drift.

In practice, such studies try to "get under the skin of an organization" (Johnson 1987: 70–77). In Johnson's case this involved interviewing staff at different levels (both individually and in groups), reviewing personal documents as well as a wide variety of company material (from annual reports to departmental memos), and making extensive use of secondary sources. The varying results were cross-checked against each other, making explicit use of the differences between accounts. What occurred was a linking of "the reasoning of the managers with the understanding of the researcher as guided by the concepts and theory with which he or she is familiar" (78).

Johnson's study is a clear example of inductive analysis. Unlike exclusively positivist research, the study was not designed to test a set of hypotheses. His account shows how he was forced to define critical concepts, examine multiple instances of the behavior in question, and continually test propositions to see how far they explained the data. It was through the classic juxtaposition of different data with existing theory and research that Johnson's dynamic social understanding of the management process was constructed. Given the author's departure from conventional wisdom, he had no established propositions to examine. Instead, the qualitative method was ideal for the opening of a new stance on strategic change and the emergence of fresh explanations.

Overview

The advantages of using qualitative techniques in the three cases I have discussed are marked. Kunda is able to present an account of work in a high-technology organization that is more critical and subtle than the official company line or the received wisdom of the industry. Above all, he offers an understanding of work that exposes contradictions and disjunctions. Knights and Morgan show how qualitative approaches yield alternative accounts. Their study epitomizes the way such techniques produce genuinely novel insights. In this instance they question the assumed neutrality of the technical language used in an entire sector. Johnson's work, while academically rigorous, shows how a qualitative orientation, based on multiple sources and induction, can produce *practical* results. His approach supplied the most convincing explanation for the performance of the focal firm according to industry experts.

Future of Qualitative Analysis

Studies that offer qualitative analyses of the employment relationship have a promising future. If the social relations of the workplace are the product of the joint creativity of individuals, then this process of creation continues to produce diverse forms of organization and control. Two examples present themselves. Those involved in the current debates over the fate of human resource management (HRM) initiatives (for an overview, see Mabey and Salaman 1995: chap. 5) will learn much from closely focused studies. The meaning of organizational learning in HRM and the operation of single-union, no-strike agreements in the face of changing commercial circumstances have yet to receive the full weight of qualitative research. Conversely, the identification of social networks that can support new forms of market activity (Biggart and Castonias 1996) poses new challenges for established techniques such as ethnography.

The growth of postmodernism in the social sciences may have specific relevance to workplace relations. Advocates of postmodernism attack orthodox theoretical structures (positivist or realist) as products of capitalist logics; they are regarded as means of domination in modern cultures through their espousal of rationalism and scientific knowledge (Friedman 1996: 653).

While the debate rages over the general significance of postmodernism, it is apparent that some of its assertions have relevance for students of the employment relationship. Language is a prime example. Postmodernists highlight the way language is used as a bearer of dominant logics and as a means of legitimization and exclusion via a process of discourse. Their deconstruction of the use of language and signs has made inroads in the study of strategy (Knights and Morgan 1991). The meanings and assumptions of the workplace are ripe for similar investigation by means of such new approaches (see, for example, Godard 1993).

The impact of theoretical upsurges elsewhere in the social sciences on our understanding of the employment relationship is hard to predict. More certain, though, are the prospects for a synthesis of techniques from the positivist and interpretive orientations. There is no necessary reason for the strict separation of qualitative from quantitative methods. On the contrary, they often complement each other. At this point, it is in the international sphere that the most striking potential for such combined approaches appears. The impetus is part technical and part cultural in origin. As Kochan argues in chapter 2 of this volume, international comparative research on industrial relations will need both qualitative and quantitative methods if the subject is to move beyond descriptive accounts or national systems typologies. Paradoxically, Hyman (1996:402) contends that, in contrast to the fragmentation and insecurity among western scholars of the employment relationship, the prospects for revival in the field appear greatest where the orthodoxies of the subject are least established: in Eastern Europe and in many "less developed" economies. The prospects for multimethod studies have never been greater. Perhaps these settings will yield fresh conceptions of research and novel, hybrid applications of techniques for which the qualitative tradition has been noted.

CHAPTER FOUR

Quantitative Methods: It's Not What You Do, It's the Way That You Do It

Keith Whitfield

Q uantitative methods have been used increasingly in industrial relations research in recent years. This has resulted from, first, a substantial increase in appropriate quantitative data. Workplace surveys, for example, have proliferated, and quantitative data sets have been developed in areas in which they were previously negligible (see, for example, chapter 10, "Employee Attitude Surveys"). Second, the range of statistical techniques available has expanded enormously, aided by the phenomenal growth of computing power.

A review of six leading industrial relations journals indicated a wide variation—from 12 to 82 percent—in the percentage of articles that rely on quantitative methods (Whitfield 1994). American journals were especially likely to publish quantitative articles. There was a high propensity for quantitative papers in industrial relations to use data the authors collected on their own, in contrast to economics, for example (Leontieff 1982). The approach taken and methods used in such articles were seen to be more heavily influenced by economics than by other cognate disciplines, although there was an increase in the percentage of articles on human resource management, which might be expected to increase the influence of psychology on quantitative methods in this field.

In principle, the application of quantitative methods adds rigor to research. It allows hypotheses to be tested, orders of magnitudes of the relationships between key factors to be established, and patterns to be uncovered. In practice, however, if insufficient care is taken, the use of quantitative methods can potentially seriously mislead the research process. In such a situation the estimates made of the key relationships under investigation can be biased from their true values. Such bias can emanate from a variety of sources—poor data, wrong techniques, bad modeling, and the use of inappropriate structures for statistical equations. How to identify and respond to such issues is the focus of this chapter.

After briefly defining the approach and distinguishing it from others, the chapter focuses on the elements of a typical quantitative study. This is followed by an overview of the main types of quantitative data and statistical techniques available. Thereafter, the focus turns to how quantitative methods are used, concentrating on the development of statistical models and the structure (functional form) of estimating equations. The next section looks at attempts to move beyond single studies to increase both validation and the effectiveness of quantitative research. The chapter concludes by discussing some implications for future research in industrial relations using the quantitative approach.

Definition and Distinction

Quantitative analysis can be defined as the application of statistical techniques derived from the principles of statistical inference to the empirical investigation of a research question. It should be distinguished from mathematical analysis, which is concerned with the development of theoretical models using mathematical concepts. Although the two are related and quantitative analysis is often used to test hypotheses derived from mathematical analysis, they are not the same.

Much research undertaken in industrial relations involves some form of quantitative technique. By contrast, mathematical analysis has been used to a very limited extent in this area, largely reflecting a widespread belief that the complexities of the subject matter cannot be reduced to a set of mathematical formulas. The mathematical analysis of industrial relations phenomena has predominantly been undertaken by economists and has largely been ignored by industrial relations researchers. The prime area of industrial relations in which mathematical analysis has been used is wage bargaining (see, for example, Manning 1987).

Functions of Quantitative Analysis

Quantitative analysis serves three main functions: (1) to uncover patterns that may suggest new hypotheses and theoretical constructs; (2) to test hypotheses that are generated by received theory or prior reasoning against empirical fact; (3) to establish orders of magnitude for the key relationships suggested by theory. To some extent these functions suggest a logical progression, and it can be expected that the greater the "maturity" of a research area, the greater the emphasis will be on the third function rather than the first. Whether such a link exists in reality is, however, the subject of some debate (Godard 1993).

The relative importance of these functions also depends on the dominant methodological stance in the discipline/field concerned. In particular, the more the field emphasizes a deductive approach (Cappelli 1985), the more weight is given to the second and the third functions. In contrast, the more inductive the stance, the more that the first function will be emphasized.

Elements of Quantitative Analysis

Quantitative analysis typically involves explaining variations in a given variable (the dependent variable) by variations in other variables (independent variables). In most situations the aim is to estimate the "pure" (other things being equal) relationship between the dependent variable and a key independent variable (often termed the explanatory variable). The other independent variables (the control variables) are introduced to allow for factors other than the explanatory variable that influence the dependent variable (the *ceteris paribus* clause). (Chapter 5, "Experimental Methods," discusses an alternative means of undertaking such an analysis.)

Most quantitative analyses involve four elements: (1) a *quantitative data set,* measuring the key factors under investigation; (2) a set of *statistical techniques* for estimating the numerical relationships between the variables; (3) a *statistical model* that reflects the processes that are generating variations in the data; and (4) a *functional form* for each equation, which reflects the key properties of the relationship between the dependent and independent variables.

An example is provided by a study in which Mulvey (1986b) estimated the union wage differential in Australia. The data set was an Australian Bureau of Statistics Survey of thirty thousand households. Each respondent was asked for information on personal characteristics (including whether he or she belonged to a union), jobs, and earnings. The statistical model estimates equations in which earnings is the dependent variable, union membership is the explanatory variable, and personal/job characteristics are the independent variables. Separate equations are estimated for males and females to allow for different relationships for each group between the dependent and independent variables. The statistical technique used is ordinary least squares analysis. The set of variables allowing for factors affecting earnings other than union membership is very comprehensive and includes terms allowing for a nonlinear relationship between the dependent and independent variables.

Each of these four elements of quantitative analysis will be examined in turn.

Types of Data Sets

A major problem for the quantitative analyst is obtaining data that are appropriate to the research question at hand. It is rare that the quantitative information available to industrial relations researchers will be perfectly suited to examine all the relevant research issues. Unless this is taken into account, serious errors of interpretation may occur.

Industrial relations researchers use four main types of data sets: cross-sectional, time-series, pooled, and panel. Each type raises distinctive questions for the quantitative researcher. These relate both to the collection of information, the interpretation of the results generated, and the approach taken to statistical modeling.

Cross-Sectional Data

Cross-sectional data are based on a given population at a specific point in time (e.g., Bain and Elsheikh's 1979 study of variations in unionism between industries) and are typically obtained from surveys. An issue of particular importance for the analysis of such data is whether the respondents to the survey are a random sample of the population from which the sample is drawn. Substantial levels of nonresponse will typically indicate that this is not the case, and inferences for the general population should not be made. Moreover, it is generally difficult to check whether the respondents are randomly distributed.

Information about the background characteristics of the full sample can sometimes be compared with that of respondents, but the information that is generated is typically extremely general and may not relate to the key differences between the two groups. Thus, for example, establishments in the original and respondent groups may be similar in size, sector, and industry but differ in, say, country of ownership or the locus of decision making. These may be crucial explanators of variations in industrial relations outcomes (e.g., Marginson et al. 1988). Techniques for minimizing such bias are outlined in chapter 9, "Large-Scale National Surveys for Mapping, Monitoring, and Theory Development."

Time-Series Data

Time-series data report the change in given variables through time and are typically highly aggregated, focusing on, for example, union membership, the incidence of industrial action, and wage change. The main problems with time-series data stem from the small samples used, the tendency for time-series variables to vary in a similar fashion though time, and changes in the definition of key variables (often implicit) over time.

Small samples pose difficulties in applying standard statistical tests. Many of these tests are appropriate only for the analysis of large samples in which the "law of large numbers" applies. Used out of that context, they can seriously mislead. The main problems are that small samples may violate key assumptions on which statistical tests are based and are heavily influenced by "rogue" observations. There is no "magic" number for determining whether a sample is sufficiently large for a given analysis, but bigger is usually better. This is often difficult to achieve in time series, especially those based on annual data. The same also applies to cross-sectional work using data on different countries (see chapter 11, "Comparative International Industrial Relations").

The high levels of correlation that are typically found in time-series data often make it difficult to disentangle the separate effects of the independent variables on the dependent variable. This can result in spuriously high statistics indicating how much of the variation in the dependent variable has been caused by variations in the independents or misleading indications of the strength of the relationships between given independent variables and the dependent variable (this is termed multicollinearity). To some extent such interdependence among the variables is akin to reducing the sample size and is therefore best "cured" by collecting more data. When this is not possible, great care must be taken in choosing an appropriate statistical technique for the analysis so as to minimize the problem (see, for example, Maddala 1988: chap. 7).

Poor measurement introduces "noise" into the data set and can thereby bias the results or reduce their precision. This also applies to cross-sectional data but is especially problematic for time series in that both the definitions of variables and the nature of the factors on which they are based often exhibit a tendency to change over time. For example, the definition of a union used by statistical authorities has changed markedly through time, as has the range of organizations commonly regarded as unions (see Bain and Elsheikh 1976).

Pooled Data Sets

Pooled data sets result from the merging of cross-sectional and time-series information and typically result from undertaking repeated cross-sectional surveys of similar populations. An example would be information taken from similar questions in each of the three British workplace surveys. Pooled data sets are particularly useful in extending the scope of analysis using just a single cross-section. A frequent problem, however, results from change in the sample population through time, either because of definitional changes or variations in the population at large, for example, in the distribution of industry. This raises the question of whether the sample's respondents (and therefore the data) in the different time periods can be regarded as comparable.

Panel Data

Panel data are based on questions asked of the same sample at different points in time, thereby providing a number of observations on each member of the sample. Among the most used of these sets are the U.S. National Longitudinal Surveys of Labor Market Experience. The British Workplace Industrial Relations Surveys also have a panel element.

The main advantage of panel data is that they allow causal processes to be investigated. For example, numerous studies have indicated that firms introducing "new" work practices perform better than those that do not (MacDuffie 1995). It is debatable, however, whether this reflects the effect of such practices on performance or the greater propensity of high-performing firms to invest in them. If the strongest relationships are between practices at an early date and higher performance at a later date, there is a strong possibility that the former cause the latter. This can be investigated only if there is a time element to the data set and ideally data are available on the same firms at different points in time.

Although panel data sets allow the drawing of stronger inferences than do simple cross-sections, they typically suffer from *panel attrition,* that is, the dropping out of sample members between the first and subsequent sweeps. For example, respondents in sweep one might refuse to be interviewed in sweep two or may not be contactable because of a change of address or in the case of employers because they went out of business. If this process is not random, any estimates derived could reflect, in part, the nature of the attrition process. Disentangling the influence of sample attrition and other factors requires special statistical techniques.

Types of Variables

Quantitative variables take a variety of forms. The most tractable, in the sense that they can be easily analyzed, are those that are *continuous, parametric,* and *nonlimited.* In such cases, quantitative analysis can generally be undertaken using the more readily accessible statistical techniques, such as ordinary least squares analysis (also known as classical linear regression). Where variables, particularly the dependent variable, do not take this form, more complex techniques are usually required.

Continuous Variables

Many of the techniques used in quantitative analysis are predicated on the concept of continuity; that is, the values of the variables vary over a wide range by small amounts (e.g., earnings), rather than in large (discrete) steps. Many variables are far from fully continuous, however; these are often termed qualitative variables.

Lack of continuity can take a variety of forms. In the most extreme case, the variable is dichotomous, meaning it can take one of two values; gender and union membership are examples. A variable can also be polychotomous, meaning it can take more than two discrete values. An example would be an attitudinal variable based on, say, a seven-point Likert scale ranging from "not satisfied" to "very satisfied." Such variables can be either "ordered" or "unordered." For example, the attitudinal variable mentioned above is ordered, but variables related to ethnic background or voting in a multicandidate election are unordered.

Limited Variables

Some variables are limited in that only part of their distribution can be observed (see, for example, fig. 4.1). Such variables can take a number of forms, the main ones being truncated and censored. Truncated variables are those for which information is available for only a limited range of the potential distribution. For example, in a negative income tax experiment in which information is collected only from households with an income below a threshold, truncation would occur at the upper bound since no data are collected from high-income households.

A variable is censored when some observations (typically on the dependent variable) are not observable. An example is the earnings of married women. Many do not participate in the labor market because their potential market wage is below the minimum wage at which they are prepared to

Figure 4.1a: Censoring/Truncation at the Upper Bound

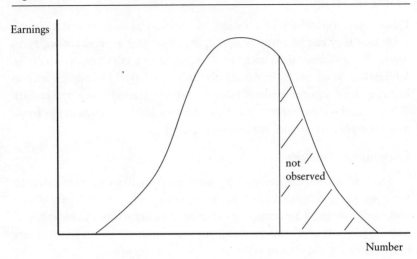

enter the workforce. In this case there is censoring at the lower bound, as in figure 4.1b.

The major difference between truncated and censored variables is that in the former case there is no information on the variable(s) generating the truncation, whereas in the latter case there is such information. Thus, when data are censored we know something about the characteristics of those about whom we do not have information concerning the variable in question and thereby possibly the factors causing the censoring. We know nothing about those who are excluded from a truncated sample.

Nonparametric Data

Nonparametric data are those that are either not drawn from sample populations with normal distributions or those that are ordinal/classificatory. The earnings distribution is an example of a nonnormal distribution; it is typically highly skewed, with more people earning income below the mean than above it (Phelps Brown 1977). Rank-order data, such as a ranking of countries by their incidence of industrial action, are examples of ordinal data. In both cases parametric methods, such as t-tests and ordinary least squares analysis, can be inappropriate and other methods termed nonparametric (see Sprent 1989) must be used.

Figure 4.1b: Censoring/Truncation at the Lower Bound

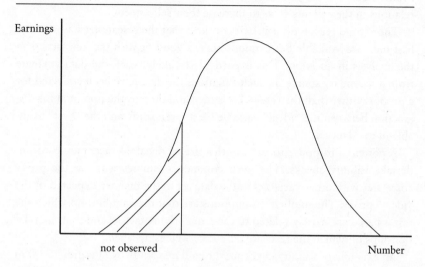

Proxies, Noise, and Validity

By their very nature, the variables entered into a quantitative analysis are representations (proxies) for the factors that are the focus of the research. Some are better proxies of the underlying factors than others. For example, if the objective of a research project is to examine the effect of training on earnings, it is better to have a proxy for training incidence that reflects both the duration and the quality of the training than one that simply indicates whether the individual concerned has undertaken training or not.

Where a variable is a poor proxy for the underlying factor, it introduces *noise* into the analysis. If such noise is randomly distributed, it is termed *white noise,* which will reduce the overall explanatory power of the analysis. If the noise is not random, it can also introduce *bias* into the estimates made of relationships within the data set. This is particularly serious if the bias affects key independent variables in a multivariate analysis. In this case there will be bias in estimates made of the relationships between dependent and independent variables. Thus, the effect of noise on quantitative analysis depends on whether it is white noise and whether it affects any independent variables.

Poor proxies occur for two main reasons. The first is bad measurement. This can be caused by inadequate measurement techniques or by bias in the reporting of information. The latter can be systematic, as in cases in which unions overreport their membership figures to gain extra votes in peak councils or in which personnel managers overrate the climate of industrial relations in their plants so as to increase their self-esteem.

The second reason poor proxies occur is that the researcher has used the best measure available but cannot obtain a good fit with the key factors in the analysis in question. This is particularly likely when the data emanate from a secondary source. In such situations the data have been collected for a purpose other than the researcher's own and there is the potential for disjunction between the "ideal" variable for a given study and the "best" available in the data set.

A potential response to proxies that are of debatable accuracy is to undertake validity checks. The most common examines whether the proxy correlates with other variables in the data set in the manner expected of the "ideal" proxy. The implicit assumptions are that the variables on which the test is based are closely related to these underlying factors and that the relationships on which the tests are based are well established.

An example of validity checking is found in a study by Huselid (1995) in which he investigated whether the introduction of "high-performance work practices" improves company performance. A scale proxying the intensity of adoption of such practices was constructed. This yielded two main factors that Huselid labeled "employee skills and organizational structures" and "employee motivation." Huselid found not only that these factors corresponded to his conceptual model but that they also correlated closely with two external measures indicating the degree to which firms value their employees—the ratio of human resources staff to total employees and whether human resources was emphasized in company reports. The factors were thereby deemed to be valid.

Validity checking is rare, however, in quantitative industrial relations research. The implicit assumption in most studies is that the proxies used are closely related to the variables in the underlying theoretical model.

Statistical Techniques

A plethora of techniques is available to the quantitative analyst. Which is chosen depends on a number of considerations. The first is the objective of the analysis, particularly whether a hypothesis is being tested or an empirical regularity is being uncovered. The second consideration is the complexity of the relationship being investigated, especially whether the phenomenon under examination is influenced by just one or (more usually) a number of underlying factors. The third consideration is the nature of the data being used and, in particular, that of the dependent variable.

Statistical techniques vary on a number of grounds but can be categorized as (1) univariate, bivariate, or multivariate; (2) if multivariate, whether they are based on least squares or maximum likelihood estimation techniques; (3) these can be further divided into techniques such as multiple regression, which estimate partial relationships among sets of variables, and other techniques, such as factor and cluster analysis, which identify patterns within a data set.

Univariate, Bivariate, and Multivariate Analysis

Univariate analysis is mainly concerned with whether the means for two populations differ significantly. An example of a univariate technique is the t-test, which indicates whether two mean scores are significantly different at a given confidence level. The test is based on the theory of probability and the drawing of random samples. An example of its use is found in a study by Noon (1990) that tested the hypothesis that newspapers owned by publishing groups are less likely to conclude new technology agreements (NTAs) with unions than those are not part of such groups. After estimating an NTA score for each newspaper, Noon shows that three of those in groups have significantly lower scores than those not in groups but that a fourth does not.

Bivariate analyses focus on the simple correlation between two variables. They show whether two variables have a tendency to move in the same or opposite directions, that is, whether they are positively or negatively correlated. For example, Brown Johnson, Bobko, and Hartenian (1992) divide job insecurity into two types—high source (caused by reorganization and decline) and low source (caused by arbitrary supervision and technological change). To test whether the two types are found in the same workplaces, they estimated a correlation coefficient, which indicated that the two types were positively but not strongly correlated.

Multivariate analysis is based on the principle that variations in a dependent variable are usually the result of variations in a number of underlying variables. It is therefore important to control for the influence of all these other variables on the dependent variable to uncover the "all other things being equal" or "pure" relationship between the explanatory variable and the dependent variable. Most multivariate analyses use a variant of the least squares technique, which is based on the principle of minimizing the sum of the squares of the vertical distances between a set of observations and a regression line (see fig. 4.2).

Figure 4.2: Principle of Least Squares

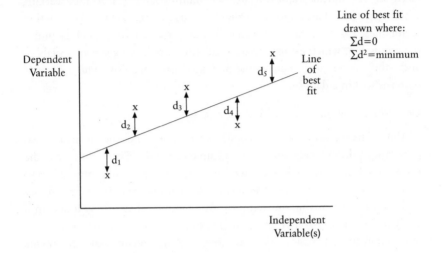

Least Squares and Maximum Likelihood

In many situations least squares analysis may not be appropriate. For example, if a dependent variable is not continuous or limited, a technique based on maximum likelihood estimation is generally more appropriate. Maximum likelihood estimation chooses the values of the estimates of the relationships between the dependent variable and the independent variables that are *most likely* to have generated the observed distribution of the dependent variable.

The main examples of statistical techniques using maximum likelihood estimation are *probit* and *logit* analysis. Where the dependent variable is dichotomous, either the binomial probit or logit models are used. If the dependent variable is polychotomous, the multinominal probit and logit models can be used.

The main principles underlying probit and logit analysis can be explained by reference to the example of estimating the determinants of individual union membership. In such a study the dependent variable indicates whether an individual is a union member or not. This is seen to be the outcome of an unobserved underlying index that can be termed "unionateness." Individuals with a unionateness score greater than zero become union members and those less than zero do not. An individual's unionateness is a reflection of a set of his or her personal and environmental characteristics, such as income, education, and family background. Thus, maximum likelihood estimation searches for the distribution of these characteristics that is most likely to have generated the observed division of individuals between union and nonunion members—that is, its maximum likelihood. From this it is possible to derive the unionateness score of each individual in the sample. For an example of such a study, see Stewart 1983.

Censored dependent variables can be estimated using the *tobit* model (Maddala 1983: 151–65), which uses information relating to the explanatory variables for those for whom the dependent variable is censored, in addition to information for those for whom it is not, to explain the distribution of the dependent variable between "1" and "0." Green (1990) uses tobit analysis in his examination of sex discrimination in job-related training. This is because the large majority of persons in his sample spent no time in training, causing the dependent variable to be censored. Estimating truncated dependent variables is more problematic and can be undertaken only following the invocation of strong assumptions about the distribution underlying the dependent variable (see Maddala 1983).

Correlations and Clusters

A crucial distinction between quantitative studies is between those that are focused on estimating correlations between variables and those such as factor and cluster analysis that are centered on uncovering patterns in a data set. Whereas the former focus on the size and direction of correlations between individual variables, the latter attempt to identify those groups of variables in a data set that are highly correlated.

Examples of the use of factor analysis can be found in the literature on labor market segmentation. The aim of this work is to ascertain whether labor markets exhibit a tendency to divide into distinctively different segments. Factor analysis is often used to test whether the variables suggested to differentiate labor market segments (such as capital intensity, establishment size, and product market concentration) are typically found together (are highly correlated) (Buchele 1983). If they are, it is suggested that there is a prima facie case that the industrial structure is segmented.

Statistical Modeling

No matter how good the data and how sophisticated the statistical technique used for estimation, they will yield good estimates only if the statistical model on which the analysis is based is compatible with the processes generating the data used. A statistical model is essentially an attempt to represent in an empirically analyzable form the processes that have generated the dependent variable under investigation.

A statistical model is composed of two main elements. The first element is the structure of the equations that are to be estimated. It could involve the estimation of just a single equation, reflecting a simple cause-and-effect relationship, or a system of interrelated equations, reflecting a more complex chain of causation. An example of the latter is research evaluating the effect of training on earnings. It is usually based on a model that allows for factors other than training that might influence earnings, including the processes by which individuals are selected for training. Unless these processes are properly controlled for, the estimate on the variable proxying training could be biased from its true value. For example, if participation in training is positively correlated with motivation (and therefore the individual's earnings potential), any simple estimate of the effect of training on earnings will be upwardly biased (conflating the returns to training and motivation). To achieve unbiased estimation requires that the separate effects of training and motivation on earnings be disentangled. If the selection process for training is random, estimation using a simple model involving just ordinary least squares could suffice. If not, a more complex model is needed, incorporating the process of selection into its structure.

The second key element in a statistical model is the method deployed to estimate each equation. This depends on interrelationships within the data set. For instance, in time-series analysis it is often the case that once-for-all events that affect dependent variables in one time period (e.g., an earthquake) also influence them in other periods (this is termed serial correlation or autocorrelation). In this situation the use of the ordinary least squares technique would yield estimates that would not be optimal. An alternative technique that allows for the correlations across time periods is needed.

Functional Form

Whatever statistical model is chosen, an important question that needs to be addressed is the *functional form* of each equation in that model. Functional form can broadly be defined as the manner in which the independent variables are entered into an equation. Key questions include the following: Should the variables be estimated in linear or nonlinear form? Is there potential for interaction between the explanatory variables? What is the direction of the causal relationship between correlated variables?

Nonlinearity

The majority of statistical relationships are modeled as linear; that is, the nature of their interrelationship can be viewed as taking the shape of a

Figure 4.3:   Typical Age-Earnings Profile

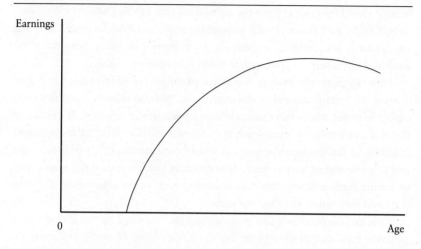

straight line. It is clear, however, that this is often only a crude approximation of the true relationship. Unless potential nonlinearity is properly allowed for, empirical estimates can be seriously biased. In practice, however, nonlinear relationships can take a variety of forms and it is rarely obvious which is most appropriate. Theory might suggest an appropriate form, but it is typically a poor guide in this respect. Furthermore, many nonlinear relationships are extremely complex and may not take the form that is most readily addressed.

In most cases researchers use one of a small number of nonlinear functions to convert nonlinear relationships into a linear form (thereby allowing estimation using linear techniques). An example is the use of the quadratic function in earnings analysis. The age-earnings profile is typically concave (see fig. 4.3), suggesting a nonlinear relationship between the two variables. To allow for this, researchers usually introduce both age and age squared (a quadratic function) into earnings equations. An alternative nonlinear transformation that is often used is to estimate the equation in the logarithm of the original variables. The prime example is in the estimation of the Cobb-Douglas production function in analyses of capital and labor productivity (see, for example, Freeman and Medoff 1984: chap. 11).

Interaction Effects

Many relationships in industrial relations are interdependent rather than independent. For example, it has been suggested that work practices promoting greater worker involvement are more effective if introduced in a mutually reinforcing bundle rather than in isolation. If so, the effect of the bundle could be greater than the sum of its parts (MacDuffie 1995). Similarly, Levine and Tyson (1990) suggest that employee-involvement schemes are typically successful in improving a company's performance only if introduced alongside an appropriate gain-sharing mechanism.

Thus, to properly analyze the effect of employee involvement and gain sharing on organizational performance, one should include variables indicating whether a firm has none, either, or both of the schemes. If the last of these is not explicitly examined, the estimate of the effect of the schemes could be biased because the analysis would conflate the effect of having just one scheme and of having both. This estimate is valid only if the joint effect of having both is simply the sum of having each of the schemes in isolation (i.e., additive rather than multiplicative).

Such interdependence can most simply be identified by the introduction of terms into an equation proxying the interaction. Typically, these are dichotomous (or dummy) variables taking the value of one if both elements are present and zero otherwise. If variables are also introduced for each of the factors in the bundle indicating whether they are present (either singly or jointly), it is also possible to estimate the effect of the presence of the factor on its own. It is thereby possible to see if the joint effect is greater than the two single effects. Thus, if an equation examining differential financial performance has positive and significant coefficient estimates on its interaction variables but on the noninteraction variables, it can be said that the joint effect is greater than the single effects (i.e., there is a multiplicative interaction).

Causality

Much industrial relations research is concerned with the identification of *causal relationships*. Many models that are estimated, however, are appropriate only for establishing *correlations* between variables. Such correlations could result from forces operating from the designated independent variables to the dependent variable, the reverse, or (more typically) a mixture of the two. A prime example is whether unions are able to establish a wage premium for their members over nonmembers. Many studies have found that union members earn more than otherwise similar nonmembers. The extent to which this difference is caused by the ability of unions to raise wages or by the fact that it is easier for unions to organize high-wage employees cannot be answered by simple correlation alone.

Causality can sometimes simply be inferred from the underlying theoretical model; in some cases it can also be tested. In time-series analysis the temporal patterns in a data set permit the construction of causality tests. An example is the Granger test. In its simplest form, current values of the dependent variable are regressed on lagged (previous time) values of both the dependent variable itself and the independent variables. If the coefficient estimates on the latter are not significantly different from zero, it can be said that the independent variables do not "Granger-cause" the dependent variable.

In cross-sectional analysis, it is more difficult to test for causality, since there is no inherent time element. Consequently, it is necessary to collect and analyze longitudinal information, such as panel data. As noted above, this information is difficult and expensive to collect, however, and is associated with numerous methodological problems. Good panel data are therefore rare.

In recent years there has been an increased propensity among industrial relations researchers to use the principles of causal modeling to test for causality. This has been associated with the development of the LISREL statistical package. The essence of this approach is that alternative causal models are specified and these are compared using various goodness-of-fit measures. Those models that are judged "best" are then tested to see if their goodness of fit can be improved by introducing variations into their causal structures. Bacharach, Bamberger, and Conley (1990) used this technique is their analysis of teacher militancy. (For further analysis of the use of LISREL in industrial relations research, see chapter 10, "Employee Attitude Surveys.")

A standard defense of those using cross-sectional data in a situation of potential multiple causality is to infer that the causing variable is established independently of the caused. For example, those inferring that unions cause the union wage premium rather than the reverse often assert that union organization is typically determined well in the past, whereas wage differentials are determined in the present. Union organization can therefore be regarded as being determined prior to and hence independently of wage differentials.

Beyond Single Studies

Meta-analysis

Increasingly, researchers are recognizing that single studies can rarely provide definitive tests of a hypothesis or ascertain unambiguously the "pure" relationship between factors. This has led to the practice of cumulating research findings across studies, or *meta-analysis* (Hunter, Schmidt, and Jackson 1982). Meta-analysis is extremely effective when there is a substantial body of research addressing similar questions but using different data sets or techniques and thereby obtaining varying results.

Meta-analysis attempts to explain why seemingly similar empirical analyses reach different conclusions. In some circumstances it can be used to correct for key differences (such as the techniques used for estimation or the variables used to hold all other things equal) and to produce a set of more comparable results. If a substantial difference in results still exists, the next step is to consider whether appropriate measures or techniques were used in the first place.

There are two main problems on which the typical meta-analysis focuses (Hunter, Schmidt, and Jackson 1982). The first problem is whether observed differences are due to what statisticians call artifacts. These are factors such as sampling differences, measurement differences, and different restrictions in range. The second problem is whether the variables used in the various studies are measuring the same thing. In this situation the meta-analysis involves a search for what are called moderator variables, which break the studies into subsets. Applying the techniques of meta-analysis to these subsets can uncover large differences in the mean values of these subsets, thereby allowing an assessment to be made of how much of the difference is due to artifacts and how much to measurement.

An example of the use of meta-analysis is a study by Jarrell and Stanley (1990) that examines the varying estimates of the union-nonunion wage gap. The study is based on 152 observations from 114 studies and concludes that observed differences in estimates stem from variations in the samples, the measures of wages, and the independent variables that are introduced to hold constant all the influences on wages other than union membership. Moreover, these are seen to vary across the economic cycle. By controlling for this, the authors reduced the range of estimates to 3.5 percentage points. Thus, a great deal of the variation observed is shown to stem from the time in the business cycle when the data were collected.

Triangulation

In some areas of quantitative research, there has been a tendency to cross-check (triangulate) by using alternative methods to examine the same problem (Jick 1979). An example has been work using both statistical and field experimental methods to ensure that all other things are equal. Such work has generally been undertaken to check the validity of different statistical modeling approaches and the assumptions that they make in applying different techniques, causal mechanisms, and functional forms.

Multivariate analysis enables a researcher to determine the influence of factors other than that of the explanatory variable on a dependent variable by statistical means. This usually involves the invocation of strong assumptions about the processes causing other things not to be equal. In some situations this can also be done by the use of random assignment. In this case a population is divided randomly into study (or treatment) and control groups. Those in the former group are allowed access to the "treatment" (a different tax regime or participation in a training scheme, for example), but those in the latter group are not. Thus, by design, the two groups are random samples of the original population except that members of one group experience the treatment and the members of the other group do not. Any difference in outcome (e.g., earnings) between the two groups can therefore be ascribed to whether they undertook the treatment (see chapter 5, "Experimental Methods," and Maynard 1994 for more detail on this technique).

Undertaking such a random experiment can potentially allow for triangulation with nonexperimental techniques that have used statistical methods to invoke the *ceteris paribus* clause. Such triangulation has been particularly important in evaluating evaluation studies. An example is a study by LaLonde (1986) that focuses on the impact on earnings of participating in a temporary employment program. The major issue addressed is how to allow for the effect on earnings of factors other than program participation. This is especially difficult because, as noted above, the factors influencing the propensity to participate are likely to be correlated with earnings potential—for example, motivation. Unless this is controlled for, any estimate of the "pure" relationship between participation and earnings will be biased. To allow for this, a variety of alternative statistical models have been suggested. These have yielded a wide range of estimates of the training effect.

LaLonde compares estimates derived from a random assignment experiment with those obtained using different statistical models. The assumption here is that the experimental estimates give the pure estimate. LaLonde finds that most statistical estimates of the training effect differ substantially from the experimental estimate but that some models differ less than others. Additionally, he shows that the size and direction of this difference vary systematically between demographic groups. His results can therefore potentially be used to choose between statistical models and to adjust for any inaccuracy in statistical modeling caused by invalid assumptions.

The use of field experiments to check the accuracy of different statistical techniques, models, or functional forms is potentially extremely important to the development of the quantitative approach. Field experiments are not unproblematic, however. First, such experiments are costly to conduct and in many cases impossible to construct. Second, they often raise ethical questions concerning the morality of denying access by some individuals to a "treatment" that could benefit the persons concerned. Third, it is possible that the outcome of the experiment might not be the "pure" (other things being equal) effect. For instance, factors other than the "treatment" might vary between the two groups, as in the Hawthorne experiment (see chapter 5, "Experimental Methods").

Conclusions and Implications

Quantitative methods have had and continue to have a major impact on research in industrial relations. Like any research method, however, quantitative analysis must be handled with care. Moreover, the poor application of quantitative methods can promote erroneous results and thereby misdirect policy formation and future research.

There are many elements to a good quantitative analysis. Four are outlined in this chapter—appropriate data, correct techniques, accurate modeling, and correct functional forms. Industrial relations researchers have generally been at the forefront in the use of the first of these but have tended to lag behind those in cognate disciplines in the other areas.

The high use of quantitative methods based on the strong logical positivist bedrock of economics is to some extent at odds with the more subjectivist approach to methodology that is found in industrial relations (Godard 1993). Such a disjunction suggests that the quantitative tail may be wagging the methodological dog. This is not to say, however, that much of the quantitative research undertaken in industrial relations has been wasted but simply that it might not have been guided by a sufficiently clear view of the role that such analysis can play in a subject area such as industrial relations. If the field is to respond strongly to the challenge that some have made to its academic status, there is an urgent need to pay more attention to such matters.

CHAPTER FIVE

Experimental Methods

Jan Bruins

E xperimental methods have been used in industrial relations mainly to
investigate questions at the level of individuals or small groups, such
as job satisfaction, turnover, job performance, group decision making,
coalition formation, and especially bargaining. The experimental method
enables researchers to test hypotheses about causal relations and as such
forms a key part of the scientific process of gaining knowledge. Since only
valid theories can provide us with meaningful ideas about how to redress
situations such as suboptimal outcomes in negotiations, low job satisfaction, and escalating conflicts, experimentation is an essential research tool.

In this chapter I first explain the nature of experimental methods. Then,
I describe how these methods work and why they should be used. Next, I
discuss the concepts of internal and external validity and describe specific
threats to both in laboratory and field experiments. Following this discussion, examples of research in industrial relations will be given to illustrate
the previous material. Finally, I discuss the contributions and limitations of
experimental methods.

What Is the Experimental Method?

The essence of the experimental method is that it allows us to determine if
a causal relationship exists between two variables by manipulating one (the
independent variable) and examining if there is a change in the other (the
dependent variable) while holding everything else constant (the *ceteris
paribus* principle). An example would be an investigation of the effect of
the size of one party's initial demand in a pay negotiation on the final out-

come of the negotiations. Such an experiment might involve a simulated negotiation in a laboratory. The independent variable might be manipulated by instructing half the participants to make a high initial demand and the other half a low demand. The dependent variable would be the final negotiation result. Keeping all other variables constant by giving all participants the same standardized instructions (apart from the manipulation), randomly assigning participants to the two experimental conditions, and using a standard laboratory setting enables the investigator to make the inference that if there is a difference in the final result negotiated by the two groups, it must be due to the manipulation of the size of the initial demand.

Some, but only some, of the advantages of the experimental method can also be obtained by using multivariate statistical analysis. The researcher using this approach would closely observe a large number of negotiations and for each negotiation record the initial demands made, the final result, and as many other potentially relevant variables as possible. Using statistical techniques such as regression analysis, path analysis, and structural equation modeling, the researcher would also be able to establish whether a relationship exists between initial demands and final outcomes. But because it is not possible with multivariate analysis to control the situation as stringently as is feasible in experimental settings, one cannot be entirely sure what the exact causal relationships are. For instance, it is always possible that the relationship between initial demands and final outcomes is due to the influence on both variables of a third unmeasured variable (e.g., mutual trust between the parties).

There are two types of experiments: laboratory and field. Laboratory experiments are carried out under standardized and controlled circumstances, as for the simulated negotiation described above. Field experiments are investigations carried out in "the field," that is, in the specific setting in which the phenomenon under investigation occurs. For example, a new approach to employee supervision might be tried out with real workers on a factory floor.

Internal and External Validity: Control versus Generalizability

Internal validity refers to the extent to which "we infer that a relationship between two variables is causal or that the absence of a relationship implies the absence of cause" (Cook and Campbell 1979: 37). High internal validity can be achieved through rigorous control of the experimental situation. The more certain we can be that an experiment was conducted under controlled circumstances, and therefore that "all else was held constant," the more confident we can be that our manipulation of the independent variable is the cause of differences found on the dependent variable, that is, the higher the experiment's internal validity.

Manipulation of the independent variable(s) is guided by the experimental design chosen by the researcher. One of the most frequently used experimental designs consists of two groups (usually referred to as the experimental and the control group), which for each dependent variable are compared on two measures: measures taken before the experimental induction is introduced and measures taken after the experimental induction is introduced. Although there are many other experimental designs (see Cook and Campbell 1979), in this chapter we will limit ourselves to this so-called untreated control group design with pretest and posttest.

External validity refers to the extent to which "we can infer that the presumed causal relationship can be *generalized* to and across alternate measures of the cause and effect and across different types of persons, settings, and times" (Cook and Campbell 1979: 37; emphasis added). High external validity can be achieved by using multiple operationalizations of the independent and dependent variables, sampling participants from the various populations to which we want to be able to generalize findings, and carrying out the research in different settings and times. Since establishing external validity in this way will often require multiple experiments, external validity can be thought of as a topic of investigation rather than as a feature that can be built into each separate experiment. In practice, external validity most often refers to generalizations to specific populations (e.g., managers, union members, workers) or settings (e.g., organizations, negotiation settings, the work floor). The main issue thus becomes the extent to which the participants in an experiment, and the setting in which the experiment was carried out, are representative of the real-life situations to which one wants to generalize the results of the experiment.

In general, experiments carried out in laboratories are highly *internally valid* because the setting enables the researcher to maintain considerable *control* over all relevant aspects of the situation that is being investigated, thus enabling the researcher to find *causal relationships* between variables. This control is achieved at the expense of *external validity,* however, which is hampered by the type of *participants* in the experiment and the limited *reality* of the experimental situation, making it harder to generalize the results to real-life situations. Thus, the high internal validity of lab experiments is achieved at the expense of their external validity. Field experiments, by contrast, allow for less control (lower internal validity) but are more realistic and therefore allow for wider generalization of the results (higher external validity).

Threats to Internal Validity

One feature detrimental to internal validity is that a third variable provides an explanation for the presence of a relationship between two variables. An example was indicated in the negotiation study above, in which mutual trust influenced both the initial demands made *and* the final negotiation result. Two ways to deal with this threat are (1) to measure the possible third variable and statistically control for its effect through an analysis of covariance and (2) to manipulate the possible third variable to investigate the extent to which its effect is distinct from that of the independent variable. In general, threats to internal validity can be dealt with satisfactorily in lab experiments. Field experiments, however, are quite susceptible to such threats.[1] The main threats to internal validity are history, maturation, testing, instrumentation, selection, and mortality.

History

History occurs when something other than an intended manipulation happens between pretests and posttests, rendering it uncertain whether an observed change is due to the experimental manipulation or to the unforeseen occurrence. For example, if two companies with different management styles are compared on employee job satisfaction and one company unexpectedly has to go through a reorganization process, an eventual difference in job satisfaction could be due to either the difference in management styles or to the reorganization.

Unfortunately, unexpected events can occur during the course of field experiments. Especially in lab experiments, however, there are ways to prevent history. Through rigorous control of the experimental situation, the researcher can make sure that participants experience exactly the same things under all conditions except for variations in the independent variables. The behavior of the experimenter can be controlled by keeping him or her ignorant ("blind") of the specific condition each participant has been assigned. The use of lab controls for most environmental factors (e.g., ensuring that there are no distractions) and standardizing (e.g., computerizing) the experiment can provide exact control over the experimental procedure.

1. Space limitations do not allow a full description of these matters, but an excellent book on this topic is Cook and Campbell's *Quasi-Experimentation* (1979).

Another tool that may be used is deception. Usually this takes the form of misleading participants about the actual aim of the study. The reason for doing this is that in research situations people usually try to make good impressions on the experimenter by bringing about the result that they think the researcher wants to obtain. Because of ethical considerations, however, deception should be used only when essential, and once an experiment involving deception is over, participants should be told about the nature of and reasons for the deception.

Maturation

Maturation occurs because participants get older, wiser, and more experienced over the course of an experiment and this may have differential effects on an experimental and a control group. Maturation is particularly problematic when there is a long period between pretest and posttest or when the participants are themselves changing fast (as in the case of new members of an organization) *and* participants in the experimental and control groups are maturing at different rates. Because lab experiments are usually fairly short-lived, maturation is hardly ever a problem, and even though field experiments may be carried out over a fairly long period of time, it is unlikely that people in the different conditions will mature at different rates.

Testing

Testing occurs when dependent measures such as questionnaires are administered more than once and the participants' answers change because of boredom, annoyance with the measure, or any other such tendency. Answers to job satisfaction questionnaires could become more negative among members of a control group if the participants in this group saw less reason for taking these repeated measurements than workers in the experimental group. Again, in lab experiments, control of the experimental situation can strongly reduce testing. In both lab and field experiments, testing can be further minimized by using unobtrusive dependent measures, such as video recordings of negotiation processes. If this is not feasible, dependent measures should be used sparingly.

Instrumentation

Instrumentation occurs when the measuring instrument changes between the pretest and the posttest. The "measuring instrument" should be considered broadly to include, for example, observers who during the course of an experiment may become more experienced, sensitive, or bored. For example, when observing negotiation processes over time, raters may learn to pick up subtle nonverbal cues that they did not notice at the start of the investigation. It is therefore recommendable to provide observers with specific instructions, thorough training, and prestructured observation schemes that provide clear categories for the various events they have to record. In general, researchers should always define their dependent measures clearly and derive from their definitions unambiguous measuring instruments, for example, rating scales for measuring satisfaction, time for measuring negotiation efficiency, or observation schemes for measuring behavior.

Selection

Selection occurs when there are unintended differences between the two groups of participants stemming from the procedure used to assign people to the various groups. These differences can be minimized in two ways, both of which are harder to implement in field than experimental settings. One way is to assign participants randomly to the two groups, thus ensuring that on average they have the same characteristics. If this is not feasible, another strategy is to match participants in the control group with those in the experimental group. Matching should be done on characteristics relevant to the research question under investigation. In a study on work productivity, workers could be matched on motor skills; in a study on bargaining, organizations could be matched on trade union membership among their workers.

Mortality

Mortality occurs because people drop out of the experiment. An example is a bargaining study in which the bargaining process is longer for the experimental condition than for the control condition. This could result in more experimental than control participants not finishing before the end of the experiment. Because the slower participants who did not finish in time may differ systematically from the faster ones who are included in the study (e.g., slower participants may have tried to drive a harder bargain), it remains uncertain what the outcome of the experiment would have been had all the participants been included in the final sample.

Because lab experiments are highly controlled and fairly short-lived, mortality is rarely a problem. It may be a problem in field experiments, however, and once it has occurred it cannot be repaired. Nonetheless, it is still possible to investigate the extent to which mortality forms an actual threat (see also Cook and Campbell 1979: 360–63). First, the researcher should compare attrition rates under the various conditions. If these rates are similar, the chances that there is a mortality problem are slim if it can be assumed that the reasons participants dropped out of the experiment are the same under all conditions. Second, the participants who remain should be compared with each other on background data such as demographic characteristics to establish the extent to which they were similar at the outset of the experiment. Similarity will strengthen faith in the internal validity of the experimental results. Third, and finally, by extending the experimental design, participants remaining in the experiment should be compared with those who dropped out, using the pretest measures as dependent variables, to find out if differences in the characteristics of the dropouts and the survivors might have affected the final results.

Summary

In sum, field experiments are prone to many threats to their internal validity. The challenge for the researcher is to conduct the experiment so that problems can either be avoided or controlled. In general, the two main ways to avoid threats to internal validity are to choose the experimental design with care and to try to measure all relevant variables. With regard to the experimental design, using the untreated control group design with pretest and posttest will usually enable the researcher to deal with a number of the threats, especially if it is possible to assign participants to conditions randomly (matching is a second-best option). With regard to the second solution, measuring relevant variables will enable the researcher to maintain statistical control over the results so that if unforeseen changes occur, he or she will be able to keep track of their effects and statistically control for them by partialing out their effects using analysis of covariance.

Issues concerning External Validity

External validity can refer to generalizations to many different domains, but in practice the main ones concern the type of people and the specific settings to which experimental results can be applied. As far as generalizations to specific populations are concerned, the crucial issue is how and from which population the participants in the experiment were sampled. Random sampling from a certain population (students, citizens of Amsterdam, rowers) will enable us to generalize our findings to that specific population. It is important to remember, though, that especially in the case of a field experiment, random samples are hard to obtain because of problems in getting access to and recruiting sufficient numbers of suitable people who are able and willing to participate in the experiment.

Stratified sampling involves taking random subsamples from the different populations to which we want to generalize our results. The subsamples can differ on various dimensions such as socioeconomic status, gender, or age. Again, drawing subsamples on a random basis is extremely hard to do.

With sampling procedures other than random and stratified sampling, one has to be careful when attempting to generalize results and should generalize only to populations that are similar in relevant characteristics to the obtained sample. Similar generalization problems exist with respect to the time at which the data were obtained and the specific setting in which the experiment was conducted. Economic conditions may change through time, rendering it questionable whether results obtained before a period of economic growth or decline are still valid. Also, results obtained in one type of organization (e.g., banks) may not apply to other organizations (e.g., transport).

Survey research does not usually involve experimental control or manipulation and is generally not particularly engaging for participants. Thus, for this type of research, the sampling procedures and generalizability of results are not usually serious problems.

Results obtained in field experiments usually are generalizable to real-life situations similar to the field in which the experiment was carried out. Also, the participants in field research are usually people who "belong" in the settings in which the research is carried out (employees on the shop floor, union leaders in bargaining situations, arbitrators involved in conflicts). Nonetheless, results obtained in one field setting should be generalized to similar settings only and may not be generalizable to a different time period.

In contrast to field experiments, lab situations and participants in lab experiments are usually quite different from those found in daily life. Lab experiments thus have limited generalizability.

The most thorough approach to obtaining external validity is to make it the subject of investigation. The generalizability of results can be checked by using stratified sampling or by carrying out similar experiments using participants from different populations. Similarly, we can check generalizability through time by replicating a past experiment. This is necessary only if there has been a change in, for example, cultural or social circumstances that might affect the validity of previously obtained results. Results from field research on bargaining carried out in a time of economic growth might not apply during a recession, for instance.

Finally, generalizability beyond a specific setting can be investigated by repeating the original experiment in a new setting. For instance, the best way to find out if results on the effects of a new worker participation scheme in a large metal works are applicable to small restaurants is to repeat the original experiment in the restaurant business.

Illustrative Examples

Workplace Change

Around 1930, several field experiments were carried out in the Hawthorne plant of the Western Electric Company (Roethlisberger and Dickson 1939). These yielded dramatic findings and also had great influence on industrial relations research and practice. These studies were carried out in different parts of the plant. The relay assembly test room study investigated the effects of (among other things) the introduction of a new incentive system, a simpler task, rest breaks, a shorter working day, and (later) the replacement of two out of five workers with more motivated people. After these changes were made, productivity increased dramatically.

Since they were carried out in a field setting, the Hawthorne studies had good external validity. There is evidence that they lacked internal validity, however. For instance, there was no control group with which the task performance of the experimental group could be compared. The only comparison that could be made was between performance before and after the introduction of the changes, leaving open the possibility that the change in performance could have been due to the effect of an extraneous variable. Also, the study was carried out over such a long period (six years) that maturation may have affected the results. Over the six years, workers' attitudes, expectations, or skills may have changed considerably. The replacement of two workers by more motivated people is evidence that history occurred. Finally, the simultaneous introduction of several changes makes it hard to say which one was ultimately responsible for the increase in productivity (but see Franke and Kaul 1978). Thus, critical evaluation of the studies suggests that they were not as definitive as some have suggested (Carey 1967 and Franke and Kaul 1978).

Worker Participation

Coch and French (1948) investigated how different degrees of participation in job design in a pajama factory affected work performance and the learning of new job skills. One of the frequent occasions in which employees' tasks were changed was used to set up the field experiment. Three experimental groups were created. Workers in the full participation group—pajama examiners—attended a meeting at which a new way of working was devised. Those in the limited participation group—pajama folders—were represented in the decision-making meetings by a few of their colleagues. Finally, those in the control group—hand pressers—were simply told about the new job arrangements by management.

The three groups of workers were roughly matched on pretreatment efficiency ratings, the degree of change involved in their tasks, and the amount of pretreatment group cohesion. It was found that fully participating workers learned more quickly (and increased their performance more quickly) than the other two groups of workers.

Even though, in this case, the workers in the three groups were matched on certain variables, one can never be sure that an important variable was not overlooked. There is at least one concurrent variable, namely, the worker's task. Although workers were matched on the degree of change in their tasks, that their tasks were different may have affected how fast the workers learned their new skills. Without appropriate control groups, this alternative explanation cannot be ruled out.

That Coch and French carried out their research in a field setting gives the study good external validity. Generalizability can never be assumed, however, without careful consideration of the specific setting in which the research was undertaken. This was demonstrated in an attempt by French, Israel, and Ås (1960) to replicate Coch and French's findings in a Norwegian shoe factory. In this latter study, no difference in production was found between (unmatched) experimental and control groups. The possible reasons French, Israel, and Ås cited for their failure to replicate the earlier findings were the stronger group production norm in Norway; the stronger union tradition in Norway, which may have resulted in a different attitude toward worker participation; and the fact that the decisions in which the workers could participate were more important in the U.S. study, resulting in a stronger manipulation of participation. Thus, even with field experiments, external validity can never be taken for granted.

The Coch and French (1948) findings are in line with what might be expected. An experiment that yielded rather counterintuitive results was carried out by Mulder and Wilke (1970), who showed that participation in decision making by less powerful people does not always lead to a decrease in differences in influence and power but that this reduction is contingent on the relative expertise of the parties involved. Mulder and Wilke invited students from a high school for teachers' training to their lab and told each participant that, together with someone else who was in another room, they would be deciding on the location of a hospital as part of a town planning project. Communication with the "other" would be by means of written messages. In fact, the other did not actually exist, and the messages were prepared in advance to control for the partner's behavior. The partner's *expertness* was manipulated by varying the amount of task-relevant information the partner allegedly provided to the participant. The amount of *participation* was also manipulated. In the high-participation condition, twice as much time was available to exchange information as in the low-participation condition.

The results indicated that under both participation conditions participants were more strongly influenced by the partner and accepted the partner's power to a larger extent when the partner had high expertise than when the partner had low expertise. This difference was much more significant, however, under the high-participation condition than under the low-participation condition.

The internal validity of this experiment was very high. In a lab environment participants were randomly assigned to conditions, given standard instructions, and deceived to some extent; dependent measures were taken by means of standardized questions, and there was no mortality. Thus the researchers could be fairly certain that they had uncovered causal relationships between participation, expertise, and influence. The findings cannot be readily generalized, however. First, the participants in the experiment were students, and it could well be that (older) workers and managers in real organizations would deal with this type of situation differently. Second, the task was very specific, and different tasks might generate different interpersonal processes. Also, the fact that a lab setting was used where participants were seated in separate cubicles and communicated through written messages is different from real-life settings and communication processes. Third, and finally, the participants' responses were restricted to answering standard attitude questions, whereas outside the lab people of course have many ways of responding to attempts to influence their behavior and to interpersonal communications.

Arbitration

Research suggests that in discipline cases arbitrators tend to be more lenient toward female than toward male grievants. Bemmels (1991) examined two explanations for this finding: (1) arbitrators attribute less blame to female than to male grievants or (2) arbitrators attribute equal blame but are more lenient toward female than toward male grievants.

Written scenarios describing a discharge case were mailed to a sample of arbitrators, who completed a questionnaire that asked them to indicate the extent to which they thought management was responsible for the incident that led to the discharge, the extent to which the grievant was responsible, and their preferred decision. High internal validity was achieved by introducing manipulations of independent variables by varying certain wordings in the scenarios, such as the indication of the gender of the grievant, and by randomly assigning participants to experimental conditions. External validity was achieved by conducting the experiment among people who were active arbitrators.

The results indicated that arbitrators treated male and female grievants in the same way as far as attributing blame was concerned, but that with blame held constant, arbitrators gave smaller penalties to female than to male grievants. Although participants were randomly sampled from the membership lists of professional arbitrator organizations, the fact that only 53 percent of the questionnaires were returned still raises the question of the extent to which *these* arbitrators were representative of the population as a whole.

Olson, Dell'Omo, and Jarley (1992), in a novel approach, combined two different research methods to investigate decision rules employed by arbitrators of union-management contract disputes. In a lab experiment, professional arbitrators decided thirty-two hypothetical disputes between a police union and a city that were described to them in scenarios that varied in several respects (e.g., employee working conditions and cost of living). A field study investigated nineteen arbitrators' actual decisions in 208 real-life teacher disputes in Wisconsin that differed from each other on aspects similar to those in the police disputes.[2]

When the authors compared the factors that influenced the arbitrators' decisions in the disputes in which one particular issue (wage) was at stake, the two approaches were found to lead to very similar results: union offers were chosen more often the higher the wage increases in comparable bargaining units and the lower the community tax rate. This research has high internal and external validity. Because of its internal validity, the lab experiment reveals causal relationships, and the strong resemblance between the two sets of results indicates that the findings have considerable external validity as well.

---

2. Formally, this field study was not an experiment because the researchers used archival data on the disputes and thus did not manipulate any independent variables.

Bargaining

Bargaining partners usually differ in their abilities to use coercive power. Lawler, Ford, and Blegen (1988) investigated two theoretical ideas that predict different results in the use of coercive power and concessionary behavior. They invited participants to a lab and had them negotiate in dyads. Participants negotiated over points, and, depending on the coercive power condition, they had the capacity to take away either 10 percent or 90 percent of the points owned by the other party. Dependent measures consisted of the frequency with which participants took away points, the amount of concessions made to the other party, and questionnaire measures. The results indicated that higher mutual power led to a lower expectation of the other party using his or her power, less use of actual punitive power, and more concessions.

The internal validity of this study is very high, but the extent to which the results can be generalized to real-life work settings is questionable. The two parties are equal to each other except with respect to the aspects manipulated by the researchers. In actual bargaining situations, there is always one major difference between parties: unions and management have clearly distinct roles.

The effects of these roles on how members of the two parties perceive both themselves and the other party and how their different roles might influence bargaining behavior has been investigated by Haire (1955). Haire built on previous experimental research (Asch 1946) that had found that people rated others who were described by a number of adjectives including the word "cold" much more negatively than others described with the *same* adjectives except that "cold" was replaced by "warm." Haire investigated whether describing someone as "a local manager of a small plant which is a branch of a large manufacturing concern" or as "secretary-treasurer of his union" would have similar effects on both a group of workers and a group of managers. Not surprisingly, the results showed that union people perceived other union people more positively than they did management people—and vice versa.

With regard to bargaining behavior, a subsequent analysis of verbal protocols from actual bargaining sessions revealed that union members made more tentative than definite statements and more often made requests than nonnegotiable statements. Exactly the opposite pattern was found for managers.

Haire's (1955) study illustrates how experimental findings from one study, which has little apparent relevance to industrial relations, can suggest other experiments that do have direct relevance to industrial relations. The crucial issue is to replace a core characteristic of the original experiment with a *similar* but more specific element that plays a role in industrial relations. For example, a large number of experimental studies in social psychology address intergroup phenomena in general terms (for an overview, see Messick and Mackie 1989); however, interesting (and highly applicable) findings could be obtained by replacing the "minimal groups" used in many of these studies by "workers" versus "managers," in a way similar to the approach taken by Haire (1955).

Contributions of Experimental Methods to Industrial Relations

The potential contributions of experimentation to research in industrial relations are twofold. First, experimentation enables causal relationships to be discovered. Although still subject to criticism, the studies by Mulder and Wilke (1970), Bemmels (1991), and Lawler, Ford, and Blegen (1988) are good examples. Knowing that A *causes* B provides not only more precise information than merely knowing that A and B covary; it also provides a tool for *change*. If we know what causes bad negotiation outcomes, worker dissatisfaction, or low performance, we can use this knowledge to improve matters. Without knowledge about causation, attempts to alleviate undesirable conditions will remain a process of trial and error.

Second, experiments allow us to investigate underlying psychological processes. Bemmels (1991), Lawler, Ford, and Blegen (1988), and Haire (1955), for example, revealed the importance of attributions, expectations, and interpersonal perceptions. Thus they helped us understand *why* people behave as they do. Again, this knowledge can be used to implement change. The Lawler, Ford, and Blegen (1988) study, for instance, indicates that during negotiations the parties may be more encouraged to make concessions when they indicate to each other that they will not use their coercive capabilities, thereby reducing mutual expectations that "the other" might use its power and in so doing reduce the probability of its detrimental use.

Limitations of Experimental Research

To some extent, the advantages and disadvantages of experimental research are related to each other through a trade-off between internal and external validity. High internal validity requires tight experimental control but reduces generalizability. Thus, there is a trade-off in that the more applicable we want our results to be, the less sure we can be about causal relationships, and vice versa. Keeping this in mind, the main limitations of experimental research in industrial relations are twofold.

The first limitation is that several external influences that have an impact on processes in industrial relations fall beyond the scope of experimental research. The effects of various economic, social, and cultural factors are too large scale for internally valid experimental research because they cannot be controlled. Other factors that are smaller in scale but equally hard to control include market forces, technological change, and changes in government regulations. Investigation of the impact of these matters clearly demands a different methodological approach.

The second set of limitations is more relevant to lab than to field research. Much lab research is very short-lived, and participants are not as highly involved as they are in real-life settings. Moreover, in most experiments nothing is at stake for the participants, contrary to real life. Finally, subjects are typically undergraduate students, suggesting caution in generalizing results beyond an undergraduate population.

In principle, some of these drawbacks can be dealt with. In practice, this is not usually done. Issues of generalizability are often mentioned as aims for future research, but the internal dynamics of the scientific cycle seem to be a more powerful inducer of research that deepens our understanding than of research that broadens the limits of its applicability. Research always provides both answers to the original research question and new questions. Instead of researching how and where the obtained answer can be applied, the more usual observation is that subsequent research needs to address one of the new questions.

Among the examples described in this chapter are a number of studies that, although their internal validity leaves something to be desired, are generalizable to real-life problem situations (e.g., Coch and French 1948; Olson, Dell'Omo, and Jarley 1992; Roethlisberger and Dickson 1939). That these studies were carried out in the field makes it easier to generalize their results to practical situations. This jump is much bigger for lab experiments, although these are typically more valid internally.

Conclusions

Experimental methods have made a significant impact on research on the world of work. They are not easy to use, however, and typically result in findings that are difficult to apply. They are especially powerful, though, when allied with other methods, particularly when their role is to check the internal validity of studies yielding highly externally valid results. The reverse is true also: the generalizability of causal relationships found in experimental research can be established in subsequent research using other methods described in this volume. Thus, either as a stand-alone method or in combination with other approaches, experimentation has much to offer industrial relations research.

CHAPTER SIX

The Role and Challenge of Case Study Design in Industrial Relations Research

Jim Kitay and Ron Callus

A case could be made that the case study is the most favored research design used by industrial relations researchers. The use of cases in industrial relations research goes back at least to the Webbs (1902), whose seminal work in the United Kingdom was based on an intensive study of the histories and practices of several trade unions. Similarly, Kaufman (1993: 33) notes that case studies were an important device used by the early institutionalists in the United States. While theoretical and methodological fashions have changed in industrial relations over time, the case study continues to be widely used.

The ongoing popularity of case studies reflects the multidisciplinary character of industrial relations research. More important, it manifests the desire by industrial relations researchers to provide explanations and an understanding of complex social phenomena, for which case studies are particularly well suited. In addition, the importance of institutional analysis in industrial relations lends itself to the use of case studies because of the complexities of institutions. Industrial relations deals not simply with "objective" facts but with values and perceptions and therefore requires methods that are able to access a range of information sources and so assist in making sense of the subjective elements of social and economic life. Another reason for the popularity of case studies is that they can be conducted with limited resources, although this by no means is meant to suggest that they can be done properly with little training, planning, or effort. Indeed, good case studies often require a great deal of time and effort.

Case studies have helped shape the work of successive generations of industrial relations researchers. Early case studies included Lipset, Trow, and

Coleman's (1956) investigation of democracy in one union, Gouldner's (1954b) work on a wildcat strike, and Flanders's (1964) analysis of the Fawley productivity agreements. More recently, Batstone, Boraston, and Frenkel (1977, 1978) examined workplace trade unionism and the process of industrial action in one enterprise.

Many of the key insights into the changing nature of work in the mass-production and continuous process industries were based on case studies (Goldthorpe et al. 1968; Beynon 1984; Nichols and Beynon 1977). More recent debates continue in the same vein (Mathews 1994; Berggren 1992). Kochan, Katz, and McKersie ([1986]1994), who have had such a significant impact on industrial relations research in the United States, relied heavily on material based on case studies. As Stoecker notes in a different context, given the importance of case studies as a source of ideas and explanations, it is difficult to understand the tendency of some researchers to treat them with disdain, as "barely better than journalism" (1991: 88).

This chapter explores the nature of case studies and how they are conducted. It will be argued that case studies are a research strategy rather than a specific technique and as such can serve a variety of purposes and make use of a range of techniques. An outline is given of some of the activities involved in undertaking case studies, including project design and the selection of cases, gaining entry to research sites, and collecting and analyzing data. There are no clear protocols for their use, but there are many potential traps for the unwary.

What Are Case Studies?

There is no agreed-upon definition of "case study." Some writers, such as Orum, Feagin, and Sjoberg (1991), suggest that they are typified by the use of qualitative research methods. On occasion, however, quantitative techniques may be used and indeed may constitute the primary means of data collection (Goldthorpe et al. 1968). Yin (1994) restricts his definition of case studies to contemporary phenomena, but this is an unnecessary limitation, particularly in view of the significant contribution to industrial relations made by historical studies of workers and unions (Commons 1909; Turner 1962) and more recently management (Gospel and Littler 1983).

According to Platt (1988: 2), more than one case may be included in a research project, but each case should be treated as an individual entity, and the sheer number of cases is not a primary consideration. Placing phenomena in their wider context is an important element of case studies (Yin 1994).

Thus, the case study can be defined as *a research strategy or design that is used to study one or more selected social phenomena and to understand or explain the phenomena by placing them in their wider context.*

In adopting this definition, we suggest that to understand a phenomenon in its context, a range of information needs to be collected. Therefore, although case studies do not inherently involve several techniques, in practice they often require researchers to make use of more than one, and often many, different research methods. This highlights a common misconception—that the "case study" is a method or research technique in itself. Similarly, case studies are often confused with the technique of observation, or with qualitative methods more generally. Although case studies often use qualitative methods, more accurately case studies should be seen as a research strategy (Yin 1994) that uses one or more techniques or methods. As such the case study often involves all or some of the following techniques: semi- and unstructured interviews, archival work, structured questionnaire surveys, and observation.

Elements of a Good Case Study

Despite the popularity of case study design among industrial relations researchers, there are no universally accepted standards for its use. What makes one case study complete and rigorous and another superficial and unacceptable is often not readily apparent. In some instances case studies may cover an extensive range of sources using a variety of techniques but none of them intensively, while others may use fewer data sources but exploit them more fully. It remains an open question as to the relative merits of these often opposing approaches. Like many research issues, achieving the right balance requires judgment and experience and depends on the time and resource constraints facing the researcher. Case study research remains more of an art than a science, notwithstanding attempts by some authors to inject a greater degree of rigor into the approach (e.g., Yin 1994).

The lack of well-established protocols for case research explains the wide variation in the approach. For example, some studies rely mostly on information supplied by key informants, such as managers and union delegates, while others are based largely on employee surveys. However, most case study researchers rely on a range of methods. It can be argued that there is no "best" method in research; rather, there are simply techniques that are better suited to generating some types of data than others (Zelditch 1970).

In evaluating case studies, it is possible to evaluate the techniques that are used according to the well-established standards of those methods; however, whether the researcher's choice of particular techniques was appropriate to obtain the necessary information also needs to be addressed. For example, a case study examining consultative committees may shed light on the impact of the committees on employee attitudes or work practices, but this is inadequate if no attempt is made to examine the minutes of the committees over the past few years, the ways in which decisions were reached, or the purposes for which the committees were used. Similarly, intensive observation of the relations between management and employees in one workplace is likely to provide deep insights into the processes that generate conflict and cooperation, but the task of ascertaining how widely these conditions prevail among various workplaces would remain.

The great strength of case study design is not simply that it is a way to gather information efficiently but that it allows the researcher to place the information in a wider context. In other words, it helps us understand complex social situations and processes. Case studies can also promote the generation of new ideas and theory development. Thus, although an important use of case studies is exploratory, they can also be used in combination with other approaches for explanatory purposes or quite adequately serve the purposes of explanation in themselves.[1]

Case Study Design

When does a research topic lend itself to case study? In addition to the important practical considerations of time, access, and resources, the choice of a research strategy depends largely on the research question being posed. Yin (1994: 6) suggests that case studies lend themselves best to answering "how?" and "why?" questions. In other words, they are most appropriate for examining the processes by which events unfold, as well as for exploring causal relationships. The case study is particularly well suited to researching motives, power relations, or processes that involve understanding complex social interactions.

A key issue in deciding to undertake a case study is whether a holistic understanding of a phenomenon is required. Case studies, by their nature, deal with the complex relations within a unit as well as the interaction between the unit and its wider environment. Often the distinction between a phenomenon and its context is unclear. In *Working for Ford,* most of

---

1. For an excellent discussion of possible purposes of case studies and a justification of their use for explanatory purposes, see chapter 1 of Yin 1994.

Beynon's (1984) data were gathered through interviews and observation at one site, but he found it necessary to use other methods to gain information on the operations of the company as a whole, without which the activities and perspectives he encountered would have been difficult to understand.

Another key issue is the extent to which questions of interpretation may be involved or if the answer to the research question concerns a complex chain of causal events. Certainly discrete incidents, such as a particular industrial dispute, require a case study approach almost by definition. More important for much present-day debate, it is difficult to know whether organizations are responding to changing product market conditions by introducing more flexible working arrangements and greater levels of employee involvement without at some point undertaking detailed analyses of particular enterprises (Kochan and Piore 1990).

In embarking on case study research, one must decide the boundaries that will define the case. This includes the unit of analysis on which the case will be based and how many cases will be involved. By "unit of analysis," we mean the object of the case study. This may be, for example, events (Krause 1992), individuals (d'Alpuget 1977), workplaces (Edwards and Scullion 1982), occupations (Ouellet 1994), organizations (Smith, Child, and Rowlinson 1990), industries (Cappelli 1985), communities (Patmore 1997), or even nations (Turner 1991). It is possible, however, that the unit of analysis that the case study is "about" may be understood only when information is obtained from case studies conducted within other units of analysis. For example, a case study of the changing nature of industrial relations in an industry may require detailed case studies to be undertaken of particular organizations within those industries (Berggren 1992; Kitay and Lansbury 1997). Similarly, Turner's (1991) comparison of Germany and the United States was based largely on case studies of plants.

Thus, specifying the boundaries of the unit or site of analysis does not artificially restrict the study, in that one of the key features of case study research is the ability to explore the relationship between a unit and its wider environment in considerable detail. It is essential, however, that the researcher not attempt to generalize from one unit of analysis to another without strong grounds for doing so. There are no clear guidelines on this matter, and much will depend on the design of the study and the nature of the units of analysis in a particular instance. For example, most major banks have elaborate regulations about branch operations, which make it likely that a study of a small number of branches will yield information that can be generalized with a fair degree of confidence. This is less likely to be true in, for example, multidivisional manufacturing enterprises. Similarly, it is well known that the branches of a trade union may differ considerably in different locations.

Selecting Cases

Although the selection of cases in case study research is not based on the same sampling logic that is used in surveys (although a survey conducted as an integral part of a case study should adhere to the appropriate sampling protocols), nevertheless, a set of criteria similar to the process of stratified sampling is often employed.[2] In other words, the researcher may wish the case study or studies to reflect particular characteristics of the population, such as its size, level of unionization, management style, or technology. It is important for the researcher to know what the case study is seeking to highlight or explain.

In most instances the selected case study will represent some aspect or feature of the population. This does not mean that the case study is representative of the population. The case study may in some cases be atypical or illustrative. To this extent it is important to have a sound knowledge of the characteristics of the population. A good example of the use of a nonrepresentative case was Goldthorpe et al.'s (1968) study of affluent workers in the automobile industry. To examine whether the process of embourgeoisment—the adoption by working-class individuals of middle-class attitudes and practices—was occurring, Goldthorpe and his colleagues selected a research site on theoretical grounds where the phenomenon was most likely to be found. If evidence of the phenomenon was not found at a site most suited to its manifestation, it would be a strong indication that the theory of embourgeoisment was incorrect. Indeed, the three volumes of *The Affluent Worker* study called into question common views about the British working class on the basis of a small number of case studies and one site in particular.

To determine the number and type of cases to be selected, it is first necessary to have a sound understanding of research sites that might be examined. This information can come from a variety of sources, including existing documents or studies, published statistics, or personal knowledge. One of the most important sources, frequently used in industrial relations research, is the advice of key informants who are able to direct the researcher to likely sites. For example, a researcher wishing to conduct a de-

2. For a theoretical discussion of the selection and use of cases, see Ragin and Becker 1992.

tailed analysis of the process of introducing new working arrangements might first approach experienced union officials, who are likely to know which enterprises are making these changes. The next step might be to approach selected companies, since the appropriateness of particular enterprises as research sites could be determined at this point from discussions with key informants such as managers.

The number of cases that are studied depends on the objectives of the study and such practical issues as time and resources. An exploratory study can easily get by with one case, since it may generate ideas for further research. Burawoy's (1979) study of a single machine shop, *Manufacturing Consent,* for example, yielded a wealth of insights that had a significant influence on the direction of labor process theory in the early 1980s. Similarly, Yin (1994: 38) notes that a single case may be appropriate when it is a critical case, as in *The Affluent Worker* study. An unusual or deviant case, such as the International Typographical Union, which Lipset, Trow, and Coleman (1956) studied, can illuminate more general processes by highlighting the conditions under which common tendencies are not manifest.

The use of more than one case, however, can produce greater confidence in the reliability of the findings. Cases with similar characteristics might be examined to ensure that a single case was not atypical. Many researchers select cases with different characteristics, which can provide a rudimentary form of stratification with a similar logic to that used in sample surveys. The selection of cases with different features does not replicate the sampling logic of a survey, and it is inappropriate to generalize to a population (since a population has not been sampled); however, virtually all writers on case studies assert that the findings of a well-conducted case study can be used to refine or test theory,[3] which gives case studies a generalizability beyond the individual instance.

Gaining and Maintaining Access

Having identified suitable case study sites, a range of issues must then be addressed.[4] One, the question of gaining access, is not unique to case studies. What is distinctive about case studies is the commitment that is often required on the part of all concerned. Unlike a survey, in which each re-

3. In addition to Yin (1994), who argues this position strongly, see, for example, Eckstein 1975, Hammersley 1992, Platt 1988, and Sjoberg et al. 1991.

4. We can provide only a selection of the issues that can arise in case study research, especially field research. For a discussion of a good range of the problems that arose in particular organizational research, see Bryman 1988.

spondent is likely to spend no more than a few hours, and usually far less, talking with researchers or completing a questionnaire, in case studies the researcher and at least some respondents typically establish ongoing relationships. This may involve a considerable commitment of time and, in some cases, resources.

Time and resource implications also arise because the information necessary to conduct a case study is not necessarily available using a single technique or from a single source of information. Where there are many individuals who can provide different viewpoints or different types of information, it may be necessary to interview many or all of them or to observe a range of sites. Because case studies are potentially open-ended, there is no obvious point at which "enough is enough." An advantage of the case approach, of course, is that missing pieces of information might be collected at a future date. The amount of information, the level of detail, and the decision as to when the data collection phase of the case study is complete are a matter of judgment.

It is not possible to start a case study with a predetermined research plan. The art of a good case study is in being able to follow leads and pick up on interesting issues as they arise. This is a key difference between case studies and other approaches, such as surveys or experimental design, in which the research design is determined before entering the field.

A common initial step is to identify key informants within the unit of analysis or those outside the unit who have a sound knowledge of the issue being investigated. The researcher will need to make judgments about who should be treated as key informants (Johnson 1990). As the research proceeds, it is likely that new key informants will be recruited. Apart from the obvious issue of the validity and reliability of the information they impart, it is important to be aware that the perspective of any key informants will be tempered and limited by the positions they hold.

Failure to take this issue into account poses a serious danger to the validity and reliability of case studies, particularly when senior managers are used as informants in organizational or workplace studies. One reason that senior managers make useful informants is that they typically have a broad overview of the organization and are able to provide a great deal of information quickly. Typically, they are also articulate and persuasive. In that industrial relations research is increasingly commissioned by governments and enterprises for their own policy purposes, however, the danger of lapsing into a managerialist explanatory framework is evident and becomes critical if too much weight is given to the information and perspectives provided by management informants. Unless the research objective is limited to the narrow topic of managers' work (e.g., Smith 1990; Dalton 1959; Watson 1994), industrial relations research that relies on management informants alone must be considered fundamentally suspect.

Because case studies are often longitudinal, the issue arises not only of how to gain access but of how to maintain and extend the foothold in the unit. In a small-scale case study, the agreement of one gatekeeper—often a senior manager or union official—may be sufficient to ensure the cooperation of members of the organization. In longer-term studies, however, the researcher will need to deal with multiple gatekeepers, many of whose roles are due to their informal rather than their formal influence. Typically, "snowballing"—working through networks of personal introductions, for which gatekeepers are key figures—will be necessary.

Just as case studies themselves are not based on a statistical sample, neither is the process of selecting those who will be interviewed. The main criteria that must be taken into consideration are the need to cover all relevant viewpoints (again, a rudimentary form of stratifying applies), identifying who possesses special knowledge, and determining how to gain access.

When the case study involves fieldwork, such as in-depth interviews or observation, the members of a unit will try to place the researcher in social space. The researcher must therefore be aware of how he or she is being identified. Gaining the imprimatur of senior management may be necessary to gain access, but if the researcher is then associated with management in the eyes of other members of the organization, difficulties may arise with supervisors, union delegates, and employees. Similarly, there may be factions within the organization. If the researcher wishes to gain access to all areas of the unit, it is essential that the research make clear his or her impartiality. Many researchers experience the difficulty of having individuals or groups within the unit try to recruit them to their side in organizational conflicts as they become aware of the sensitive information to which researchers have access.

Confidentiality

The issue of confidentiality arises in all forms of research but may be particularly acute in case studies. The first problem is that a researcher who delves deeply into any social unit is likely to unearth sensitive information, and work organizations or unions may be reluctant to permit an outsider to gain access to secrets or information about shortcomings. There is a danger in organizational-level case studies that the case study will be vetoed by the gatekeepers and permission to publish or use the case study data withheld.

Access may be denied to key individuals or parts of the organization. In a case study of performance pay systems undertaken by Australian researchers, management refused access to branch managers who were critical in implementing the scheme. These managers were also union members, however, and access was arranged through the union. Understandably, the employer under study felt betrayed and it took some time for the researcher to rebuild trust with the organization.

A related issue is that the researcher is likely to use the information gained from one respondent as the basis for questioning other respondents. Researchers who do this run the risk of betraying promises of confidentiality and of identifying behaviors that later respondents might view negatively. In some cases, such as the revelation of inefficient work practices, negative attitudes, or illegal behavior, officials within an organization might act on information gained by the "unaffiliated" researcher under promises of confidentiality. Fortunately, industrial relations researchers are seldom confronted with the ethical and legal dilemmas involved in studying criminal activities (see, for example, Klockars 1974), but a range of "offenses" may still be uncovered in the course of conducting case studies in work organizations, such as failure to observe all provisions of health and safety legislation, industrial awards, or contracts.

Organizational secrecy becomes particularly sensitive when researchers wish to publish their findings. Increasingly, academic researchers must enter into confidentiality agreements to gain access to research sites. These often include provisions allowing the host organization the right to vet the published findings. In some cases, this is a simple undertaking on the part of the researcher to ensure the accuracy of the findings. In other cases, an organization may claim the right to censor some material or even stop publication altogether. Some researchers, such as Kriegler (1980), who published a study highly critical of personnel practices in a shipyard operated by Australia's largest company (BHP), have been threatened with legal action. Anonomyzing the details of the case may reduce this problem, but the danger remains that some individuals in the organization may not approve a critical or "bad news" study.

One way to minimize this risk is to have a memorandum of understanding with the organization as to what right of review and input the organization has into the researcher's report; this may also cover the anonymizing of the organization. The danger is that requesting to formalize the process may be too threatening to the organization and cooperation may not be forthcoming or may be terminated. Once again, judgment, luck, and the quality of the researcher-participant relationship are critical.

Organizational sensitivities are likely to vary depending on the nature of the research. The possibility that material gathered by student researchers will come to public attention is less likely to be an issue for research subjects than if the material is being gathered by senior researchers, particularly if the research is being undertaken for the purposes of policy formation or evaluation.

Validity and Reliability

One of the advantages of case studies is that the amount of information that is collected and the ability to probe beneath the surface enhance the validity of the information that is obtained. Nonetheless, case studies are often viewed as less reliable than other approaches to research, because of the difficulties of replicating the findings (Kirk and Miller 1986). Each case study is unique, and even in the case of the most dispassionate investigator, much will depend on the individual researcher. The possibility of bias or gullibility must always be considered. Furthermore, it is difficult to subject the findings of case studies to rigorous external scrutiny. Case studies often go unchallenged, because of the time and effort that would be required to replicate the study—if, indeed, this were possible at all, given limitations of access and the fact that another researcher will necessarily encounter a situation that has changed in at least some respects.

When more than one researcher are involved in a case study, and particularly when multiple sites are being studied, it is essential that there be a common protocol to ensure that similar issues are addressed. This does not necessarily mean that each interview or observation must be replicated at each site, but the issues studied must be the same and the information must be comparable. This question of comparability is particularly acute in the case of cross-national case studies, which have become increasingly common in industrial relations.[5] Often such studies will involve common interview schedules—which may have to be translated into a number of languages (see chapter 11, "Comparative International Industrial Relations").

It is tempting to be critical of case study design because of the lack of accepted techniques or procedures. Further, there are few published articles based on case studies, particularly in journals, that detail the techniques adopted. Often the reader is left guessing whether or not the research findings are based on interviews with only the CEO during one or two meetings

---

5. Kochan and Piore (1990) discuss methodological issues arising in a multinational, multi-industry project involving case studies.

or the result of an exhaustive process of investigation and interviews. The evaluation of case studies would be improved if there were better documentation of the techniques utilized and data on the sources of information, such as interviews and archival material.

Conclusion

Case studies remain one of the favorite research strategies among industrial relations researchers. Curiously, among other social scientists, case studies continue to be largely out of favor. There is a trade-off for researchers trying to understand complex social phenomena. The case study strategy provides information that can best be understood by locating it within the social situation in which it was collected. In contrast, sample surveys accept the information collected at face value, and the data are presumed to speak for themselves, with the assumption is that there is no need to explore the context that gives them meaning.

As industrial relations research moves into new areas, such as globalization and the creation of such supranational structures as the European Union, the Association of Southeast Asian Nations, and the North American Free Trade Agreement, researchers conducting case studies will need to adapt to these increasingly complex arrangements. They raise challenges for case study researchers in defining the unit of analysis and in identifying sources of information. The flexibility inherent in the case study strategy makes it well suited to meet these challenges.

CHAPTER SEVEN

In the Eye of the Beholder: Ethnography in the Study of Work

Raymond A. Friedman and Darren C. McDaniel

Zuboff's (1988) pathbreaking book on the impact of computers on work does not contain a single correlation, t-statistic, or regression model. Nonetheless, it is filled with hundreds of pages of data, including extensive and richly textured descriptions of paper mill operators and clerical employees at work, drawings by workers portraying how they see themselves on the job, and direct quotations from workers themselves. In one quote, a paper mill operator explains his feelings about computers:

> Doing my job through the computer, it feels different. It is like you are riding a big, powerful horse, but someone is sitting behind you on the saddle holding the reins, and you just have to be on that side and hold on. You see what is coming, but you can't do anything to control it. You can't steer yourself left and right; you can't control that horse you are on. You have got to do whatever the guy behind you holding the reins wants you to do. Well, I would rather be holding the reins than have someone behind me holding the reins (64).

Throughout the book, *workers'* views are interlaced with Zuboff's as she shares with the reader the data that brought her to her conclusions. It is this personal interaction with the subjects of study, on the part of both the author and the reader, that is the unique contribution of ethnographic research. Only by being with and talking to workers could Zuboff have learned how they reacted to new technologies, and only by having them tell their own stories could the reader gain direct access to their understanding of the changes they faced. Ethnographic research methods provide a richness of detail, a sensitivity to perceptions, and an opportunity to discover important new issues that cannot be achieved through a priori theorizing.

Ethnography has played a critical role in the study of work. In the 1930s, Roethlisberger and Dickson (1939) discovered the importance of social relations for workforce motivation by finally talking to the workers who were not responding to experiments as predicted. In the 1950s, Roy (1954) discovered the social norms that governed workers' rates of production by working in a factory himself, and Sayles and Strauss (1953) documented the political dynamics of local unions after years of observation and informal interviewing. More recently, by spending two years as a mediator-trainee, Kolb (1983) was able to discover that mediators do not let their analysis of particular disputes determine what role they should play. Rather, mediators begin with an understanding of their preferred role in mediation and shape their analysis to fit that role. In each of these studies, ethnographic research methods provided insights that could not have been derived from questionnaire surveys or analyses of wage rates or voting patterns.

This chapter provides an overview of the ethnographic approach to research. First, we describe the basic elements of ethnographic research. Second, we describe its advantages and disadvantages. Third, and finally, we describe some of the practical challenges that face those who choose to do ethnographic research. In the process, we hope to encourage readers to consider ethnographic research, but also to help them know better when this method is—or is not—feasible and appropriate.

Basic Elements of Ethnography

According to Hammersley and Atkinson, ethnography "involves the ethnographer participating, overtly or covertly, in people's daily lives for an extended period of time, watching what happens, listening to what is said, asking questions—in fact, collecting whatever data are available to throw light on the issues that are the focus of the research" (1995: 1–2). The objective of ethnographic research, they add, is "to describe what happens in the setting, how the people involved see their own actions and those of others, and the contexts in which the action takes place" (6). Similarly, Conklin notes that ethnography requires "a long period of intimate study and residence in a well-defined community employing a wide range of observational techniques including prolonged face-to-face contact with members of local groups, [and] direct participation in some of the group's activities" (1968: 172).

Underlying these comments are four distinctive features of ethnography. First, ethnography requires direct and personal observation of the people and situations being studied. Ethnography is at its core a hands-on process that involves interacting with people, often over extended periods of time. Exactly how that is done varies across studies. Roy (1954) and Graham (1995) took jobs at the companies they studied. Kanter (1977) spent five years consulting to the organization she studied. Kolb (1983) and Friedman (1994) directly observed negotiators and mediators in action. And Batstone and his colleagues (Batstone, Ferner, and Terry 1983 and Batstone, Boraston, and Frenkel 1977) attended company board meetings and followed union stewards through a strike. In addition, many of these same authors interviewed dozens or even hundreds of workers and managers. Ethnographers gather their data firsthand, directly from their subjects.[1]

Second, ethnographers make their observations in the *context* of people doing their jobs and interacting with others at work. Unlike experimental research, which takes subjects out of their actual social world, ethnography focuses explicitly on the social context. Fetterman (1989) refers to this as "naturalism," or the study of the world in its natural state. Such naturalism enables the researcher to assess "cultural patterns across and within societies, and their significance for understanding social processes" (Hammersley and Atkinson 1995: 9). From an ethnographic perspective, unique cultures are considered worthy of study and critical to understanding action: "Whether we are examining the organizational worlds of middle managers, tramps, stockbrokers, high school principals, police officers, production workers, or professional crooks, we are certain to uncover special languages, unique and peculiar problems, and, more generally, distinct patterns of thought and action" (Van Maanen 1983: 13). Naturalism also allows the researcher to see the cumulative effect of multiple forces on people's actions. This perspective stands in sharp contrast, again, to experimental research, in which the focus is on individual factors that are carefully isolated and little attention is paid to whether the same effects occur in real situations.

---

1. Some stricter definitions of ethnography include only *participant* observations. We choose to be somewhat more expansive in our definition, including research based on direct field observations but excluding research that uses only formal interviews or company records. Many researchers combine ethnography with other methods. Fantasia reports: "I would broadly characterize the approach I have taken in these studies as an ethnographic one, which variously combines participant observations, oral history through structured open-ended interviews with participants, and extensive use of informants, as well as archival research" (1988: 248).

Third, ethnography gives prominence to the words, interpretations, and experiences of the people studied. The goal of the researcher is to gain access to their understanding of work and work relationships, both at the level of what is explicitly expressed and at the level of what is taken for granted or expressed nonverbally. According to Schwartzman, ethnography provides researchers with

> a way to examine the cultural knowledge, behavior, and artifacts that participants share and use to interpret their experiences in a group. . . . Ethnography also requires researchers to examine the taken for granted, but very important, ideas and practices that influence the way lives are lived, and constructed, in organizational contexts. Because ethnographers are directed to examine both what people say and what people do, it is possible to understand the way that everyday routines constitute and reconstitute organizational and societal structures (1993: 4).

In ethnographic research, subjects' experiences are considered not only valid but absolutely primary to understanding social action.

Fourth, the ethnographer shares his or her observations with the reader. Readers not only learn the ethnographer's interpretation of a situation but, as much as possible, are put into the situation and allowed to experience it themselves. At a minimum, ethnographies include extensive quotations from the people studied and detailed descriptions of their situations, places of work, and social contexts. Some ethnographies go further. Van Maanen (1988) not only describes the situation but helps get readers involved through storytelling. In one study, he places the reader with him in the middle of a police chase for a robbery suspect. For ethnography, *how* information is portrayed is of central importance. The role of the ethnographer is to stand between the social world of the reader and the people studied—to "decode one culture while recoding it for another" (Van Maanen 1988: 4). The best ethnographers are skilled, not only at research, but also at writing in a way that is nuanced, creative, engaging, and insightful.

It is worth noting that much research of this type has not in fact been labeled ethnography. Historically, social anthropology was the first field in which extensive, direct observations were made of social systems. This approach was most dominant in the empiricist tradition of British anthropology, which was heavily influenced by Malinowski's studies of the Trobriand Islands and New Guinea in the 1920s. Shortly thereafter, scholars began to apply some of the same techniques to the study of communities in the United States. This led to the creation of the Chicago school of sociology, which was largely interested in social change in urban areas caused by immigration and industrialization. Well into the 1950s, much of sociology was based on direct observation of people in communities, including research on work and occupations, but these studies were typically referred to as "participant observation" or (less often) "applied anthropology." The founding studies of the human relations school of organization studies were also based heavily on direct observation (Roethlisberger and Dickson 1939; Whyte 1959). Only recently—in the past ten to twenty years—has the term "ethnography" been used frequently outside anthropology, and then predominantly in the United States. Indeed, much of what we consider ethnography is still not explicitly labeled as such.

Strengths and Weaknesses of Ethnography

Advantages

The particular characteristics of ethnography suggest a unique role for ethnographic research in social science. Unlike research methods that emphasize deductive theorizing or structured questionnaires, ethnography enables researchers to discover new issues and forces them to incorporate into their analyses the perspectives and concerns of their subjects. In this way, ethnography helps researchers enter the "black box" that separates a presumed cause from a presumed effect. Conversely, when researchers begin to examine topics about which there has been little or no research, ethnography provides a way to identify critical issues and map out uncharted territory. Ethnography is also uniquely suited to addressing certain research questions, such as those that require an understanding of culture, social interaction, or other aspects of complex social systems that cannot be reduced to individual actions or attitudes. Whenever researchers are interested in studying emerging issues in the workplace or the cultural or social aspects of existing problems, ethnography is an appropriate research tool.

Ethnography's openness to discovery is apparent from a number of studies. Zuboff (1988) describes how one of the central questions of her book emerged only after she began field observations, not before. While studying job enrichment, she asked workers about technological change and was surprised by their responses: "Many people voiced distress, describing their work as 'floating in space' or 'lost behind a screen.' They complained that they were no longer able to see or touch their work. Many felt that they no longer had the necessary skills or understanding to function competently. I did not know how to make sense of these comments, but I could not stop thinking about them either" (xii). This discovery became the focus of her research. Similarly, Friedman (1994) reports that his study of the negotiation process began with an unexpected discovery. During interviews with negotiators about the 1979 United Auto Workers strike at International Harvester, several expressed anger and frustration that the opposing negotiators did not follow the traditional negotiation process. The public ritual was apparently more important and meaningful than the researcher expected, and his later research was designed to ascertain why this was the case.

Finally, when Piore (1983) began his research on the acquisition of new-technology skills, he planned simply to compare the engineer-created "manning tables" for newer and older factories. By listening to workers, however, he found out that those tables were irrelevant. What mattered, he found, were the social relations among workers, who depended on each other to acquire new skills. There is much more room for discovery, he adds, and less chance of missing the real issues, when subjects have a chance to tell their stories rather than being forced to provide codable answers to preset questions. All of these cases highlight the degree to which ethnographers discover not only the answers to questions during their fieldwork but also the questions themselves. As Hammersley and Atkinson put it, "Ethnographers do not automatically assume that they know the right questions to ask in a setting" (1995: 24).

The role of ethnography in discovery, and its focus on inductive learning, make it especially important as a vehicle for entering new domains of study and examining areas under change. Much of the ethnographic work in labor relations was done during the 1950s, when the labor relations system had not yet been institutionalized and was therefore not well understood (e.g., Gouldner 1954a; Sayles and Strauss 1953; Wilensky 1956). More recently, as industrial relations has undergone tremendous changes, some ethnographies have sought to investigate this uncharted territory. For example, Friedman (1994) has examined the logic of the negotiation process, trying to understand its lack of response to changing economic pressures, while Graham (1995) has examined worker reactions to the emergence of Japanese styles of management in the United States. Ethnographies have been critical in opening up other areas in the study of work, such as the role of emotions (Hochschild 1983), diversity in organizations (Kanter 1977), and organizational culture (Kunda 1992). In many cases, ethnographic research raises new research questions and provides the initial data for new avenues of inquiry.

Ethnography is also especially useful for studying certain theoretical and research domains, particularly those that involve aspects of *culture,* broadly construed, and *social organization.* An ethnographic approach is not needed, for example, to determine the distribution of money and promotions in organizations since that information is easily visible and requires only individual-level data; archival and survey research do just fine. Ethnography is essential, however, if one wants to examine collective understandings of how rewards should be allocated or taken-for-granted assumptions about whose work is valued. These deeper layers of assumptions, understandings, and perceptions are not easily visible (they are not identified in policy statements and may never be stated verbally by anyone in the organization), and they are inherently collective (they are not individual views but rather collective norms expressed and reinforced through social interaction).

For those who are interested in studying such collective understandings and believe they have a significant impact on work and labor relations, ethnography is an essential research tool.[2] Kolb (1983), for example, was interested in the way in which mediators' unconscious model of the role of mediators in a dispute shapes their analysis of the dispute (even though they claim to shape their role in response to their analysis). Friedman (1994) was interested in uncovering the logic behind deeply held loyalties to traditional negotiation rituals that he had discovered. And as Hodson and his colleagues explain, "Worker solidarity has resisted study by conventional survey techniques because solidarity is a complex phenomenon that emerges from specific situations and histories. Worker solidarity is also a group phenomenon and such phenomena resist exploration with face-to-face interviews or telephone surveys that entail an inherent methodological individualism" (1993: 398). Ethnography is uniquely suited to examine these types of interests.

Disadvantages of Ethnography

These strengths of ethnography also represent weaknesses. To the degree that questions emerge from the research process itself and attention is paid to what is unique in a particular context, ethnographic studies are not easily amenable to replication. With the exception of Burawoy's research (1979) at the same machine shop where Roy (1954) had worked some twenty-five

2. Although it is not necessary to operate out of a particular social science paradigm to use ethnographic methods, ethnography is used especially heavily by those who are influenced by phenomenology (Schutz 1967) and ethnomethodology (Garfinkel 1967), two branches of social thought that emphasize the primacy of culture in understanding how people perceive reality and act on those perceptions.

years earlier, few attempts have been made to reproduce previous findings, and with the exception of Gallie (1978) and Burling, Lenz, and Wilson (1956), few studies have been comparative. Thus, although ethnography serves as an excellent way to discover deep patterns in social interaction and to generate new insights, it is not a good way to prove theoretical statements. This weakness has led some to question the validity of ethnographic research findings and their applicability to situations other than those studied.[3]

Hodson and his colleagues (1993) argue that to test propositions using ethnographic studies, it is necessary to conduct a meta-analysis across known cases using coding and statistical analysis.[4] Others suggest that theory validation is simply not a task that can or should be accomplished by ethnography. Piore (1983), for example, argues that there is a trade-off. Open-ended field research offers the benefit of greater *plausibility* for the theories it produces, but it does so at the cost of theory validation. We would suggest that the best ethnographers have, through insight and great writing, provided lessons about social interaction that extend beyond the particular case, yet there is certainly a great risk that a scholar doing ethnographic research may never get beyond the level of description or that the theories generated may be inaccurate.

These problems are made worse by the lack of a clear and exact method for translating careful observations into generalizable and parsimonious findings. Some guidance is found in the writings of Glaser and Strauss (1967) and of Fetterman (1989), but in general the ethnographer is on his or her own when turning observations into insights. Moreover, given the inability of ethnographers to cite established methodological steps as sources of reassurance about their findings, it is up to the individual researcher to convince the reader that the research was done properly, that the insights generated are accurate, and that the researcher truly does understand the phenomenon under study. As Golden-Biddle and Locke (1993) put it, one must convince the reader that the research is *authentic* and that the interpretations are *plausible*. The risk here is that findings may

3. Katz (1983) calls these the problems of representativeness, reliability, and replicability. He also talks about reactivity, or the tendency to get too personally involved in the situation.

4. In the hope of encouraging cross-case comparisons of anthropological research, the Human Relations Area Files was created at Yale University in 1949, but comparisons across cases proved more difficult than expected since even studies of the "same" topic usually began with different theoretical assumptions and therefore involved the collection of very different kinds of data (Agar 1986).

be influenced by the researchers' own biases and expectations: they may have looked only at evidence that supports their own theories and interpreted the data only in ways that support their arguments.[5] We are left, then, with the individual ethnographer as the primary source of credibility. Both the actual research and the credibility of the results are extremely dependent on the person who does the research and on his or her analytical, rhetorical, and—most important—writing skills (Van Maanen 1988).

The final weakness of ethnographic research is the practical difficulty of doing direct observation. Ethnographic research is extremely time-consuming, access to sites can be difficult, and managing the relationship with the individuals and organizations being studied requires a great deal of political skill and interpersonal sensitivity. Gullahorn and Strauss (1954) discuss the need to avoid being identified with labor or management, and Friedman (1994) reports that it took dozens of requests before he was given permission to attend labor negotiations. Even though we believe that ethnographic research can be among the most engaging and fulfilling ways to learn about the workplace, surmounting these logistical problems requires a great deal of effort. Successful fieldwork requires persistence, trial and error, and a certain amount of luck.

Trends in Research

Given these strengths and weaknesses, ethnographies have been done less often in recent years in the United States, especially in the field of labor relations. As the institution of labor relations stabilized in the 1960s and 1970s, the emphasis in research shifted from discovering new insights toward testing and replicating existing theories. Changes in the institution of academia also contributed to this transition. Since the 1960s, there has been a much greater emphasis on theory building and testing, quantitative methods (made feasible with the arrival of computers), and—correspondingly—the use of journal articles (rather than books) as the primary vehicle for publishing scholarship. In industrial relations, the shift away from case studies and participant observation was also a result of the increasing dominance of labor economics (Kaufman 1993). All of these factors have made it hard for people to establish their academic careers using ethnographic re-

---

5. We would argue that the same problem exists for quantitative research. Quantitative data analysis is really much more of an art than is typically admitted. It is just that ethnography lacks the veneer of science that comes from a priori hypotheses and correlation tables, as well as established conventions to guide the analysis and provide reassurance that proper steps were taken.

search. Sutton (1994) argues that reviews are weighted so heavily against inductive, field-based research that he actually hides from reviewers the fact that his research began that way and advises others to do so as well. Although ethnography is critical for research, and is probably used more often than is admitted, the only acceptable way to report the research, says Sutton, is to claim that one's arguments are derived deductively from existing theory.

The pattern outside the United States has not been as extreme. In Britain, there is a strong and continuing tradition of extensive cases studies based, in part, on direct or participant observations (Edwards and Heery 1989; Batstone, Ferner, and Terry 1983; Batstone, Boraston, and Frenkel 1978), much of which is associated with the industrial relations center at Warwick University. Similar work is being done in Australia (Frenkel and Coolican 1985) and on the European continent. (Edwards, Collinson, and Dell Rocca 1995 summarizes the findings of several studies on workplace resistance.) Although the differences among these countries cannot be definitively explained, one factor may be the continued strength of unions outside the United States and in fact that the shift toward deductive theorizing and quantitative methods is much stronger in the United States. Looking at the difference from the American point of view, Cappelli describes the British tradition of scholarship in industrial relations as an "approach to research . . . characterized by the aphorism 'a pound of facts and an ounce of theory' " (1985: 91).

Practical Challenges for the Ethnographer

For those who do ethnographic work, the first major hurdle is obtaining access to the research site. Some researchers, such as Roy (1954) and Graham (1995), have bypassed this issue by simply taking jobs at the places they wanted to study. In most cases, however, it is necessary to gain permission from those in control to enter the workplace, observe work processes, and interview employees. As with any research, those in power will want to know the purpose of the research and how the information will be used. Their degree of concern is often heightened when the researcher is an ethnographer because ethnography involves reporting data that are very personal and the research is usually very open-ended (which makes it difficult to predict with great certainty the nature of the output). These concerns can be dampened somewhat by promises that all information will remain confidential and that neither the organization nor individuals in the organization will be named in the final report.

People may still be concerned, however, about the presence of the researcher in the organization. While other researchers may want access to wage data, archives, or the opinions of top-level managers, ethnographers ask to have access to many employees, often in unstructured settings with no controls. Managers may therefore be concerned not just about the final product but also about the possibility that the researcher will interfere with the work being done, have an impact on the opinions and actions of individual employees, or convey information among employees that would not otherwise be shared among them. Given the ethnographer's access to the organization, those in charge must be convinced that the individual researcher is sensitive, sensible and has good interpersonal skills. Yet even the most sensitive ethnographer may change the behavior of those being observed simply by being around them, so it is nearly impossible to eliminate all risk to organizations being studied. The problem is even more severe in the domain of labor relations, where much information is kept confidential, the environment is highly politicized, and strained relations can easily be disrupted. Extra effort is needed to ensure that the researcher is perceived as politically neutral, and to gain support for the research from both sides.

One way to compensate managers and workers for the risks they take being research subjects is to offer to provide feedback to the organization or to suggest ways in which workers or managers could benefit from the knowledge produced. Whyte (see chapter 8 in this volume) goes further, suggesting that ethnographers should engage in participatory action research in which the researcher is actively involved in changing the organization being studied. In these ways organizations get something in return for the risks they must take.

Getting access to a work site is only the first step in doing ethnographic research. The ethnographer still has to gain the cooperation of all the people being studied. In that sense, access must be negotiated repeatedly with each individual on each day of observation. Just because someone's superior has allowed a researcher on site does not mean that that worker will accept the researcher's presence. Workers are often suspicious that the researcher might be a "spy" for someone, many will be confused about why the researcher would spend time researching the organization, and others will simply dislike being watched all the time. McDaniel (1994) reports that it took months before the janitorial staff at a university accepted his presence at the daily lunchtime washer-tossing ritual, and Friedman (1994) had to convince each new person he encountered during his study of labor negotiations of both the importance of the research and his neutrality. Both

Friedman and McDaniel report that there were times when they became very comfortable in the field—believing that everyone had finally accepted their presence—only to be challenged by yet another person who wanted an explanation of who they were and what they were doing.

The next practical challenge the ethnographer faces is how to collect and record observations. Some researchers have been able to tape-record events or interviews. This ensures that comments and interactions are not forgotten and provides the most complete set of records from which to draw quotations. Tape recorders should be used, however, only when there is an extremely high level of trust between the researcher and the subjects and the presence of the recording device will not interfere with the research process or with the subjects' willingness to be open and honest.

When tape recorders are not appropriate, the researcher has to take copious notes—of the events observed and what was said, as well as about his or her own feelings and theories of what these events might mean and how the participants might be interpreting them. Even when a tape recorder is used, the ethnographer still has to keep track of his or her own interpretations and feelings. Note taking is less obtrusive than tape recording, but it is still obtrusive. People will notice when a researcher pulls out a note pad and when the researcher starts and stops writing. If the researcher is going to take notes during observations, it helps, therefore, to write consistently—even when no information really needs to be recorded—to minimize drawing attention to the writing process. Note taking can also be obtrusive in that it makes it harder for researchers to attend to the interpersonal dynamics between themselves and their subjects. Finally, for those engaged in full-blown participant observation, note taking must be done after hours and out of sight. Graham (1996) was luckier than most. Her job required that she carry a clipboard so that she could take notes on damage to car bodies, making it much easier to take her own notes without drawing undue attention.

The hardest part of ethnography comes next—organizing the data and ideas accumulated during observations into a coherent story with a conceptual purpose. During the research process the ethnographer is fully embedded in the complex reality faced by the subjects of study. He or she probably is at the peak of understanding the situation. The problem is that the ethnographer has more information than can be conveyed in any text and more than would be useful for the reader. Ethnographers would be well advised not to publish hundreds of pages of notes or transcripts, as Ann Douglas (1962) did in her study of negotiations. However, there are no easy rules for knowing which information to present and which to ignore. It is at this point that researchers have to slowly extract themselves from the situation they have been studying and switch their attention back to theory development and research questions. They have to engage in "selective forgetting" of much of the information they have collected so that a pattern may emerge and a story line be created. Either implicitly or explicitly, they must begin to code their data and organize them around emerging themes or explanatory schema.

Much of this process occurs during the actual writing of the ethnography, during which the ethnographer faces several additional challenges. There is no standard format for presenting ethnographic data as there is, for example, in experimental social psychology. Should the data be presented as a complete story, with conceptual analysis organized around the story, or should the analysis provide the basis for organizing the text and the data be used to support those arguments? A more philosophical concern is the degree to which the writer presents information as objective data or emphasizes that the report is based on his or her perceptions. Thus, should the ethnographer and his or her reactions be reported in the story, or should the ethnographer be invisible to the reader? These questions are addressed extensively by Van Maanen (1988), whose book is devoted to the options ethnographers face when presenting data, or, as Van Maanen calls it, "telling their tales." The point here is that the pulling together of the story and the creation of a conceptually powerful research product depend heavily on the author's ability to write his or her observations so they come to life and connect to questions of theoretical and practical concern.

Use of Ethnography

Ethnography is an extremely time-consuming and high-risk way to do research. It requires months and sometimes years of fieldwork and entails the risk that one might lose access to research sites or have the findings rejected as unscientific. Moreover, it all comes down to the researcher's ability to reduce years of observation into a coherent story that readers perceive to be authentic and plausible. For these reasons, the use of ethnography has diminished in many fields, and for those same reasons we do not suggest that scholars venture lightly into this territory.

At the same time, ethnography still has an important role in research, lest we collectively become deaf to changes in the workplace, unhealthily enamored of our own theories, and overconfident that our surveys and regressions have conveyed complete and unbiased truth. To ensure a certain level of vigor and the generation of new ideas, we must remember to continually examine the perceptions and experiences of the people whose actions we are trying to explain. Moreover, we must make sure that social context and collective understandings are not ignored as an unintended consequence of the dominance of quantitative research methods. Ethnography provides no inherent access to truth (as is the case for more quantitative methods), but it does provide a set of strengths and benefits that complement those of the more common research methods described elsewhere in this book.

CHAPTER EIGHT

Participatory Action Research: Getting Involved and Creating Surprises at the Workplace

William Foote Whyte

*P*articipatory action research (PAR) has become a popular research strategy, yet there continues to be confusion about what researchers mean by the term. The confusion arises because some researchers have described *action research, participatory research,* and *participatory action research* as if they were all the same phenomenon. To clear up this confusion, I suggest the following set of definitions:

> In *action research,* the professional researcher seeks to maintain as much control as possible of both the research process, the actions resulting from the research, and the documentation of results.

> In *participatory research,* some members of the community or organization being studied become involved in the research process but the process aims at increasing knowledge rather than generating action.

> In *participatory action research,* one or more of the members of the community or organization being studied participate actively in the research process and in the actions that grow out of this process.

For some applied research projects, PAR has special advantages over conventional approaches. PAR tends to expand the disciplinary base of social research, gets members of the organization being studied committed to advancing the practical implications of the research, and yields what I have called creative surprises.

Where and When Were PAR Strategies Introduced?

Although I have publicized the use of PAR (Whyte 1991), I don't claim to have invented the term, and it is unclear who first used it. The historical question of when and where PAR was first used cannot be answered easily either because some projects that meet all the definitions of PAR were not identified as such by the researchers reporting on them. For example, in the 1960s Norwegian social psychologist Einar Thorsrud (1971) led what he called the industrial democracy project, a collaborative effort by behavioral scientists and practitioners in the Norwegian maritime industry that involved government officials, members of management of one of the major shipping companies, and ships' officers and sailors.

During World War II, Thorsrud had worked in Norway's underground opposition movement with men who later became prominent government and business officials and union leaders. Since the lives of these people depended on their maintaining the trust of the other members of the underground, a basis of trust was established that carried over the years and into new joint activities. Thorsrud organized the industrial democracy project from his social research base in the Institute for Social Research at Oslo. When he learned that leaders of the maritime industry were worried about the declining position of their industry, Thorsrud approached the president of a leading maritime firm to explore the possibilities of a social research solution.

The aim of the maritime project was to improve the international competitive position of Norwegian ships and the quality of life on board them, as well as relations between engine room and deck crews. The program also involved cross-training whereby members of the deck crew, whose jobs gave them no useful experience for employment on shore after they left the sea, could learn some of the essentials of engine operation, which would be useful in many jobs on land.

The behavioral scientists working with Thorsrud guided the process from initial interviews with a wide range of maritime personnel, through discussions of possible changes in technology and the social organization of work, to ship-to-ship conferences in which representatives of several ships exchanged views on the changes that were necessary. The program led to the construction of a new ship that could be operated efficiently with a sharply reduced crew and that was structured so as to minimize the status and other differences between engine room and deck crews and between officers and seamen.

Practitioners were heavily involved in designing new technologies, writing job descriptions, and developing training programs. Behavioral scientists structured the total process but did not seek to control the outcomes.

Not only did the program produce major changes in the Norwegian maritime industry, but it was also studied by other behavioral scientists and practitioners and led to changes in the maritime industry throughout the world. Furthermore, the Norwegian project later was influential worldwide in the development of work teams.

Use of PAR at Xerox

I first became aware of PAR while learning about a transformation in labor relations at the Xerox Corporation. Relations between the company and the Amalgamated Clothing and Textile Workers Union had been relatively harmonious for some years, and in the early 1980s Xerox and the union had begun to encourage worker participation in decision making through an ambitious training program, supported by outside consultants and facilitators.

After some initial successes, the program encountered a crisis when Xerox announced its intention to shut down the wire harness department and buy the harnesses from a vendor, thus saving $3.2 million. After a period of discussion among management and union leaders and consultant/facilitator Peter Lazes, the parties agreed to set up what we called a cost-saving team (CST) in the wire harness department. The team, which included workers in the department, their supervisor, and a management engineer, worked together for six months searching for ways to save the $3.2 million and keep the jobs in-house. The success of the wire harness CST and of other departmental CSTs stimulated the development of a real partnership between the union and management in solving major problems facing the corporation.

Consultant/facilitator Peter Lazes, who has a doctorate in social and community psychology, played a key role in guiding the discussion toward the establishment of the CST in the wire harness department. He served as a facilitator during the organization and discussion stages of that team, but the research in engineering and cost accounting that ultimately led to the CST devising ways to save more than $3.2 million and protect the 180 jobs in the department was done entirely by the workers, their foreman, and consultants in management they called upon (Whyte, Greenwood, and Lazes 1989; Whyte 1991).

Use of PAR in the Mondragón Cooperatives

I introduced social anthropologist Davydd Greenwood of Cornell University to the Mondragón cooperatives, but he needed no introduction from me to the Basque culture, since he was a well-recognized authority when we met. We started working together when I was writing a book on Mondragón (Whyte and Whyte 1991). Although we often discussed his PAR project, my involvement was only incidental.

While Greenwood and I were discussing social research possibilities, personnel director José Luis González invited Greenwood to give a course on social research methods for members of the personnel department of FAGOR, the largest group of cooperatives in Mondragón. Greenwood agreed to conduct a month-long seminar in July 1985.

The personnel people arrived for the first meeting with notebooks and pens, ready to make notes on what the professor said. There was some initial confusion when Greenwood announced that he would keep the lectures to a minimum and that his purpose was to help them understand and improve their own organizations.

Working particularly with José Luis González, Greenwood led a team of personnel people from the FAGOR group through a PAR project that focused on how they could perform their functions more effectively. At first the members of the group were overwhelmed by the challenge of doing social research, but as they got into it, they developed an extraordinary commitment to the process. They concentrated first on Ulgor, the first and largest of the cooperatives, and then on FAGOR. Besides achieving some useful practical results, Greenwood's program led to the publication of two books on the organizational culture of FAGOR. These were jointly written by Greenwood and five members of this group of cooperatives (Greenwood et al. 1991 and 1992).

From Conventional Research to Creative Surprises

In a conventional sociological research project, the researcher goes through several standard steps: a search of the research literature, specification of several hypotheses that seem worth testing, design of the project (usually a survey), field study (or getting a graduate student to do it), and finally the creation of a report on the results for an academic journal. Whether the researcher will ever report on the results depends on his or her having guessed right in developing hypotheses that could be confirmed by data at a particular level of statistical significance. From the standpoint of *learning* and *action,* this conventional approach is highly inefficient.

If the researcher already has some training in survey methodology, he or she learns nothing throughout the research process until the final results are available. Then, if the hypotheses are not confirmed, the researcher has to start over with new hypotheses or abandon the line of research.

In contrast, in PAR, the researcher is constantly being tested by new challenges and dilemmas as he or she follows through from the initial organization of the project to the final stages of carrying out actions that emerge from the research. This reality testing is a powerful stimulus to learning.

I have never yet encountered a statistical correlation that led directly to a line of action. The most general favorable result is action that arises out of a combination of factors, so that no clear line of action is revealed.

In PAR, the ultimate test is in the actions emerging from the research. If no actions result, the researchers may learn much from the experience but the project cannot be considered successful. In the cases described above—and in many others in the rapidly growing PAR literature—the resulting actions have been impressive.

PAR contrasts with conventional research in offering creative surprises (Whyte 1991) that jar the researcher out of conventional ways of interpreting the research world. In the case of the Xerox project, an important surprise was the discovery of new trends in industrial cost accounting, as reported by researchers in that field. None of the behavioral scientists involved in analyzing the Xerox case had had any academic background in accounting, and it would not have occurred to us to challenge management's methods of measuring labor costs. The wire harness CST made this challenge, however, with the result that management refigured those costs and substantially reduced them. Although we did not learn from this case how to do industrial cost accounting ourselves, we did learn that the first question to ask a management group that claims that its labor costs are too high is "In figuring labor costs, how do you allocate indirect or overhead costs to labor?"

Another creative surprise emerged out of our rethinking one of the most frequently studied industrial relations questions: the relationship between job satisfaction and worker productivity. As we studied the productivity gains achieved at Xerox, we recognized that they arose out of a combination of changes in management—especially a reduction in the number of supervisory personnel—and increases in the workers' responsibilities. To arrive at a more realistic picture of these gains, we shifted from measures of worker productivity to the relation between costs and productivity. On this basis, we found that increased job satisfaction and productivity growth came together through the measurement of costs. Economists call this measurement *total factor productivity*. We had not expected even to attempt to resolve the satisfaction-productivity relationship, but the PAR process led us to this result.

In the Mondragón case, the initial focus of the PAR project was on learning ways to improve the functions of the personnel department. As interest shifted toward understanding the culture of the FAGOR group of cooperatives, the parties arrived at a new and challenging formulation of the meaning of organizational culture. Among the members they interviewed individually or in groups, the project participants found that there was extraordinary consensus on the basic *values* underlying the cooperatives but that there were frequent disagreements on the *means* being used to maintain these values. In other words, the agreement on values left open a wide field of argumentation on how the belief in these values should be expressed.

Strategies for Organizing a PAR Project

The initiative for starting and structuring a PAR project is in the hands of the research professional. How do we begin? Let us review what happened in the cases described here.

Although we do not have a play-by-play report on the beginnings of the PAR process in the Norwegian maritime industry case, it appears that social psychologist Einar Thorsrud structured the process so as to ensure there was full participation by representatives of government, a major maritime company, the maritime unions, and the officers and crew members of ships. Thorsrud and his fellow behavioral scientists at the Norwegian Institute for Social Research proposed the composition of the working groups and wrote the research publications, but the practitioners (the members of the maritime industry) contributed to the design of the project. Thorsrud's aim was to establish as extensive participation as was possible for progress to occur in discussions and in practice.

In the Xerox case, Peter Lazes switched his role from consultant/facilitator to social researcher as he, Davydd Greenwood, and I got together to retrieve records of the events surrounding the crisis in the wire harness department and to create its cost study team. To secure the involvement of the principal actors in interpreting the case, I asked Anthony Costanza, shop chairman for the union, and Dominick Argona and Larry Pace of

Xerox's organizational effectiveness department to write their own interpretations of the events. I worked closely with them as they drafted and redrafted their reports, but I sought to confine my role to offering editorial criticisms rather than injecting my thoughts. Nor did any members of the cost study teams contribute any writing to these practitioners' reports.

In the FAGOR case, Davydd Greenwood assumed the role of teacher but transformed what started as a personnel department seminar into an applied research project by introducing the PAR process. Five members of the seminar group worked with Greenwood in writing two books, the first in Spanish, the second in English. Of the three cases discussed here, the FAGOR case went far beyond the others in securing the full involvement of the practitioners in writing the final reports.

In none of these cases did the social researcher begin by announcing that people were to participate in a PAR process. Thorsrud never attached that label to the maritime industry project. He had broader aims—to advance participatory processes throughout industry. It is the focus on applied research that brings a project within the PAR framework.

In cases I have followed in agricultural research and development in Latin America (Whyte 1991), professionals took the initiative in farming systems research and extension. Small farmers participated actively in structuring new approaches and keeping records of their experiences, but the social scientists wrote and published the results.

Based on these experiences, I continue to believe it would be helpful to the PAR process to have more practitioners involved in writing their versions of events. In practice, we usually have to settle for less. In one case, for example, a practitioner I asked to write his version of events replied, "I'd like to do it, but I am not a writer." In such cases, one solution is to interview the practitioner and then give him or her a rough draft of the report to check facts and meanings.

Can PAR be used for applied research in any field of study? In general, its use is confined to the social sciences. At Cornell University, however, Reynolds (1994) used the PAR process to redesign an introductory physics course. Graduate students and teaching staff worked with four undergraduates in choosing a new textbook and developing new exercises. The research design represented here could just as well be used in courses in sociology or economics.

Can the PAR process be used in evaluation research? Within certain limitations, it can be. To start the process, applied researchers may want to discuss with the people carrying out the program to be evaluated what they are trying to achieve to make sure that the major aspects are reflected in the research design. This could limit defensiveness in the face of later discussions of negative comments.

The applied research process generally begins with exploratory interviewing. During this stage, we learn that all informants are not created equal. The researcher will find that some can contribute little beyond their personal experiences, whereas a few will seek to place their experiences in a broader organizational framework. Those in the latter category are the ones the researcher should cultivate and eventually involve in the PAR project. They can contribute ideas as well as information, and they will enjoy the challenge of participating in PAR.

Conclusion

As Argyris (1952) pointed out, by treating informants as passive subjects, social researchers are simply manipulating and distorting reality. PAR provides an important avenue to gain the active participation of members of the organization being studied.

Compared with standard research methods, the PAR process involves the researcher in learning through fieldwork rather than simply waiting for survey findings to be available. PAR enables researchers to extend the interdisciplinary scope of their research beyond the social sciences into such diverse fields as engineering, business administration, and plant science. Venturing into these extended fields produces creative surprises—discoveries that the researcher had not sought or expected—that can be powerful forces in jarring us out of familiar academic routines.

As the appeal of PAR has spread rapidly across many academic fields, this action research strategy has been used in agricultural research and development (Whyte 1991), in investigating the relations between public schools and the university (Greenwood, Whyte, and Harkavy 1993), and in studies in many other fields. A catalogue of the uses to which PAR has been put would be out of date as soon as it was printed.

In this chapter, I have not attempted to summarize the PAR literature, even within industrial relations. It seemed more useful to concentrate on a few cases and to focus particularly on the underlying logic of PAR, which offers both scientific and practical advantages over conventional research strategies.

CHAPTER NINE

Large-Scale National Surveys for Mapping, Monitoring, and Theory Development

Neil Millward, Paul Marginson, and Ron Callus

*I*ndustrial relations as a field of study has benefited enormously from the development of large-scale surveys based on statistically representative samples. National surveys of employing units—the focus of this chapter— have provided comprehensive mapping of the structures, practices, and policies of industrial relations at workplace and enterprise levels; have progressively enabled key changes in practice and important continuities to be identified; and have enabled researchers to confirm or challenge conventional industrial relations wisdom. Advances in computer technology and statistical software have turned these publicly available data sets into a resource of unparalleled richness. Both the strengths and limitations of this resource deserve to be more widely and better understood.

Although national surveys of employees are commonplace in most countries, surveys of employing organizations are uncommon and economywide examples are rare. Yet employer-based surveys have a long history in industrial relations research. In many industrialized countries employer-based surveys were undertaken by government statisticians in the late nineteenth century. Only recently, however, has the combination of statistical sampling theory, adequate sampling frames, and electronic data processing permitted the adoption of survey techniques for national investigations of industrial relations.

In this chapter we focus on national surveys in Britain and Australia, where the record of comprehensive surveys with high response rates is

The authors wish to thank Roger Thomas of the Survey Methods Centre at Social and Community Planning Research in London.

strongest and longest. National surveys of employers in the United States have had lower response rates and less comprehensive coverage. Probably the closest to our examples are Osterman's 1992 survey of private-sector establishments with fifty or more employees (Osterman 1994), the 1987 survey of employee-involvement programs and practices by the U.S. Government Accounting Office (Lawler, Ledford, and Mohrman 1989), and Lawler, Mohrman, and Ledford's 1990 survey of employee-involvement and total quality management programs (Lawler, Mohrman, and Ledford 1992), of which these last two surveys were conducted in Fortune 1000 companies.

In focusing on Australia and Britain, we draw on our experiences as the lead researchers on three major surveys: Callus's with the first Australian Workplace Industrial Relations Survey (AWIRS); Millward's with the three British Workplace Industrial Relations Surveys (WIRS); and Marginson's with the two British Company-Level Industrial Relations Surveys (CLIRS). The issues that we discuss are applicable, however, to other employer-based surveys, not just the large, national ones with which we have been involved.[1]

Strengths and Limitations of Employer-Based Surveys

Knowledge of the employment relationship in a wide diversity of settings has been built up over many years by means of a variety of research methods but most extensively as a result of detailed case studies of workplaces or companies carried out by individual researchers or teams. This rich tradition is on the wane, however, in large part as survey data become more widely available (Brown and Wright 1994; Kaufman 1993). Some argue that surveys are overresourced because they are methodologically less appropriate to grappling with the texture of industrial relations within the workplace or enterprise than detailed case studies (McCarthy 1994). In our opinion this argument is unfounded, in that it views different methods as substitutes for each other, instead of asking which method is most appropriate for the research in question. Morris and Wood (1991) provide a rare example of a study that assesses the relative strengths and limitations of the use of survey and in-depth case study methods within the ambit of a single research project.

Case studies inherently lack two vital ingredients: generalizability and

---

1. A fuller discussion of the issues and descriptions of the surveys are contained in Millward, Marginson, and Callus 1996.

transparency. By contrast, large-scale surveys possess both these features. With proper statistical sampling and rigorous fieldwork procedures, they can produce results that apply to a well-defined population of employment units. And if there is thorough documentation of the methods of data collection and processing, the results can have almost complete transparency. Moreover, survey data sets that are publicly available have the overwhelming advantage that any published analysis can be checked and replicated; only on matters of interpretation need there be dispute.

At the same time, surveys are blunt and inappropriate instruments for understanding the social processes that underlie employer-employee relationships and in particular the bargaining processes that have been the focus of many case studies. Morris and Wood (1991) comment on the inability of the survey to detect the processual changes occurring within industrial relations structures and institutions, while noting the success with which the survey maps the institutional landscape. Surveys, then, are unrivaled in producing findings of broad generality using a transparent methodology.

There are several principal uses of national, employer-based sample surveys:

- to provide an economywide snapshot of the structures, practices, and outcomes of industrial relations in organizations or organizational units;
- to identify the differences in industrial relations between parts of the economy or between organizations with different characteristics, as in size, location, and ownership;
- to track over time changes that have occurred and in which types of unit;
- to learn more about the nature of change through panel designs;
- to provide the empirical platform for hypothesis testing, model building, and theory development; and
- to provide an efficient and transparent means for evaluating public policy and the policies of organizations.

In the case of hypothesis testing, surveys are often used for purposes far beyond what their designers originally intended or envisaged and occasionally for purposes for which some consider them inappropriate. A case in point is the recent British controversy involving practitioner organizations as well as researchers over the use of a single question in the 1990 WIRS on the industrial relations climate, from which the researchers drew inferences about the ineffectiveness of employment practices associated with human resource management (Fernie, Metcalf, and Woodland 1994).

The versatility of survey research is evident from the uses that have been made of the British WIRS. Millward and Woodland (1995) list about two hundred publications using data from the WIRS in academic fields as diverse as labor economics, management, geography, sociology, and statistics.

Olsen, Romeyn, and Alexander (1995), in reviewing the literature that used the 1990 AWIRS, concluded that "the papers reviewed clearly suggest that the first AWIRS has made a considerable contribution to industrial relations research in Australia. It has stimulated informed debate on a broad range of issues and provided a data base unique [in Australia] in its statistical reliability and breadth."

The links between research and policy outcomes are often tangential and difficult to make, but the availability of data sets such as AWIRS and WIRS creates the potential for better-informed policy making by governments, employers, and trade unions. For example, the AWIRS data were used by the Australian union movement to understand and remedy its declining membership base; the results challenged the conventional understanding of union organization, showing that in most workplaces unions were inactive or active only sporadically.

As evident from the initial publications based on these surveys and the stream of secondary analysis, WIRS, CLIRS, and AWIRS have transformed what is known about the structures and practices of industrial relations in Britain and Australia. Some findings and a few analyses have been controversial, but this is no surprise. For example, the primary analysis of the 1990 WIRS revealed, through comparisons with earlier surveys, the extent of the retreat from collective bargaining over the previous decade and concluded that collective bargaining no longer constituted the dominant model of British industrial relations (Millward et al. 1992: 350). Analysis of the 1990 WIRS also exploded the myth of the single-union agreement as growing and significant between employers and trade unions (Millward 1994a). Furthermore, the 1990 WIRS threw distinct light on the prevailing nature of industrial relations practice in the absence of collective bargaining, a situation Sisson (1993) more accurately characterized as "bleak house" than as human resource management. A key way in which the findings of CLIRS have had an impact is in demonstrating the extent of corporate management intervention in establishing the budgetary and other parameters for pay settlements in what at first sight appears an increasingly decentralized and fragmented system of pay determination within Britain (Brown, Marginson, and Walsh 1995).

Because of the resources needed to conduct large-scale employer surveys, they are generally funded, wholly or partly, by governments. This raises the possibility that the research may be compromised by government officials, especially through the choice of questions and the selective reporting of results. Several factors serve to limit this influence. First, survey research requires skills generally found among only the professional researchers and subject specialists who form the core of the research team. Their professionalism militates against, for example, the inclusion of leading questions that policy advisers might suggest. That there is public access to the research instruments helps ensure that this professionalism is maintained. Second, voluntary surveys require the cooperation of large numbers of managers and employees. If the survey design and analysis were obviously subject to political bias or interference, that cooperation might well be withheld. Third, because the surveys discussed here are archived and used by other researchers, any attempts to misrepresent the findings would run the risk of being exposed through public scrutiny of the data and survey instruments.

Design Issues

Choice of Survey Instruments

The three main methods for conducting surveys—face-to-face interviews, telephone interviews, and self-administered questionnaires—can be used separately or in combination. The choice of method has a major impact on the amount and type of information that can be collected and on the number, length, wording, and sequencing of questions (Dilman 1978). WIRS and AWIRS used face-to-face interviews with managers and union representatives, supplemented, in the case of managers, with self-completed questionnaires when obtaining information that might have required referring to organizational records. AWIRS also used telephone interviews to administer a less complex questionnaire to managers at small workplaces.

Each approach has its place. Face-to-face interviews allow more in-depth probing and open-ended responses and often produce higher response rates than the other two methods but are extremely time-consuming and resource intensive and require highly trained interviewers. Self-administered questionnaires are useful for obtaining precise statistical information but are less likely to achieve high response rates, the maximum time required has to be shorter than is necessary for a face-to-face interview, and the researcher has little control over who completes the questionnaire or the quality of the information that is provided. Self-administered questionnaires are, however, cheaper to administer and process than interviews. Finally, telephone surveys are a relatively efficient and cost-effective way to obtain a limited amount of information. Modern computer-assisted interview systems allow, indeed require, skip questions to be programmed in, and they reduce interview errors by incorporating range checks and other logic checks as the interview proceeds. Processing time is also substantially reduced.

Choice and Definition of Units

Any statistical survey requires well-defined units as the focus for data collection and analysis. In surveys of persons few such difficulties arise. In social units such as households, however, problems of definition and identification emerge. In organizations or employing units, these problems proliferate. Complex organizations, such as business enterprises, may be conceptualized in differing ways, creating a pressing need for clear and consistent definitions.

In using surveys to study employment relationships, there are two types of units that have a strong claim to primacy: at one extreme the *workplace* or establishment, representing a single but spatially whole employing unit; at the other extreme a complete *organization* (or enterprise in the business sector), representing the worldwide collection of employing units under common ownership or control.

In between these extremes there may be a variety of other definable units, such as legally defined companies or divisions of a national enterprise. The most relevant intermediate unit for many surveys may well be the legal entity corresponding to an employer. In some instances, however, an individual employing unit may fit more than one definition. For example, a small business may have a single site and thus fit the definitions of both a workplace and a complete organization.

Most populations of employing units include both simple and complex units. To be able to generalize from the sample to the population, it must be clear what the units are.

How, then, are units chosen? This depends on the research issues and the researchers' prior knowledge of how the phenomena of interest vary across units of the population. If the research question concerns the practicalities of management-employee relations, the workplace seems to be the natural sampling unit. Of course, there may be variations within some workplaces that require additional questioning at the subunit level; there may also be uniformity across workplaces within some organizations and hence sampling more than one of their workplaces may be somewhat inefficient. But it is dangerous to assume this uniformity without secure prior knowledge.

If the research question largely concerns matters of policy and strategy and the structures through which they are formed and implemented, the enterprise or organization is the most relevant unit. Again, there may be variety between subunits; for example, product or geographically based divisions may have sufficient autonomy to formulate different policies and implementation structures, in which case additional questioning about these subunits will be required.

Focusing on practice at the workplace level or on policy at the enterprise level assumes too clear-cut a separation. Ideally, a survey concerned with either practice or policy would adopt a multistage design encompassing data collection from enterprises, workplaces, and individual employees. In reality, resource constraints, the burden of response on informants, and the complex logistics required to administer such a design militate against its use.[2]

Sample Design and Sampling Issues

Sampling frames for employing units share many of the problems of the more familiar frames for individuals and households: outdatedness, incompleteness, and partial or inaccurate information. In addition, there are problems unique to surveys of organizations, notably:

1. the unavailability of the frames constructed by government statistical agencies (usually the best frames available) because of legal restrictions or matters of confidentiality;
2. all or some units in the frame do not correspond to the statistical unit defined for the survey;
3. doubts about whether the unit still exists—for example, dormant businesses and those with no employees;
4. the high rate of turnover in very small units;
5. mergers, amalgamations, and fragmentations of units;
6. geographical clustering of some types of units, such as head offices in capital cities and primary industries around concentrations of natural resources and energy;
7. the vast range in the sizes of employing units in virtually any population that one might wish to study.

Any of these problems can be considerable. In relation to the second item, none of the potential sampling frames that were publicly available for the CLIRS research team contained usable data on the employment size of

2. For the second AWIRS, conducted in 1996, a multilevel design was used that involved interviewing both workplace managers and randomly selected employees within each workplace. This design was also adopted for the fourth WIRS in 1997.

U.K. enterprises. Consequently, the team had to compile its own frame, working from a list of enterprises that included information on worldwide employment. The seventh item takes on particular importance when the researchers intend to make estimates about employees in addition to estimates about the employing units in which they work. The almost universal practice, as in statistical surveys of economic phenomena (Sigman and Monsour 1995), is to sample larger units with higher probability than smaller units.

The most common method is to stratify the frame into size strata and oversample units in the larger strata. For the 1990 WIRS, for example, the sampling fractions varied from one in one hundred for units with twenty-five to forty-nine employees up to one in two for units with one thousand employees or more. Roughly equal target numbers were set within each size band so that comparisons across size bands could be made with greater precision. Further stratification variables may be introduced to improve the accuracy of estimates among categories on other variables, but adding more than two or three additional stratifying variables complicates the sample design while producing little additional benefit.

Access to Sampled Units

Approaching units that have been selected for a sample requires a tailored approach. In surveys of enterprises there is often little doubt about whom to approach, once the roles have been specified. In workplace surveys an important practical difficulty is that the person or persons who need to be interviewed may not have the authority to give an interview without receiving permission from a senior manager, often at the head office; yet when managers do request such permission, head office managers may take offense that they were not approached initially by the researchers. Highly clustered nonresponses can be the result. Hence, in both WIRS and AWIRS different approaches have been used for different parts of the sample: approaching head offices in organizations with several or many units in the sample and what are thought to be centralized personnel functions, and approaching establishment-level personnel otherwise (Millward 1991; Callus et al. 1991). This process is resource intensive but helps ensure the collection of high-quality data.

Operationalizing the Definition of the Survey Unit

Moving from an employer's name and address on a sample list to identifying the precise unit where the survey will be administered is fraught with difficulties. The contrasting approaches adopted by the WIRS and AWIRS research teams illustrate these well. In both cases the survey unit was defined as an establishment, by which was meant the operations of a single employer at (or from) a single site or address.

Where the surveys differed radically was in the way they dealt with organizational complexity at selected employment locations. The WIRS interviewers were instructed to cover *all* the employees of the named employer working at or from the employing unit, whether or not the employer had uniform or separate arrangements, practices, and management structures. Occasionally this required that two respondents answer for separate sections of the workforce. The AWIRS team, following Kelly (1990), adopted the opposite approach. They took the view that the activities of an employer at an address

> may be so varied that, in practice, there are a number of co-existing industrial relations sub-systems. Each may be managed and operate independently and have distinct rules, customs and culture. When a workplace address housed complex and diverse organisational structures or administrative units, in terms of industrial relations, it was regarded as consisting of several separate workplaces . . . [and] the survey reviewed the industrial relations structures and practices of the workplace [or sub-unit of a workplace in WIRS terminology] . . . with the largest number of employees (Callus et al. 1991: 9)

Selection of Respondents

Surveys of employing units rely on individuals whose responses are ascribed to the workplace or broader organization. In choosing these key informants, a central presumption is that their role within the employing unit places them in a position to be well informed about the issues addressed by the survey. Given the focus of workplace surveys, senior workplace managers responsible for personnel and industrial relations have been key informants in both the Australian and British series.

Under many circumstances the breadth of the issues being addressed has required multiple respondents. Thus, the researchers for both the Australian and British surveys interviewed up to three union representatives at each workplace because a manager could not be expected to be well informed on matters of union organization and activity in the workplace. The second CLIRS investigated the implications of the framework of budgetary control in large corporations for the management of industrial relations, using a senior finance executive as an additional respondent.

A common problem is whether there is any role holder at an employing unit who can act as a reliable informant. Much industrial relations practice occurs beyond the workplace, before tribunals (Australia and Canada) or at the industry level (Austria, Germany, and the Nordic countries), for example, whereas in many larger organizations top management may play pivotal roles. The key point is that questioning needs to focus on industrial relations matters that are within the purview of respondents at the employing unit identified.

Another potential problem is that the role of the preferred informant may not exist in all units within the sampling universe, or the incumbent cannot be interviewed. In such cases, if practicable, an alternative informant needs to be identified. For the 1990 WIRS, for example, in 18 percent of the workplaces either no manager responsible for personnel and industrial relations was found or the person could not be interviewed and the interviewers were obliged to find an alternative informant at a level above the workplace (Millward et al. 1992: 377).

In each of the WIRS, interviews were sought with representatives of the employees in establishments with recognized unions. In a minority of cases in each survey, the role of the preferred informant was found not to exist (Millward et al. 1992: 377). In some of these cases the position existed but was vacant; in others the representative worked elsewhere.

Not only are respondents informants but they are also actors in an organization who have their own perceptions of events and practices, and they may be prone to exaggerate their own roles and to downplay those of other actors. Hence, one rationale for utilizing more than one informant within an employing unit is to identify differences in perceptions between role holders. This was an explicit objective of the first British CLIRS. Concerns had been expressed (Purcell 1983) that earlier workplace surveys (WIRS 1980 and its predecessors) that relied on the accounts of workplace-based managers had given an exaggerated impression of their autonomy. Consequently, the CLIRS research team interviewed the managers responsible for personnel and industrial relations at two or three different levels, ranging up from the workplace, through the division, to the corporate head office. Differences in the accounts of the managers at the different levels were evident, and regarding some specific events workplace managers appeared to claim more discretion than was attributed to them by their higher-level counterparts. There was, however, no general systematic bias in the accounts of the managers at any particular level (Marginson et al. 1988: 227–57).

Not surprisingly, the accounts of managers and union representatives in workplace surveys have differed too, even over such fundamental matters as whether industrial action occurred in the recent past (Daniel and Mill-ward 1983). This was dealt with by taking either respondent's report that an incident had occurred. On most other matters there was little difference in the aggregate, and managers' accounts were used because they were available for the whole sample.

For some variables the aggregate distributions for two groups of respon-dents may be very similar even though substantial within-unit discordance exists. For the 1990 WIRS, in 59 percent of the workplaces where both management and union representatives were interviewed, both groups of respondents reported the presence of a joint consultative committee. In 28 percent, however, there was discordance on whether such a committee ex-isted (Cully and Marginson 1995). These differences in view would be an interesting topic for analysis in their own right.

Survey Instruments for Heterogeneous Populations

To conduct national employer-based surveys requires administering a standardized survey instrument to all units within the sample. In designing this instrument, survey researchers confront two particular problems: first, the diversity of structures, institutions, and practices across employing units means that potentially whole sections of questions may not be applicable to a sizable number of units; and second, differences in structures, institu-tions, and practices may exist among employee groups within an employing unit.

The usual solution to the first problem lies in routing respondents through the questionnaire in such a way that they are asked only about matters that are applicable. For instance, questions about union organiza-tion would be asked only where there were members present. In this way respondents' attention is more likely to be held, and the quality of the data collected is likely to be higher.

The more heterogeneous the population being sampled, the more diffi-cult it is to design a standardized questionnaire that is appropriate for use in all units in the sample. Hence, in AWIRS, which covered some establish-ments that had only five employees, a separate questionnaire was designed for workplaces with fewer than twenty employees because it was felt that many of the more structured relationships that are a feature of larger work-places did not exist in smaller ones.

It is common for industrial relations structures, institutions, and prac-tices to vary among the workforce of a particular employing unit, especially when companies or enterprises are being considered. Important differences may exist between subunits defined by occupational status or group; whether the groups' terms and conditions are determined through collective bargaining; employment status (full time or part time; continuing, fixed term or temporary); and whether the groups work at the same or different sites. The designers of the questionnaire need to recognize these differences; otherwise, respondents will find questions difficult to answer or will make generalizations based on one subunit about the whole workforce without informing the researcher.

One solution is to adopt an exhaustive approach that asks about each group in the workforce. This practice is time-consuming and therefore costly, and it may put respondents' goodwill at risk since questions will need to be repeated for different groups. Another solution is to ask about whichever group is numerically dominant or in some other way typical or most salient. Industrial relations in employing units is then characterized based on a subgroup, albeit typical, within the workforce, and generalizations from employing units to employees become problematic. WIRS and AWIRS have tended toward an exhaustive approach because of the importance attached to generalizing the findings to employees as well as employing units. In contrast, because the company-level surveys aimed to be able to generalize findings to (large) employing units and not to employees, the 1992 CLIRS focused on the numerically largest groups as defined by occupational status.

Turning Concepts into Questions

A major challenge in all surveys is operationalizing concepts to ensure that questions capture the phenomena that are being examined. For example, researchers may be interested in measuring the extent to which workplaces are managed under the precepts of human resource management. Clearly, HRM means different things to different people—respondents, as well as researchers. Accordingly, asking managers to state on a five-point scale the extent to which their workplace practices HRM would be unlikely to produce meaningful results. The researcher has to operationalize the concept by asking a series of specific questions about the components of HRM, in particular whether various practices and policies exist and some of the details.

Thus, many concepts and variables cannot be measured with a single question. The results of several questions can be combined at the analysis stage, although this will require more complex descriptive writing than just reporting on the results of the questions. This flexibility is two-edged. It gives more scope for the creation of useful derived variables, but it requires more documentation and allows more scope for dispute among researchers about the best measure of the underlying concept. Nevertheless, using more complex derived variables can often resolve initial doubts about the validity of measures. Thus, Millward's (1994a) analysis of the extent to which workplaces had consultative committees focused only on "functioning committees," excluding those that had met infrequently and those that management reported had discussed nothing of importance in the last year. This more restrictive definition strengthened Millward's conclusion that the dual system of representation, through collective bargaining and consultative channels, had been most in decline in the late 1980s.

Another potential problem in question design occurs because respondents may want to give socially desirable responses. For example, managers may feel that having an effective consultation channel with employees is socially desirable and may spuriously respond positively if asked a question framed in such a way. Such bias is less likely if the question is broken down, as illustrated above, into separate questions about the existence of a consultative channel, its frequency of use, and the issues it addresses.

Response and Data Quality

A high response rate is crucial to achieving high-quality data. Appropriate access procedures contribute to this rate; so does promising to provide feedback of the results to respondents and following through.

The scale of the resources devoted to achieving a high response rate is paramount. On both WIRS and AWIRS, these resources were considerable, resulting in response rates of 73, 77, and 83 percent on the three WIRS surveys and 87 percent on AWIRS. Response rates for the two company-level surveys were lower: 55 percent for CLIRS1 and 28 percent for CLIRS2. The requirement that interviewers needed to achieve matched interviews with managers at different levels (CLIRS1) or in different functions (CLIRS2) was an important reason for the lower rates. In the second survey securing agreement by senior finance executives to be interviewed proved particularly difficult.[3]

The value of a high response rate is twofold. First, it increases the confidence with which the sample data can be used to make inferences about the population: the higher the response rate, the lower the possibility of undetected nonresponse bias. Second, a high response rate is a general but im-

---

3. Thorough checks for nonresponse bias among the achieved sample were taken utilizing information on the wider population obtained at an earlier screening stage in the sampling process (Marginson et al. 1993: 3).

perfect indicator of overall data quality: research organizations that allocate the professional resources necessary to achieving high response rates are likely to have high standards in other areas of the fieldwork process. These considerations apply regardless of the survey instrument that is used.

Analysis of Employer-Based Surveys

Data Availability and Confidentiality

In each of the three surveys discussed in this chapter, the survey data have been made available to the public[4] so that "secondary" analysis has been an integral part of the research program. Public access was certainly facilitated by the nature of the data that were collected. Little was commercially sensitive or quantitative. The surveys did not collect precise financial figures for sales, R&D expenditures, or capital employed, for example. Nevertheless, in combination, information on a few variables, such as size, industry, and location, could have led to the identification of some large employers. In practice, the data have not been abused in this way, and the initial assurances given to respondents by the research teams were generally sufficient to allay fears of disclosure. Respondents were told that neither individuals nor their employing organizations would be identified in the published results and that the names and addresses of employing units would not be included in the data files used by the primary research team or later released for public use.

Arrangements for public access were made at the start of the projects, ensuring much wider use of the data by the academic community than generally occurs. In the cases of WIRS and AWIRS, this secondary analysis is as extensive as it is for many national personal and household surveys held by the national data archives.

Descriptive Analysis

In describing findings on the practices and policies of industrial relations, survey researchers have explored the presence and extent of differences based on the key characteristics of the employing units. These characteristics usually relate to the structure, ownership, and environment of the workplace or organization and of the workforce. The relevance of many of these characteristics derives from ex ante expectations taken from

---

4. All the relevant data sets are available from the ESRC Data Archive, University of Essex, Wivenhoe Park, Colchester, Essex, CO4 3SQ, United Kingdom.

the existing literature; that of others emerges ex post in the process of exploratory analysis.

Researchers have also sought to distinguish key institutional features that underpin marked differences in policies and practices among employing units. Not only are these classificatory variables valuable in descriptive analysis, but they are also important as control variables for multivariate analysis seeking to test more precise propositions. Each of these characteristics is considered in turn.

One obviously important structural characteristic is the size of the workforce: analyses of workplace surveys have consistently found that the size of the workplace workforce and, where applicable, of the owning organization is associated with differences in practice. So too is whether the workplace is an independent establishment or a branch of a larger organization or the head office of a larger organization.

In company-level surveys, the size of the total (national) workforce appears to be less of an influence, whereas the number of workplaces an enterprise owns is more strongly associated with differences in industrial relations structures and policy at the corporate level. At the company level too, the divisional structure (product, functional, or geographically based) has proved to be salient. Important differences in industrial relations practice and policy have also been identified with whether an employing unit is privately or publicly owned and, within the private sector, whether the employing organization is home or foreign based and, if the latter, its country of origin.

Besides the obvious differences that are evident across economic sectors (primary, manufacturing, and service) and by industry, more theoretically based descriptors have been found to be useful, such as the degree of competition in product markets, measures of the spatial scope of competition, and trends in product demand.

In differentiating between employees across units, three main characteristics have been used: occupation, personal attributes, and employment status. The two most basic occupational distinctions have been between manual and nonmanual employees and between managerial and nonmanagerial employees. Among personal attributes, the gender composition of the workforce has consistently been found to be associated with differences in practices and outcomes. Ethnic composition has been considered less frequently, perhaps because workforces with a preponderance of employees who are ethnic minorities are relatively rare in Britain and Australia.

Whether employment is full time or part time and whether it is permanent, fixed term, or casual have also been shown to have a bearing on practice. Although difficult to distinguish from the gender effect (since most part-time workers are female), the effect of working part time appears to be particularly pronounced.

In practical terms, a workplace can be classified along each of these dimensions as being predominantly either of one type or another; more illuminating categories separate out workplaces with more extreme proportions. Typologies using two or more dimensions of workforce composition have only rarely been used because the researchers run up against the difficulty of containing some categories with few observations.

Showing that there is an association between, for example, having a high proportion of part-time employees in the workforce and a low rate of unionization is only an indirect demonstration of something that could be shown directly with more specific questioning. Different groups of employees within the same workplace may be parties to different industrial relations practices; this returns to the question of whether the researchers should attempt to include in their analysis a description of practices across an entire employing unit or focus on subgroups within it. Where institutional arrangements for different workforce groups are markedly different, either parallel accounts are required or a single account based on the most significant group.

Certain features of the institutional landscape of industrial relations have long been regarded as pivotal in shaping wider policy and practice. In the WIRS series a central distinction has been made between those workplaces and workforce groups where management recognizes trade unions for the purposes of negotiating pay and conditions of employment and those where management does not. This definition of union representation stemmed from the importance of the recognition decision to the conduct of industrial relations in Britain—based, as it is, on voluntarism. In Australia, where there is no equivalent of the recognition decision, analysis of the AWIRS data suggested that the mere presence of union members in the workplace did not especially differentiate workplaces by their industrial relations practices. More important was an active union presence, defined as the presence of an active union delegate, a functioning union committee, and meetings of members (Callus et al. 1991).

On the management side, the presence at the workplace of a manager who specializes in personnel and industrial relations has been identified as underpinning some noticeable differences in practice. In workplaces that are part of larger organizations, differences have also been evident depending on whether there is a board director for personnel. Classification at the organizational level was taken further in the company-level surveys, in which the size of the corporate personnel function was found to be associated with differences in policy and practice.

The AWIRS researchers went a considerable step further and combined indicators of union presence with those of management organization and a measure of the extent to which joint arrangements existed for the conduct of industrial relations to develop a typology aimed at characterizing the industrial relations regimes of different workplaces. On this basis, five predominant regimes were identified (Callus et al. 1991); these accounted for three-quarters (76 percent) of the sample. In his survey of U.S. private-sector workplaces, Osterman (1994) differentiated workplaces according to the forms of management and work organization that supported "high-commitment" employment practices (see also MacDuffie 1995).

Weighting and Estimation Issues

A basic purpose behind any survey is to make estimates about the population from the sample. Since simple random sample designs are hardly ever appropriate for surveys of organizational units and larger units are almost always sampled disproportionately, weighting the results is invariably necessary. The range of weights is generally much larger in employer-based surveys than in surveys of individuals. In the 1990 WIRS, for example, the sampling fractions varied from one in one hundred to one in two, so that the range of weights to compensate for different selection probabilities was 50:1.

Any additional weighting, to compensate for frame inadequacies or differential response rates, increases the range of weighting values and reduces the effective sample size further. In the 1990 WIRS two types of additional weighting were used, and the final range of weights was 420:1. With such large ranges, it is clearly imperative that the weights be used for all descriptive purposes, but it must be recognized that the estimates so produced are much less precise than with a simple random sample of similar size.

Although the main use of the survey data in employer-based surveys is to report estimates and relationships for the survey units, an alternative form of description is based on employees. Here estimates are phrased in terms of the proportion of employees in survey units who have a particular characteristic. Thus, the results of the 1990 WIRS indicated that 45 percent of British private manufacturing establishments determined the pay of manual workers through collective bargaining, whereas 70 percent of manual workers were employed in establishments where their pay was determined in this way (Millward et al. 1992: 221–23). To produce these estimates, each weighted case is multiplied by the size of the surveyed unit's workforce.

While the argument in favor of weighting for descriptive purposes is incontestable, the issue of weighting for multivariate statistical analysis is less clear-cut. Almost all analysts who have used WIRS data have used unweighted estimation, but Skinner (1996) argues that the use of unweighted regressions is justifiable only if employment size is exogenous and included as a covariate and if some strong assumptions are made. He goes on to suggest checks of robustness and the use of weighted regressions where employment size is endogenous.

Accuracy of Estimates

Survey-based estimates are subject to many sources of error, most of which are not quantifiable and can be minimized only with careful survey design and conduct. The one source of easily quantifiable error is sampling error.

Sampling errors for complex, stratified survey designs are generally greater than for simple random samples of equivalent size, but computer programs for measuring errors for complex samples are not widely available or used. Moreover, accompanying every survey estimate with its standard error would add substantially to the cost, time, and length of any primary analysis, as well as give undue emphasis to sampling error among the range of sources of error. To avoid this situation and still give the reader some information with which to evaluate the accuracy of the survey results, both the WIRS and AWIRS research teams have included tables of illustrative sampling errors in their initial reports.[5]

Very few of the secondary analyses of the three surveys discussed here have reported standard errors for descriptive statistics. All of them reporting econometric or multivariate analysis include standard errors of regression coefficients, however, often to very high and clearly spurious levels of detail. It is unclear whether these reported standard errors take into account the design factors arising from the complex sample designs used. If they do not, it is likely that many relationships reported as "statistically significant" at conventional levels are not in fact so.

---

5. The calculations for WIRS included finite population corrections, especially important for the larger size bands.

Studying Change and Continuity

Industrial relations have changed rapidly in the past, and survey researchers have been much concerned with investigating the extent and nature of these changes. In a single, cross-sectional survey, these changes can be addressed feasibly only through retrospective questions. Such questioning is hazardous because respondents may not have occupied the same role over the period concerned, and even if they have, their recall of events may not be accurate. Nonetheless, by focusing on specified time periods, the WIRS have successfully addressed major issues surrounding changes in employment practice at the workplace, most notably in WIRS2 concerning new technology and innovations in work organization (Daniel 1987).

Survey series, as in the case of WIRS and now AWIRS, open up the possibilities for measuring the extent of change.[6] Provided the survey design remains constant and a core of questions remains unchanged, direct comparisons of industrial relations practices can be made at two or more points in time for the population from which the survey samples are drawn. It has thus become possible to measure the durability, decline, and rise of certain structures and practices across the population of workplaces in Britain and Australia. Perhaps most graphically, WIRS has charted the decline of union recognition and collective bargaining in Britain between the first survey in 1980 and the third in 1990 (Millward et al. 1992).

Cross-sectional comparisons reveal the extent of change across the population, but they do not enable researchers to fully apportion that part due to the changing composition of the population (the opening of new and the closing of existing employing units) and that due to changes in practice within the part of the population that has survived. The latter was facilitated by the addition of a longitudinal dimension to the design of the 1990 WIRS whereby interviews were conducted at a panel sample of surviving establishments from the previous survey. The second AWIRS also included a separate panel element. With such longitudinal data sets, the causes and effects of changes can also be investigated more readily.

Using the 1990 WIRS panel data, Millward (1994b) has assessed the extent of change and continuity in the surviving population since 1984. On the coverage of collective bargaining, for example, the panel data show a decline in the industry and commerce sector from 59 to 46 percent of employees. An important element of this decline is shown to be due to either total or partial derecognition of trade unions for collective bargaining pur-

---

6. The second AWIRS was being completed while this chapter was being written.

poses. As Millward indicates, the changing composition of the workforce within establishments has been a further influence.

Valuable information also comes from the unproductive element of the panel sample—those establishments that closed between 1984 and 1990: union recognition was no more prevalent among these establishments than among those that survived (Millward 1994a and 1994b). The new workplaces did display a lower incidence of union recognition, however. Only in this respect was the decline in union recognition and in the extent of collective bargaining coverage, revealed in the cross-sectional comparison, attributable to changes in the composition of the population.

Both the WIRS and AWIRS series have incorporated new lines of questioning on industrial relations practices that have been identified in the literature as emergent. For instance, WIRS 1990 contained more extensive questioning on employee communication and involvement practices and on performance-related pay than did its predecessors. In AWIRS, the second survey contains more questioning about enterprise bargaining, an emergent phenomenon since the first survey.

More problematic for a survey series is how to address shifts in the underlying approach taken by management in its industrial relations practices. In the case of WIRS, the breaking down of the manual/nonmanual distinction called into question the contemporary relevance of persisting with those parts of the survey design that rested on this distinction. And the decline of the collective bargaining model of industrial relations practice in Britain raised questions about the centrality of union recognition to parts of the design (Cully and Marginson 1995).

The fundamental dilemma facing the designers of future surveys in the two series is how best to reflect changes in approaches to industrial relations and elements of continuity that enable comparisons to be made with earlier survey results. Perhaps the most satisfactory solution is to have separate elements to address each of these broad purposes: a cross-sectional survey that aims to measure the current situation and a separate panel survey, tailored to measure change and continuity since the previous wave of the series. The next-best solution might be to make the panel serve both purposes with a single instrument, supplementing it with a sample of new units created since the previous survey; this would be more restrictive, however, in terms of updating the survey questions to capture recent developments.

Challenges and Opportunities

This chapter has identified the key areas in which there are challenges for those designing and analyzing large-scale surveys of industrial relations practices and policies in employing units. A further challenge stems from the growing interest in the performance outcomes of particular industrial relations practices or "bundles" of practices (MacDuffie 1995), stimulated in some countries by the spread of human resource management but also by the growing influence of a political economy perspective within industrial relations. Attention needs to be paid to developing and refining robust measures of a wider range of performance indicators used by organizations, embracing such elements as delivery, equity, and the quality of products and of the working environment, as well as profitability and productivity.

Another challenge is to realize the potential inherent in questioning two or more respondents within an employing unit. Respondents are not only informants but actors involved in the events and practices about which they are questioned. Yet most users of survey data sets have barely recognized the implications of potential discordance among respondents. Further, little direct work has been done on patterns of this discordance. The addition of an employee survey in the second AWIRS, and now in the fourth WIRS, poses a major challenge to survey researchers in this regard. To what extent, for instance, do managers and employees perceive practices and their effects in similar or differing ways? And how are employees' views to be summarized so that they can be compared with a manager's in the same workplace?

Perhaps the most difficult challenges facing survey researchers involve the conceptualization and measurement of change. Changes in the structure of employment pose one kind of challenge. For example, a growing proportion of the workforce in the industrialized economies are employed in smaller workplaces, are under more precarious contractual arrangements, or are self-employed. Such workers are less likely to be subject to the formal industrial relations practices that have typically been the focus of large-scale surveys. With the decline in collective representation, there is a new emphasis on individually oriented practices and on ad hoc arrangements. Such new and informal practices are more elusive and difficult to capture with standardized questionnaires.

Further, it has been argued that the design of workplace and company-level surveys is inherently conservative: that by focusing on structures and practices, they have tended to underline continuity while failing to uncover changes in processes and outcomes (Morris and Wood 1991). Survey instruments are likely to remain fairly insensitive to partial and incipient change of the kind uncovered by in-depth interviews; but few would consider them the most appropriate research tool for this purpose. Yet successive surveys in the British WIRS series have continued to identify change, as well as continuity, in structures, practices, and the substance of what occurs within structures. Moreover, panel designs offer considerable potential for explaining the sources of change.

Large-scale surveys benefit from being associated with more intensive research methods; they can also provide a systematic basis for selecting case studies, as has been done in the AWIRS and WIRS series and in both CLIRS studies. Comparing findings from survey and ethnographic methods, Morris and Wood found that "the survey method appears to have high validity as a way of mapping accurately the institutional arrangements of industrial relations management" (1991: 265). Considerable similarity was also found in the broad patterns of change both methods identified. Overall, large-scale surveys will continue to provide the most secure form of evidence for mapping and monitoring changes in the major contours of industrial relations structures and practices at national levels.

CHAPTER TEN

Employee Attitude Surveys

Jean Hartley and Julian Barling

*E*mployee attitude surveys are widely used by industrial/organizational (I/O) psychologists (e.g., Tetrick and Barling 1995) and have a long history of use in psychological research (see Nadler 1977; French and Bell 1990; Kraut 1996). Increasingly, they are being used by "mainstream" industrial relations scholars, for example, those concerned with labor-management relations (e.g., Edwards and Whitston 1993; Kochan 1979) and with nonunion employees' attitudes toward unionization (e.g., Getman, Goldberg, and Herman 1976).

The aim of this chapter is to explore the meanings and uses of employee attitude surveys. We provide a brief history of their use in industrial relations and I/O psychology research, illustrating the theoretical and empirical questions that this research method can be used to address. We then examine some of the research design and practical questions associated with using employee surveys. Finally, employee surveys are placed in their organizational context, an often neglected area in texts on survey design and use.

What Is an Employee Attitude Survey?

A *survey* is a "systematic collection of information from large study groups, usually by means of interviews or questionnaires administered to samples of units in the population" (Rossi and Freeman 1982: 90). A more pragmatic

Julian Barling gratefully acknowledges the financial support provided by the Social Sciences and Humanities Research Council of Canada during the writing of this chapter.

definition suggests that a survey is "a system for collecting information to describe, compare, or explain knowledge, attitudes and behavior" (Fink 1995: 1).

Across both definitions, several features are important. First, there is a link between the sample and the population. Not all those in a population (e.g., all employees in the United Kingdom or all employees in a particular organization) have to provide information for assessments to be made about them. Instead, a sample (taken to be representative in some way) of respondents is identified and contacted, and their responses are used to make generalizations about the larger group or population. While the term "survey" is sometimes taken to mean a national survey (such as the British Social Attitudes Survey or the Quality of Employment Survey in the United States), the term applies equally to a study that examines employee views in a single organization (e.g., Nicholson, Ursell, and Blyton 1981). The key issue is that the sample should reflect the specified population.

Second, the focus is on the *systematic* collection of information. Thus, identical or nearly identical questions are asked in an identical or nearly identical way of all respondents, using questions that are as precise and un-ambiguous as possible, so that comparisons between groups are justified. This concern with systematic data collection also means that methodological issues of reliability and validity are critical.

Third, data for employee attitude surveys are obtained from *self-reports*. Respondents are asked about their attitudes, knowledge, perceptions, opinions or their behavior, and all this information comes from the respondents rather than from the researcher. Surveys usually focus on respondents' own experiences. Less frequently, respondents may be asked about their perceptions of others (e.g., other team members, subordinates, their boss) or their expectations about how many other people are likely to act in a certain way (e.g., how many other people are likely to take part in industrial action; see Klandermans 1984). But even these questions are based on perceptions rather than the actual behavior of others. Surveys may also collect information of a dispositional nature, such as personality and personal characteristics.

Given the intensely subjective world with which attitude surveys deal, there are key psychological processes of which the researcher must be aware so that the least bias is introduced into the survey: how accurately respondents understand what is being asked of them how they perceive the phenomena under investigation, how well (or poorly) they are motivated to participate and to give honest answers, how well they can communicate their inner world. All these psychological processes affect the reliability and validity of the data gathered.

Even objective data, such as age and family circumstances, may be subject to social desirability and contextual effects (see Starbuck and Mezias 1996). Thus, the context within which the survey is conducted is crucial to the gathering and interpretation of high-quality data.

Attitude surveys can be used to explore a variety of psychological phenomena and behaviors, including knowledge, beliefs, attributions, opinions, attitudes, values, expectations, perceptions, satisfaction, behavioral intentions, and reported behaviors. Three sets of (overlapping) psychological phenomena can be delineated: cognitions (thoughts and perceptions), affect or feelings, and behavior and behavioral intentions.

Forms of Surveys

Given this psychological complexity, a survey may be conducted using a variety of methods. Self-completed questionnaires, with fixed questions and fixed-format answers (e.g., Likert scales), are the most frequently used method. They are also administratively the simplest, least expensive, and most popular approach. Self-completed questionnaires are usually of the pencil-and-paper variety, though there is increasing interest in computer-based questionnaire distribution and completion, through e-mail, for example (Kuhnert and McCanley 1996). Surveys may also include requests for open-ended comments.

Self-administered questionnaires can be problematic for workers who are not in physical situations that are conducive to questionnaire completion and for workers for whom reading and writing are an effort. Response rates for self-administered questionnaires are lower under such circumstances. Instead of relying solely on self-completion, researchers may opt to have the standard questionnaire read to respondents, either face-to-face or by telephone.

Focus groups are a way to elicit responses from a group of respondents (e.g., employees) who are gathered together. They were originally developed for use in market and political research but are now used in the social sciences more generally. Focus groups can be useful either for economies of scale or especially for the exploration of issues and the development of complex arguments. It is harder to be rigorous in focus group research, however, because of the tendency for the group dynamics to influence the quality and type of data that are obtained.

In projective tests, a person is given incomplete information and asked to add his or her own information or interpretation. This is then used to assess implicit attitudes. Respondents might be asked to complete sentences, as in the Twenty Statements Test (see, e.g., Nicholson and Rees 1994), or to fill in the blank speech bubbles above cartoon characters, as was used in a study of the attitudes of banking staff toward their customers (Cassels 1995). With careful use, however, both focus groups and projective tests can be used to make generalizations from sample to population.

Employee Attitude Surveys in Organizational Research and Organization Development

The long history of using employee surveys, especially questionnaires, in I/O psychology dates back to studies of personality, skill, fatigue, and leadership during and after World War I (Shimmin and Wallis 1994). The subsequent development of tests and measures for self-completion by employees led to the publication of several compendiums of tests and measures (e.g., Cook et al. 1981; Beardon, Netemeyer, and Mobley 1993). These provide not only the measures but details of their reliability and validity and their use in published studies.

Employee attitude surveys have also been used within the organization development movement (French and Bell 1990; Nadler 1977). From the 1940s onward, the Survey Research Center at the University of Michigan pioneered and promoted the use of questionnaires as one means of understanding employees' attitudes and behaviors. Early work suggested that when survey results were available only to managers and supervisors, little positive organizational change occurred. In contrast, when findings were shared in discussions with employees, more favorable changes were likely. Survey feedback techniques (based on administering surveys for the purpose of providing employees with feedback), using either standard questionnaires or questions developed specifically for the organization, are now common in organization development (Burke, Coruzzi, and Church 1996).

In practical terms, conducting employee surveys has been seen as part of good human resource management practice, enabling an organization, especially larger ones, to learn what employees are thinking and feeling about the organization and its management (Kraut 1996). A survey of U.K. managers' attitudes toward employee involvement showed that more than one-quarter (28 percent) reported that their organizations used attitude surveys and nearly half (48 percent) of large organizations (more than five thousand employees) used them (O'Creevy 1995). If they are well designed and conducted, surveys can provide researchers with valuable material about employees' views (though issues of impartiality still need to be confronted).

Within industrial relations research, the early research period, with its primary focus on institutions and rules (Edwards 1995), has meant that attention has been paid to those people such as personnel and human resource managers, full-time union officials, or shop stewards who understand and can talk about the complexities of institutional arrangements, rules, and procedures. The average employee or trade union member neither knows nor perhaps cares much about institutional matters, and until recently their views were rather neglected. The changing focus of employment relations has resulted in expanded interest in the attitudes, opinions, and reported behaviors of these employees (Hartley and Stephenson 1992).

One particular contribution that can be made through psychological analyses, often involving employee surveys, concerns the interpretation and understanding of some of the profound changes that have been taking place in employment and in employment relations over the last two decades (Hartley 1992 and 1995; Tetrick and Barling 1995). There are different views about the extent and meaning of the changes that have occurred. Nonetheless, any assessment will depend on the extent to which attitudes, values, and behaviors have changed—which in part requires researching the views of employees themselves. Employee as well as trade union or employer surveys are therefore important in understanding contemporary employment relations.

Researchers are also trying to understand the motivations, perceptions, and attitudes of employees in nonunion firms (e.g., McLoughlin and Gourlay 1992). Further, growing interest is being paid to those groups of employees that are increasing as a proportion of the workforce—women, service workers, part-time employees, and those with insecure or short-term fixed contracts (see Barker 1995; Hartley 1996). We do not yet understand enough about their experiences of work and employment. Significantly, the nature and focus of such constructs as organizational commitment, job involvement, and job satisfaction may vary between full-time and part-time employees, especially those working in more than one part-time job (Barling and Gallagher 1996), and this may affect the survey focus and interpretation.

HRM has also been a stimulus for research on employees and hence for the use of employee surveys. Research in this area was aided considerably by the development of standardized employee attitude measures, including measures of organizational commitment (Mowday, Porter, and Steers 1982; Meyer, Bobocel, and Allen 1991; Cook and Wall 1980). This development provided the technology needed to investigate this issue and inspired the theoretical and psychometric development of measures of union commitment (Gordon et al. 1980; Barling, Fullagar, and Kelloway 1992; Hartley 1992). This meant that commitment had been operationalized and could be carefully measured, beyond qualitative data derived from case studies.

Another area in which there has been increased use of employee surveys focuses on culture and changes in the cultures of organizations. There are arguments about whether culture can be measured with conventional tools, such as questionnaires, and whether individuals can provide an appropriate level of analysis of this social phenomenon (see Sparrow 1996). Some would argue that culture can only be accessed, not measured, and that this inevitably calls for the use of qualitative or projective methods. Others would say that although culture is inevitably diffuse and not susceptible to direct measurement, a similar construct that is quantifiable and accessible is organizational *climate.*

The construct climate reflects the relatively stable characteristics of the organization or group which are experienced by all or most members of the group and that affect their behavior. Researchers have also examined particular climates, such as those concerned with innovation, learning, or safety. There are several standardized measures available for assessing climate. Debate has raged over the range and depth of agreement that should exist among employees before an organization can be described as having a climate, and complex mathematical procedures have been used to attempt to determine this (Jacofsky and Slocum 1990; Payne 1990).

As organizations and employment relations have been changing, there has been increasing interest in how people perceive and value their employment. This could emerge as a topic of considerable concern to employment relations researchers. The notion of the psychological contract has a reasonably long pedigree (e.g., Schein 1980) but is now increasingly used to explain how employees are reacting to some of the profound changes taking place in their organizations, their work, and their careers (e.g., Rousseau 1995; Rousseau and Parks 1993). It has been argued that changes in the expectations of the relationship between organization and employee are leading to reduced levels of trust, commitment, and performance (Hartley et al. 1991). Quantitative measures of the psychological contract and its "violation" have been developed (e.g., Rousseau 1995). This is an important development that may influence our understanding of employees' perceptions of and the motivations affecting their relations with their organizations.

There is vigorous and growing interest in employment relations among organizational psychologists (e.g., Hartley and Stephenson 1992; Tetrick and Barling 1995; Barling, Fullagar, and Kelloway 1992). Employee surveys have been conducted to understand attitudes toward union certification (e.g., Getmen, Goldberg, and Herman 1976); attitudes toward and commitment to a union (Tetrick and Barling 1995; Barling, Fullagar, and Kelloway 1992; Hartley 1996; Nicholson, Ursell, and Blyton 1981), the willingness to take part in industrial action (Klandermans 1984); participation in the union (Barling, Fullagar, and Kelloway 1992; Kelloway and Barling 1993), attitudes toward industrial relations following a strike (Bluen and Barling 1988; Hartley, Kelly, and Nicholson 1983); and attitudes toward total quality management (Morrow 1997).

Questions Appropriate for Employee Survey Methodology

The features that make employee surveys unique—that they focus on the employee (rather than on the trade union official or HRM manager), that they are based on self-reported data, and that they attempt to elicit information representative of a larger population—create both opportunities and constraints regarding the kinds of questions that are most appropriately addressed by such a method. Surveys can be used to obtain both descriptive and inferential statistics about employees.

Generalizing from and Comparing Samples

Using careful sampling and statistical techniques, information from a sample can be generalized to the larger population from which the sample was drawn. Often this population will be within one organization (e.g., women employees, new recruits, manual workers), but it may cross several organizations (e.g., nonunion firms, small firms, or firms with union certification campaigns). More rarely, perhaps because of the resources required to devise the questionnaires and access the sample, surveys may be undertaken to generalize the findings to a whole nation (e.g., the employment questions in the British Social Attitudes Survey).

The development of standardized questions, with known psychometric properties and information that has been published from other studies, enables comparisons to be made across organizations (assuming similarity of context). For example, the measure of union commitment developed by Gordon and his colleagues (1980) has been rigorously tested for its psychometric properties and has now been used in studying union commitment across many countries.

Making Causal Inferences

Employee attitude surveys can contribute to answering theoretical questions about the antecedents and consequences of certain phenomena, using inferential statistics when quantitative data are available. For example, Gordon and his colleagues (1980) suggested that positive socialization experiences in the first year in which an employee is a union member leads to union commitment, and subsequent survey research confirmed this hypothesis: those union members who were supported or encouraged during their first year of membership were more likely to report higher levels of union loyalty, responsibility to the union, willingness to work for the union, and beliefs in unionism generally. This finding has immense theoretical and practical significance for understanding and influencing union commitment (Fullagar, McCoy, and Shull 1992; Fullagar and Barling 1989).

Equally important, employee attitude surveys have been used to explore some of the consequences of union commitment, though not as many as might be hoped (Barling, Fullagar, and Kelloway 1992). Research has linked union commitment with behavioral intentions to participate in a range of membership activities (e.g., Sverke 1995) and with reported behaviors (e.g., Fullagar and Barling 1989 and 1991; Kelloway and Barling 1993). Research has also shown that training workshops for union members can increase both union commitment and intentions to work for the union (Catano, Cole, and Hebert 1995).

By using similar instruments in different studies with different samples, a picture can be developed using inferential statistics of the antecedents and consequences of particular phenomena and a model proposed that can be subjected to empirical scrutiny. We have illustrated this with the case of union commitment (see Barling, Fullagar, and Kelloway 1992; Hartley 1992), but this process has also occurred in areas such as organizational commitment (Meyer, Bobocel, and Allen 1991), preferred styles of managing conflict (e.g., Carnevale and Keenan 1992), job satisfaction (Smith, Kendall, and Hulin 1969; Iffaldano and Muchinsky 1985); organizational climate (e.g., Sparrow 1997), and trust in organizations (Cook and Wall 1980).

There are theoretical reasons for treating some causal inferences as more plausible than others. The careful and explicit consideration of hypothesized relationships is invaluable here. Researchers have also tried to circumvent some of the problems of causation in cross-sectional research through the use of such analytical techniques as LISREL (see, e.g., Kelloway 1996). The aim is to specify which variables precede others theoretically and then test these statistically by comparing the predicted path with alternatives. For example, this technique has been used to study the transmission of union attitudes from parent to child (Barling, Kelloway, and Bremermann 1991; Kelloway and Watts 1994).

Longitudinal Research

On the one hand, surveys are particularly appropriate in research designs that depend on the collection of data over time. Both standardized measures and either panel or representative samples enable the researcher to keep the measure and the population relatively constant so that change in other variables can then be measured. Thus, Meyer and Allen (1987) were able to track the development (and, for some employees, the decline) over time of organizational commitment among newly recruited graduates working in large companies. Wall and his colleagues (1986) were able to examine the detailed impact of changes in employees' job design on their levels of job satisfaction, trust in management, and job involvement, among other variables.

On the other hand, although longitudinal research is valuable for understanding causality and establishing change over time, certain cautions should be borne in mind when using employee surveys in this way. To establish change over time requires both stability in the measure and stability in the sample. Reliability calculations are undertaken to establish the stability of the measure; however, these are premised on the assumption that the phenomenon under study remains constant in its conceptual structure.

Golembiewski, Billingsley, and Yeager (1976) argue that there are three kinds of change, which they call alpha, beta, and gamma change. These can have important impacts on measurement and measurement error. Standard measures are based on alpha changes (e.g., a higher or lower rating on a construct, which is used by the person in the same way on two occasions). But in some circumstances beta and gamma changes may occur (the employee changes the way a construct is used or fundamentally changes his or her understanding of the phenomenon). This argues for a stronger interest in social cognition (see Weick 1995) and in the meanings employees attribute to their surroundings, as well as the need to pay careful attention to the operationalization of constructs and the psychometric properties of measures.

In addition, measurement of change over time within organizations suggests there is some degree of stability in the organization itself, which may not be the case. There are clearly opportunities for research during organizational restructuring, downsizing, and relocation, but it may be difficult to sustain research designs based on such stable organizational features as departments, jobs, functions, tasks, or skills. In contexts of turbulent and rapid organizational and job change, so many variables may be changing concurrently that causal conclusions based on time-series data may be difficult to interpret. It is here, sometimes, that more qualitative approaches to employee attitudes may provide a useful supplement (see, e.g., Hartley 1994).

Meta-analysis

Survey research based on quantitative data is also able to capitalize on meta-analysis as a statistical and interpretive technique. Based on statistical developments (e.g., Hunter, Schmidt, and Jackson 1982), meta-analysis provides sophisticated techniques whereby data from more than one study can be aggregated, with adjustments made for sample size and psychometric reliability (Hunter and Hirsch 1987). The data from across the studies are then used to obtain an overall analysis of the relationships between different variables. This brings a level of interpretation to the research findings beyond the more traditional methods of literature review (in which results have to be weighed logically rather than statistically). For example, based on a statistical analysis of the data from fourteen studies, Premack and Hunter (1988) developed a model of the decision to become a union member.

Personal versus Situational Characteristics

Employee attitude surveys can also address questions about the influence of dispositional versus situational influences on organizational phenomena. Given that employee surveys are based on self-reporting, we need to be aware of the potential influence of personality or personal characteristics both on what and how information is reported, as well as the extent to which a person's views and behavior are influenced by his or her disposition.

Research on the influence of disposition is receiving increasing attention in I/O psychology (e.g., House, Shane, and Herold 1996; Schneider and Hough 1995). Dispositional factors have been found to be important in some research and may also have an impact on the quality of survey data even where disposition is not formally part of the theoretical framework. An example will illustrate this. Hackman and Oldham (1976) found that job redesign had a greater impact on employee well-being (including job satisfaction) and task performance among those employees with a higher degree of "growth need strength," that is, an interest in personal growth and development on the job.

In some research it may also be necessary to take account of how disposition affects reporting. This is particularly an issue in surveys, given that they rely on self-reports and therefore suffer from common method variance in the data. Common method variance is a term used to describe a situation in which there is an opportunity for biases in reporting that conflate independent (predictor) and dependent (outcome) variables due to the fact that the same method (self-reporting) has been used to measure both sets of variables.

Common method variance is a general problem in survey research, but it may be exacerbated by particular personality traits. For example, negative affectivity is the tendency of some people to have an affective (emotional) response that is generally slanted toward the pessimistic—fearing the worst, seeing the negative, expressing negative views, opinions, and symptoms (Watson and Clark 1984). (At the other end of the scale are those with a "Pollyanna" approach to life.) Negative affectivity can have an impact on reports of stressful events, such as unemployment or pressure at work (e.g. Payne, Warr, and Hartley 1984). Some researchers have developed techniques for aggregating data from several employees and substituting a mean score (see Semmer, Zapf, and Greif 1996). The existence of such traits or styles, however, confirms the need for caution in designing and interpreting data based on self-report.

Reliability and Validity

Designing samples, writing questions in ways that minimize ambiguity, and avoiding overly complex questions are highly skilled operations and should not be undertaken lightly (see Barling 1979; Fink 1995). Most questionnaires go through many drafts and often several pilots to ensure a high level of "user-friendliness" and researcher interpretability.

It is sometimes suggested that psychologists are overly concerned with the psychometric properties of their research instruments (notably reliability and validity), but these are key aspects of questionnaire design and hence of research design. In addition, weak reliability and validity may well affect any inferences that can be made. If a quantitative measure of a variable has poor reliability or low validity, then the researcher is not in a position to make confident interpretations about the data, because variabilities in scores may be as much a function of instrument error or random responding as "true variation" in the sample. This is a major argument for the use of standardized measures, for which the issues of reliability and validity will have been extensively probed and the results published. Although standard measures have drawbacks inasmuch as they are not situation-specific, the known psychometric properties of standard measures often outweigh the disadvantages.

There are also situations in which a researcher will modify an existing measure, and this can lead to difficulties in interpretation (Smith et al. 1986). For example, the well-known and widely used measure of union commitment developed by Gordon and his colleagues (1980) has been used with different combinations of items in the scale, leading to some confusion both about what is being measured and how to compare studies (see Hartley 1992 for a critique).

There are also important design decisions to be made: whether the survey will be conducted with standard or nonstandard questions, whether forced-choice or open-ended responses are called for, whether a questionnaire or an interview will be used, and whether questions are apparently factual or opinion based.

Organizational Context

Hardly any textbooks on survey design examine the organizational context within which employee survey research takes place, even though this is crucial if one hopes to obtain accurate data and to be ethically responsible. Equally important, many published reports either ignore the organizational context in which the survey took place or give a truncated picture of the organization (see Barling 1988). This approach to design and reporting seems to assume that, once efforts have been made to remove the ambiguity inherent in question writing and sampling, relatively objective data can be collected about employees in an organizational setting.

We challenge this perspective. If the psychological processes of the individual respondent affect the quality and type of data that are collected, then it is highly likely that the organizational context also has an impact. This is increasingly being recognized (see, e.g., Tomaskovic-Devey, Leiter, and Thompson 1994; Kraut 1996). For example, research by Griffin, Tesluk, and Jacobs (1995) showed that U.S. union members' attitudes toward bargaining-related outcomes were more homogeneous during the year the collective bargaining contract was being negotiated than at other times.

There are other ways in which organizational context can affect responses. The proximity (or perceived proximity) of layoffs, industrial action, or major organizational change will affect the kinds of responses that are given because these events can affect the ways employees interpret the situation. Also, employees may be motivated to disguise or distort some of their responses as a means of self-protection or retaliation because jobs, careers, and reputations can be under threat during periods of great change. Management extent may well be most favorable to employee survey research being undertaken at a time which it judges will reflect well on the organization.

How the data are to be used may also affect the quality and amount of data obtained. French and Bell (1994) distinguish between two ways in which organizations typically use survey findings, namely, to gather information about employees and as part of a feedback process of organization development (see table 10.1). In the latter case, the emphasis is not only on gathering data but on using it throughout the organization to facilitate and develop change at whatever level it is seen to be needed.

A major threat to the integrity of survey data arises when employees do not trust the survey and its results. If staff do not believe the survey is confidential, this can lead to low or misleading responses. Furthermore, if staff

Table 10.1 Differences in Two Types of Employee Surveys

	Informational Survey	*Feedback Survey*
Purpose	Gather information about employees	Provide employees with feedback
Source of data	Front-line employees, maybe supervisor	Everyone in the organization
Who learns results	Senior management, department heads, and perhaps employees through newsletters	All survey participants
Who discusses implications	Top management	Staff in work teams, starting at the top
Role of change agent	Design and administration of questionnaire; development of report	Working with senior management on strategy, design, and administration of questionnaire; design of workshops; intervention in workshops if appropriate
Who conducts action planning	Senior management	Teams at all levels
Probable extent of change improvement	Fairly low	Fairly high

Source: Adapted from French and Bell 1994.

do not see direct benefits arising from their taking part in the survey (e.g., few or no management actions occur as a result of the organizational problems raised by the survey), then organization-wide cynicism and distrust may increase, jeopardizing the use and benefit of future surveys.

Some research suggests that survey feedback is more effective if it is a continuous process and not merely a one-time occurrence (Gavin 1984). Consequently, the impact on employees' responses to interviews and questionnaires should be addressed. Certainly employees are more likely to respond to surveys that they perceive may better their lot, thus affecting the response rate obtained.

Conclusions

Employee surveys are becoming more popular both with academics and in organizations. This is partly a result of the increase in computing power and partly a response to the increase in individualism and social and organizational uncertainty. At the level of the organization, employee surveys are increasingly seen as integral to good HRM practice (O'Creevy 1995), and some organizations now undertake employee surveys annually as a matter of course.

Employee attitude surveys are able to examine a variety of self-reported perceptions, views, and opinions as well as reported and intended behaviors. The subjective nature of perception, motivation, and self-presentation means that care is needed in considering how, and in what contexts, self-reports of attitudes are elicited. Standardized measures help in dealing with the problems of reliability and validity but lead to assumptions being made about similarities in context and about the nature of change.

Both the organizational context and the epistemological base of survey research suggest the need to take account of the social construction of personal and organizational realities. Much quantitative survey research assumes a considerable degree of objectivity and uniformity in the data. But even a brief consideration of how employees perceive and respond to survey questions indicates that employees create meanings out of their own experiences, those of others around them, and the actions and reactions of the organization and then act on them. This means that survey research based on quantitative methodologies may need to be complemented by qualitative research that is able to tease out some of the meanings and social constructions that lie behind frequencies and cross-tabulations.

Part III

Comparative Analysis

Comparative Analysis

Recent years have seen increased interest in research based on international comparisons. This interest seems to be motivated primarily by the globalization of production, the growing importance of the multinational corporation, and a search for processes underlying industrial relations regardless of country.

Part III contains two chapters on different aspects of this research. The first explores the various approaches to comparative analysis and points out that the focus today is less exclusively on comparisons among national systems of industrial relations and the role of national unions, employer associations, and the state. The chapter concludes with a discussion of alternative research strategies in this field and a brief listing of the difficulties in collecting and analyzing data.

The second chapter focuses on the difficulties involving one form of data gathering: comparative workplace surveys. These potentially offer the prospect of "like-with-like" comparisons across national boundaries. Such analysis is fraught with difficulty, however, and can seriously mislead if it is not undertaken with sufficient care, even when the analysis is based on the primary collection of cross-national information.

CHAPTER ELEVEN

Comparative International Industrial Relations

George Strauss

C omparative international industrial relations (CIIR) has been receiving increasing academic attention throughout the world, in part because of the growing interdependence of economies. But there are a variety of other reasons. If industrial relations is to be viewed as a scientific discipline, presumably it should develop some principles that apply everywhere, not just in a single country. As Kochan puts it in chapter 2 of this volume, "Taking an international perspective broadens the range of comparisons available . . . and increases the chances of discovering the systematic variations needed to produce new theoretical insights and explanations."

Because of the high levels of abstraction required, comparative studies of national systems help us develop theory. By looking at differences, we seek uniformities—universal rules that explain these differences. For example, comparative studies help us understand the relative significance of factors such as technology, economic fluctuations, laws, and culture. Further, comparative studies place our own country in perspective and so help us understand our own system better. Arguments, for example, that corporatism and government regulation are the cause of unemployment in one country require much more support if research shows that this relationship does not occur elsewhere.

In a more practical vein, CIIR is useful for policy purposes; for instance, it highlights the great difficulty of transporting an industrial relations system from one country to another (e.g., from Japan to the United Kingdom).[1] In an even more practical vein, it is important for countries or

Thanks to Mark Bray, Roth Collier, Stephen Frenkel, David Levine, and Peter Sheldon for helpful comments.

1. See, for example, Martin's (1969) attempt to apply the lessons of African unionism to efforts to introduce Australian model unionism into Papua-New Guinea.

companies involved in international trade to understand the industrial relations systems of the countries with which they deal. Further, CIIR helps prepare prospective managers for overseas service.

Obviously the purpose of one's research, whether applied or theoretical, affects the questions one asks and the methods one uses. For the businessperson, a description of the differences may be enough. The scholar asks for explanations—and providing these are more difficult.

There is some debate whether the comparative approach is a method or a strategy. Whichever it is, it uses all the methods discussed elsewhere in this book, from laboratory studies to quantitative analysis. In so doing, it illustrates many of the issues discussed in other chapters. Rather than focusing on methods, however, this chapter is concerned chiefly with strategy, the kinds of questions CIIR studies ask, particularly what is compared, how comparisons are made, and the kinds of questions comparisons are used to answer.

Why Compare Countries?

CIIR studies compare institutions and practices across countries. The units compared may be national systems as a whole, industries, occupations, plants, or even the attitudes of individual employees. But what is unique about *cross-country* comparisons? Why not compare industries, plants, or regions *within* a single country or region?

Although there is much to be learned from other levels of comparison, the nation-state is still an important unit of analysis. Governments play important roles in industrial relations (though more so in some countries than in others). They set the ground rules for collective bargaining; they may function as key bargainers in corporatist countries; they may determine conditions of employment directly; they may have important influences on macro forces, through fiscal policy, protectionism, or training, for example; and they are important employers and so provide examples for the rest of the economy.

Thus, national laws, policies, and their administration play major roles in influencing the development of industrial relations institutions, by affecting the distribution of power within unions, for example. Codetermination in Germany inhibited the development of a shop-level union structure by establishing a different kind of shop-level representation system (which also permitted considerable employee influence, however). Similarly, interest arbitration in Australia, by centralizing key decisions, made shop-level representation disorganized, although occasionally quite powerful. By contrast, the U.S. legal system severely determines the times and extent of collective bargaining and discourages the development of centralized negotiations.

But laws don't explain everything. Phelps Brown (1983) ascribes the differences among U.S., Canadian, and British industrial relations systems in large part to history, which contributes to national culture and values. Further, history and culture influence what kinds of laws are passed. So research should go beyond the laws themselves and include economics, history, culture, and even personal values.

Faucheux and Rojot (1979) suggest, for example, that the differences in stability between northern and Latin European labor relations patterns are related chiefly to culture. In some societies, groups are more likely to express discontent collectively; in others, individually. Hofstede (1980) found people in the United States and Britain to be high in "individualism" and low in "power distance" compared, at the other extreme, with Singapore. Such differences in values may carry over into labor relations. (Warning: Caution is required when comparing "culture" studies; scholars define and measure the concept in different ways, some as sets of normative values, others as institutions.)

Cultural boundaries don't necessarily correspond with national boundaries. Even within a given geographical area, cultural differences may influence industrial relations. Harmonious relations within the U.S. garment industry during the early 1900s have been attributed to the fact that the key leaders on both sides were recent Jewish immigrants. Further, national boundaries increasingly are not coterminous with markets, especially in markets in which multinational firms operate. Additionally, countries may have two or more industrial relations systems, possibly one for large companies and another for smaller ones.

It is often suggested that national differences are likely to decline. Locke (1992) argues that as collective bargaining is decentralized, multinationals spread, and markets are internationalized, the national level will become less important in influencing industrial relations and the international and workplace levels more so. Decentralization, he argues, is weakening the forces leading to intracountry uniformity, while neoliberalism is shrinking the role of the state. The European Union's Social Chapter may be yet another influence in reducing the differences among its members.

For the moment, however, national differences in laws, history, and culture still explain a large part of the variances among union-management relations in specific situations (probably more than do economic and technical factors). So far, even in the European Union, in which the forces toward uniformity are growing, there is not much evidence of convergence in the structure of labor relations. Global economic pressures and technological changes are affecting developed countries in roughly the same way. Though these changes have affected countries to different degrees, these differences have been nowhere as great as the dramatic variations in the rate of union decline among countries (Visser 1990: 36). Though national differences may be less important at the workplace than at the economywide level, nations differ considerably in the way new technologies and work forms are introduced. Two new factories producing the same product in France and Germany may be very much alike—except in industrial relations.

Consequently, cross-national comparisons remain a proper focus of research. Indeed, a major research task is to determine the extent to which national differences are declining and to pinpoint the subjects and areas in which this decline is the greatest.

Newer Topics and Methods

Until recently, most comparative industrial relations analysis consisted of either studies of single countries or "parallel descriptions" (current examples include Bamber and Lansbury 1993 and Ferner and Hyman 1992). In the typical comparative book, one chapter dealt with Britain, another with France, and so on. Traditionally, too, the focus was on national unions and national policies. The view was from the top, which ignored both employers and everything happening at the company, plant, and workplace levels. The book was descriptive rather than analytical.

Much is changing. Parallel description is still useful, especially for teaching, as newer editions of older works testify. Recently, however, books have appeared that approach industrial relations topic by topic, rather than country by country. Examples include Clegg's *Trade Unionism under Collective Bargaining* (1976), Bean's *Comparative Industrial Relations* (1994), and Poole's *Industrial Relations* (1986), all of which include separate chapters on unions, the state, strikes (industrial conflict), and industrial democracy (worker participation). As in industrial relations generally, there has been a shift from inductive to deductive research, and often variables have at least been partly quantified.

The focus is no longer primarily on national unions and employers associations as institutions. Instead, increasing attention has been given to international comparisons among specific industries, occupations, and plants as well as to attitudes and bargaining behaviors. Not entirely coincidentally, this changed emphasis is in line with the greater decentralization of industrial relations generally.

Further, much recent work has been done by economists, sociologists, psychologists, historians, and political scientists (in addition to those who call their discipline "industrial relations"). Consistent with the wider range of fields involved, data are being gathered in a variety of innovative ways, for example, through employer surveys, attitude studies, and laboratory experiments. Increasingly, this research involves networks of teams; for example, a series of studies organized by the Massachusetts Institute of Technology covered four industries and involved separate teams in eleven countries (Locke, Kochan, and Piore 1995), and a similar series has been organized by the Cranfield School of Management (Brewster et al. 1996). All this reflects a broader approach to the field of industrial relations to include the entire world of work, not just labor-management. A representative (but by no means comprehensive) sample of these new approaches and methods is outlined below.

Management

Traditionally, unions took the initiative in industrial relations, and it was assumed that management's role was uniformly reactive and negative—and therefore not worth studying. Currently, as union strength is declining, there is greater interest in management and in employers associations (e.g., Sisson 1987; Tolliday and Zeitlin 1991). By contrast with earlier studies, which largely ignored national differences in management style, the newer studies emphasize the variety of strategic choices available to management, including alternative policies for dealing with unions (from union busting to cooperation), overall styles of management (from autocratic to participative), strategies for introducing change, and attitudes toward corporatism. Even when these differences don't affect industrial relations directly, they do so indirectly.

Specific Industries and Occupations Being Studied

Other studies focus on specific industries, such as automobile manufacturing, telecommunications, airlines, and banking (e.g., Locke, Kochan, and Piore 1995), or on specific occupations, such as dock work. For example, telecommunications companies face roughly the same economic and technological pressures throughout the developed world, but differences in how these pressures are worked out in practice can tell us a good deal about the nature of industrial relations systems.

Plants and Workplaces

At still lower levels, notable international studies have contrasted seemingly similar plants in two or more countries. Some involve intensive case studies, at times using ethnographic methods, of how workplace problems are handled on a day-to-day basis. Others focus on quantitative measures that enable multivariate analysis to take place. Burawoy's experiences actually working in U.S., Hungarian, and Russian factories led to insights that more superficial examination would have missed (Burawoy and Lukacs 1985). Dore's (1973) comparison of four plants, two in Britain, two in Japan, helped initiate intensive study of the distinctive nature of Japanese managerial practices (for a somewhat similar study of twin plants in Germany and France, see Maurice, Sellier, and Silvestre 1986).

Bélanger, Edwards, and Haiven's book *Workplace Industrial Relations and the Global Challenge* (1994) includes comparisons of General Motors plants in Germany and Austria, the plants of an auto parts company in the United States and Canada, and the plants of a drug company in the United Kingdom, South Africa, Taiwan, Malaysia, and Australia. In each case, company ownership remained constant, as did the technology and market pressures to some degree. The major differences were the national laws, cultures, and histories. These studies, in a sense, served as field experiments (see chapter 5, "Experimental Methods").

Individual case studies make generalization difficult. This problem can potentially be overcome by conducting multiplant surveys. The International Auto Assembly Plant Project focused on the relationship between workplace practices, such as the use of buffers and teams, and quality and productivity (MacDuffie and Pil 1995). Including both elaborate survey questionnaires and plant visits, the study was conducted in two rounds (1989 and 1993–94) and involved more than seventy plants in seventeen countries on four continents. Fairly precise measures of the main variables were developed, including measures for productivity. The Competitive Semiconductor Manufacturing Project (Brown 1996) involved teams of engineers and social scientists who compared sixteen plants in six countries, focusing on the impact of alternative forms of organization and human resource management. Both studies developed data susceptible to multivariate analysis.

Human Resource Policies

Other research has compared specific human resource policies (Brewster et al. 1996). The range of studies is illustrated by three examples: the first was conducted from a primarily legal perspective; the second, chiefly by psychologists; and the third, by sociologists. The first study, which was conducted by a committee of the U.S. National Academy of Arbitrators, involved a survey of employees' privacy rights (regarding, for example, smoking, health records, off-the-job conduct, and surveillance) in ten countries. Although these rights derive from a wide variety of legal concepts and are enforced in many different ways, the studies found "a surprising similarity among countries with respect to actual practice" (Gerhart 1995: 5).

"Industrial Democracy in Europe" (1981, 1993) focused on influence and participation at various organizational levels regarding sixteen somewhat different issues (e.g., task assignments and new investments). This gigantic project involved teams from twelve countries and 134 matched establishments, document analysis, extensive structured interviews, a questionnaire answered by 7,832 individual respondents, as well as two waves of studies, the first in 1975–77 and the second, involving most of the same establishments, in 1986-87.

Focusing on the differences in management in Japan and the United States, Lincoln and Kalleberg (1990) surveyed human resource policies and their influence on workers' attitudes in matched samples of workers and plants in both countries.

The growing use of national workplace surveys increases the likelihood that we will soon be able to make quantitative comparisons of human resource practices across countries (see chapter 12, "Using Workplace Surveys for Comparative Research"). The MIT studies (Locke, Kochan, and Piore 1995) provide comparisons based on what are essentially case studies.

Technological Change

Analogous to the studies of the adoption of new forms of HRM has been research on the diffusion of new technology. Countries have differed considerably in both the rate at which they adopted new technology and the uses they made of it.

Much of this work is historical. Cohen (1990) compared the introduction of power-driven textile machinery in the United Kingdom and United States during the early 1800s. The United Kingdom already had a craftwork tradition, a large supply of skilled craftsmen, a relatively small market locally, and a rapidly fluctuating export market. Consequently, the British textile industry adopted elements of the new technology that facilitated the production of fairly short runs of high-quality goods. This required skilled craftsmen and led to strong unionism. The United States, by contrast, enjoyed a large national market but lacked skilled workers. In this case, the industry gravitated to the production of long runs of uniform but relatively low-quality cloth. A concomitant outcome was the development of weak unions.

More recent comparative studies of how technological change has affected industrial relations have looked at dock work, computerization in the newspaper industry, and the introduction of robots and computers into the workplace. To give a specific example, Sorge and his colleagues (1983) compared the effects of introducing computers in Britain and Germany. In the former, it reduced workers' power; in the latter, it increased it.

Negotiation Styles

Increasing attention is being given to national differences in negotiation styles (and not just in collective bargaining). Negotiation studies have been based on laboratory experiments, ethnographic observations of actual negotiations, and questionnaires sent to participants. For example, laboratory studies based on country nationals' behavior in bargaining games indicate that there are characteristic differences in bargaining patterns among countries (Harnett and Cummings 1980).

Attitudes

A growing number of cross-national studies compare the attitudes of managers, union members, and ordinary workers. Based on interviews and employee attitude surveys, these studies have examined such constructs as worker militancy, union and organizational commitment, and individualism. In a study influenced by European postmodernism, Lash (1984) examined international differences in working-class imagery.

Cross-national attitude studies are beset with many of the same difficulties as cross-national surveys (see chapter 12). First, there is the problem of translation. There is no exact counterpart in Japanese for the English word "satisfaction" or in German for "leadership" (as opposed to "domination"). Second, constructs may apply to different referents. Unions serve different functions in Singapore and the United Kingdom, so that commitment to a union in one country is not equivalent to commitment in the other.

Developing Countries

After a considerable period during which the subject was ignored, there has been a burst of interest in industrial relations in developing and underdeveloped countries. Going beyond descriptions, they seek explanations for uniformities and differences among countries within geographical areas, such as Latin America (Collier and Collier 1991) and Southeast Asia (Frenkel and Harrod 1995). These studies emphasize somewhat different issues, but common themes are industrialization, the often unsteady hand of the state, and the impact of global competition. These studies demonstrate that even within regions, individual countries take different paths toward development.

Compared with studies of industrialized countries, those of underdeveloped countries generally place greater emphasis on relationships among the state, companies, and unions—with the state typically having the dominant role. Given their training and orientation, political scientists have an advantage in undertaking such studies.

What Should Be Compared?

What comparisons should one make? One's choice raises a host of methodological issues. An important distinction can be drawn between "splitters," who focus on explaining differences among countries, and "lumpers," who are concerned with discovering similarities (i.e., generalizations that apply everywhere) (Mill 1974; Ragin 1987; Przeworski 1987; Collier 1991). To take the example of attitudinal research, a typical "lumping" study might be designed to validate a psychological measure such as union commitment so as to determine whether this measure is meaningful across countries and further to test whether the correlates of this measure are the same in, say, Sweden and South Africa. By contrast, a "splitting" study might examine differences in values, for example, individualism, among countries.

As in other areas of the social sciences, the research methods used in comparative international industrial relations fit broadly into qualitative and quantitative modes. Unlike other areas, however, to date most CIIR research has been qualitative.

Qualitative Approaches

Trends and Predictions

A similarity-oriented approach is to examine trends that presumably are affecting all developed countries. This approach typically involves making predictions about future developments. A common assumption is that cross-national differences will decline and various systems converge over time.

During the 1960s two theories emerged that seemed quite plausible to industrial relations specialists. These were Ross and Hartman's (1960) prediction that strikes would become increasingly less common and Kerr and his associates' (1960) technology-driven prediction that industrial relations systems would converge into a form they labeled "pluralistic industrialism," something like the U.S. model. (Kerr later revised this theory considerably; see Kerr 1983.) More recently, researchers have predicted that corporatism would soon be universal and that production techniques and shop-floor labor relations would soon be Japanized throughout the world (Dore 1989; Womack, Jones, and Roos 1990). Both theories now seem overstated.

Today unions seem to be getting weaker and management stronger almost everywhere—and so it is easy to conclude that this trend will continue indefinitely. Just the opposite prediction was common forty years ago.

There are two lessons here. The first is that history doesn't follow a straight line. Sometimes there are cycles and sometimes erratic changes. The second lesson is that superficial tendencies often mask underlying differences. Decentralization in Germany takes a different form than in Italy. Though it is valuable to know that by some measures decentralization is occurring in both countries, one should avoid broad conclusions that the industrial relations systems as a whole are converging.

Limited cross-national generalizations, however, are useful. One can safely generalize that union density is declining in most developed countries today. Thus, for instance, we should not rely entirely on single-country explanations, to ascribe the plight of U.S. unions entirely to U.S. labor laws, for example. On the other hand, that the U.S. decline began earlier and went further than in most other countries suggests the importance of country-specific factors.

Comparative Case Studies

This approach views each country's industrial relations as a system embedded in a society. Its legal system, economy, culture, history, technology, and geography constitute an interlocking set of social institutions (with various degrees of internal coherence). Though the relationships among the parts vary kaleidoscopically, all affect the country's industrial relations. In turn, the country's industrial relations affect its social institutions. British industrial relations, for example, greatly influenced the Thatcher victory in 1979 and were in turn influenced by it.

Researchers using the case study approach look primarily at differences. Countries are examined one by one, but in each case the researchers ask the same questions. Phelps Brown (1983) and Sisson (1987) have conducted typical studies of this sort. They represent "parallel descriptions" at their best.

Typologies

Yet another approach emphasizes neither the international uniformities nor the unique characteristics of individual countries. It seeks to develop typologies—categories of countries that share major characteristics. One advantage of the typology approach is that instead of comparing every country with every other one (a difficult process), one can compare groups of countries. Another advantage is that one can analyze the commonalities within the groups. In fact, establishing typologies (or similarities) may be the first step toward explaining differences.

Hibbs (1976), for example, divided countries into three categories—the Anglo-Saxon, the Nordic-German, and the Latin—depending on the roles of strikes and the state, the political power of unions, and the extent to which national income was socialized. This typology seems to have stood up pretty well in that there have been important and stable differences between these groups and substantial uniformities within them throughout the post–World War II period. By contrast, another well-known typology—corporatist versus noncorporatist economies—now seems out of date.

Research can aid us in determining the extent to which countries within a given category do have characteristics in common and the extent to which these characteristics have remained steady over time. Of course, typologies may be based on different sets of characteristics, but to the extent this happens the value of typologies is reduced.

Exceptionalism

Some countries may seem unique in that important aspects of their industrial relations don't fit comfortably in any one typology. In this case, each country can be viewed as a typology of its own. With this difference-emphasizing approach, comparisons can then be made with the rest of the world in an effort to explain why the country in question is so different.

The United States, for instance, is unique among developed countries in that it lacks a labor or socialist party and arguably even a class consciousness. Over the years a large literature has developed on American exceptionalism. At various times the United States has been compared with European countries, Australia, and, more recently, Canada. Yet *every* country is unique in some way (Zolberg 1986). Arguments can be made that Britain or Germany or Australia-New Zealand are the true exceptions.

Close Pairs

Rather than comparing sets of countries that are different in significant ways from each other, some researchers compare matched pairs of countries with somewhat similar economies, cultures, and historic traditions and that therefore fit in a single typology (Przeworski and Tuene 1970). Examples include Australia and New Zealand, the United States and Canada, and the United Kingdom and Ireland. All of these countries once had rather similar industrial relations practices that now are diverging. Other pairs that might be compared include Germany and Austria, Belgium and Holland, and Norway and Sweden, as well as a variety of Latin American countries (Collier and Collier 1991).

The advantage of studying close pairs is that their similarities permit us to hold many characteristics constant while concentrating on the relatively few on which the countries differ. Such studies begin by focusing on the similarities and later shift to the differences. By contrast, the problem with studies that examine many countries or that look at countries that differ substantially (such as Germany and Spain) is that the large number of differences make it difficult to sort out the relative importance of each difference.

Questions quickly arise when one focuses on pairs. Why is it that forty years ago union density was about the same in the United States and Canada but since then has sharply declined in the United States and increased in Canada—even though the two countries have much the same economic mix, many of the same employers and unions, and until recently the same labor laws? Why has union density declined in Britain and remained roughly unchanged in Ireland? Why did Australia maintain a successful corporatist system for a decade after 1983, while New Zealand was moving rapidly to neoliberalism?

Deciding what factors to include in an analysis can be problematic, as the substantial comparative literature on the United States and Canada illustrates. In explaining the growing differences between the two countries, some authors emphasize differences in labor laws and how they are enforced. But the Canadian labor law system was originally modeled after that in the United States (to some extent, so was the Japanese). Why has the Canadian system evolved so differently? One explanation offered focuses on differences in the country's constitutional systems: the U.S. presidential system discourages third parties, whereas Canada's parliamentary system is more favorable to them and presumably strengthens pressure groups (though pressure groups are hardly unknown in the United States). Lipset (1986) emphasizes differences in culture as an overarching explanation for differences in labor legislation, employers' attitudes, and workers' propensity to unionize. Phelps Brown (1983) emphasizes both culture and history. Others point to Canada's relatively large and heavily unionized public sector. There is much room here for research and controversy.

As useful as they are, however, two-country comparisons have their limits. The factors explaining U.S.-Canadian differences are probably somewhat different than those explaining the differences between New Zealand and Australia. Penn (1990) compared skilled workers in America and Britain, two countries where their roles are very much alike. Perhaps he would have learned more if he had compared the roles of these workers with those in Germany or Japan.

Comparative History

As the literature on the United States and Canada illustrates, attempts to understand the similarities and differences between close pairs get us quickly into history. A new field of comparative history is developing that is explicitly concerned with how close pairs have evolved. Cross-national teams have compared the industrial relations histories of both individual industries and of national IR systems as a whole (e.g., Kealey and Patmore 1996; Bray and Walsh 1993).

The concept of "punctuated equilibrium" has been receiving growing interest (Visser 1990; Collier and Collier 1991; Kuruvilla and Erickson 1996). The assumption is that the industrial relations systems of most countries are reasonably stable over long periods of time (in some cases, their characters developed before the countries became fully industrialized). Pressures to change are resisted, and minor adjustments are incorporated in ways that ensure that the system's overall character is preserved. Gradually, environmental changes subject the system to increasing tension until a "critical juncture" occurs, at which time major changes ("transformations") take place rather quickly and in a difficult-to-predict manner. Eventually, a new partial equilibrium occurs. Critical junctures occurred in Australia around 1890–1905, in Germany at the end of World War II, and in the United States in the 1880s and again in the 1930s. They may be occurring in many countries today. Historians focus on these critical junctures and seek to explain why some choices are made rather than others.

Quantitative Analysis

Reflecting the trend in industrial relations and the social sciences generally, the field of CIIR is increasingly using quantitative analysis. Typical dependent variables include union density, strike rates, and wage structure, while independent variables range from changes in the cost of living to unemployment, corporatism, the political influence of labor, and union or bargaining centralization. As discussed elsewhere (see chapter 4, "Quantitative Methods"), quantitative analysis has distinct advantages over qualitative analysis but is also subject to major limitations and pitfalls. Among the purposes of creating typologies and studying close pairs is that one can hold certain variables constant so as to observe the independent influence of some variables on others. Quantitative analysis offers the same advantages but has the potential disadvantage (among others) that key, perhaps difficult-to-quantify, variables may be ignored.

Three kinds of comparative quantitative analysis are possible. The first approach is to estimate separate equations for each country and then compare the results. To test the validity of a variety of theories predicting the incidence of strikes, for example, Paldam and Pedersen (1982) ran separate regressions for seventeen countries in the Organization for Economic Cooperation and Development (OECD) for the period from 1948 to 1975. Some theories seemed to be refuted generally, while others held up chiefly for the United States and not elsewhere.

The second approach is to pool data from every country studied and analyze it in a single equation. The IDE (1992: 122) group aggregated data from eleven countries to estimate the extent to which factors such as unemployment rates and product complexity predicted the distribution of influence in eighty-six establishments. The pooled-data approach helps establish generalizations (similarities) that presumably hold to some extent everywhere; the single-equation approach highlights the countries in which these generalizations do not apply (differences).

The third approach is to estimate a single equation but use dummy variables so that each country can have separate coefficient estimates. This approach was used by Whitfield, Marginson, and Brown (1994) in a comparison of Australia and the United Kingdom in which they tested the hypothesis that a centralized regulatory system will result in distinctly different workplace industrial relations patterns than one that is decentralized (see chapter 12).

The use of quantitative methods for cross-country comparisons presents some special problems apart from those applicable to quantitative analysis generally. These are discussed below.

Differences in Measurement

Countries differ in how variables such as strikes, union density, and unemployment are measured, making comparisons difficult (see, e.g., Shalev 1978; Chaison and Rose 1991; Bean 1994) For example, in the United States only strikes involving one thousand workers or more are counted in official national statistics; Swedish records include any strike of more than an hour's duration. Some countries exclude political and public-sector strikes. Few collect data on various forms of industrial action, such as slowdowns, that fall short of being all-out strikes (Edwards and Hyman 1994).

Union density rates can be based on union self-reports, on per capita payments to union central bodies, or on surveys of individual members of the population conducted by a government agency such as the U.S. Census Bureau. In the United States and Australia, more than one series is available, each giving a different picture.

Differences in Institutions

Aside from being measured differently, union membership, strikes, and industrial relations institutions have different meanings and functions in various countries. As Reynaud (cited in Von Beyme 1980: 1) put it: "A strike is not a 'greve' nor is it a 'sciopero'; a 'Gewerkschaft' is not a 'syndicate' nor a 'union'; and 'Tarifvertrag' is neither a 'collective agreement' nor a 'convention collective.' "

In the United States, union density is often viewed as a measure of union strength, but this may be misleading elsewhere. Actual union membership in some countries may be less meaningful than the extent of union representation or the ability to raise wages. Being a union member may have a different meaning in Sweden, where (until recently) union membership was closely linked with benefits, than it does in private-sector plants in France or Spain, where at times only the activist core are actually members but nonmember workers often follow this core's leadership when strikes are called (Ferner and Hyman 1992: xxiv; Bean 1994).

Strikes mean different things in different countries. This is related to the concept of *strike shape*. There are different measures of strikes: their *frequency*, their average *duration*, and the average number of workers per strike (sometimes called *breadth*). Frequency multiplied by duration multiplied by breadth gives *volume* (or impact), sometimes computed as the number of working days lost annually per thousand employees. U.S. strikes may have the longest duration in the world. Here they are tests of economic endurance; they are serious matters and may lead to workers losing their jobs. By contrast, French strikes frequently have chiefly symbolic meaning: they are often political gestures, designed to serve as warnings to employers, or a means of expressing generalized dissatisfaction (Shorter and Tilly, 1974). In such cases strikes tend to be short (though they may be frequent and, if directed to the government, each strike may involve many workers).

Variables Difficult to Measure

There are numerous qualitative variables that scholars would like to enter into their equations but that are not easily quantified. Common examples include corporatism, union political power, and bargaining centralization. A key interest here is the impact of these variables on inflation, employment, and wage structure.

To reduce such qualitative variables to numbers, scholars have developed indexes that rate where each country stands with regard to particular variables on, say, a scale of 1 to 10. Sometimes these indexes are constructed by combining two or more subindexes, some of which themselves are based on quantitative data (e.g., average dues level); others are based on yes-no questions (e.g., Is national union approval required to ratify a contract?); and still others are based on informed but subjective judgment (e.g., the concentration of union power).

In addition to being based on subjective assessments, these indexes suffer from three weaknesses. First, in combining subindexes, how each is weighted is decided arbitrarily. For example, to construct a measure of "union encompassiveness," Visser (1990) gives equal weight to two measures, one of "horizontal integration" and the other of "vertical integration." Each of these measures is composed in turn of several subindexes (e.g., peak union membership as a percentage of total union membership), which are themselves added together arbitrarily. The problem is that horizontal integration may be more important in one country and vertical in another.

Second, concepts such as corporatism are multidimensional. A country can be low in corporatism on one dimension and high on another. Unless the various subindexes are highly correlated, the value of the overall index is suspect.

Third, and finally, from some perspectives, the indexes used may be poor representations (technical term: proxies) for the underlying concepts they are supposed to represent. Visser's measure of "union encompassiveness," for example, takes no account of the role of women or minorities. A clearer definition of the term might reduce confusion, but there is always the temptation to think of encompassiveness as representing a real concept rather than the arbitrary sum of a set of numbers.

Small Numbers

Some forms of elaborate statistical analysis require large numbers of cases. The number of developed countries is limited, and few studies look at more than twenty, thus restricting the number of observations that can be made. In technical terms, small numbers reduce the degrees of freedom, make some statistical tests unreliable, and severely limit the number of independent variables that can be included in an equation. A major problem is that an "outlier"—that is, an extreme case—can have a major impact on the results generated (see chapter 4).

Paradoxically, qualitative researchers seek to simplify their task by reducing the number of cases by focusing on typologies or close pairs. Quantitative researchers prefer large numbers.

A Final Caveat

There is always the danger that researchers will take an ethnocentric approach and assume that the analytical method most suitable to understanding their country's problems will explain those of other countries equally well. After all, the questions one asks often determine the answers one gets, and as Brewster and his colleagues (1996) and Locke, Kochan, and Piore (1995) point out, Americans often ask different questions and make different assumptions than do Europeans. A partial solution: use cross-national research teams.

Conclusions

Three themes run through this chapter. The first relates to the great variety of methods used in comparative international industrial relations research, from bargaining games to study national differences in negotiating behavior to regressions to examine the effect of unemployment on union growth in various countries.

The second theme relates to research strategy. Suppose that, based on data collected over twenty years from seventeen countries, a regression equation reveals that employment changes account for 50 percent of the changes in union density. Lumpers might emphasize this generalization.

Splitters might ask whether this relationship holds equally for every country, whether the unexplained 50 percent can be explained by country differences and, if so, what factors explain these differences. Going further, some might run additional regressions on the same data. Others might use the case study approach to compare two countries, one in which employment and union membership are closely and positively related and another in which they are not.

The third and final theme has to do with the relationships among economic and technological forces, national industrial relations institutions, and day-to-day practice. Understanding how these forces interact is perhaps the most important challenge for researchers in comparative international industrial relations. As globalization proceeds, most countries are subject to roughly the same economic pressures, and new forms of technology are more or less equally available in developed countries. By contrast, each country has a distinct set of industrial relations institutions, laws, and history. Obviously, national institutions mediate the impact of economic and technological forces. But with regard to what industrial relations issues are the national variations greatest? To what extent are national differences eroding? Why? There is much room for research.

CHAPTER TWELVE

Using Workplace Surveys for Comparative Research

Keith Whitfield, Rick Delbridge, and William Brown

R esearch in comparative industrial relations has traditionally focused on the analysis of highly aggregated national-level data, such as national strike statistics and union density figures. In recent years, however, there has been an upsurge of interest in undertaking comparative workplace studies, reflecting a recognition that it is at the workplace that an industrial relations system has its most important effects on the world of work (Bélanger, Edwards, and Haiven 1994). A similar focus can be observed in the burgeoning literature on the link between employment practices and business performance (e.g., MacDuffie 1995).

Much of this international research has involved the analysis of detailed qualitative data obtained through case studies (e.g., Gallie 1983; Mueller 1994; Frenkel 1994). Less attention has been paid to survey-based information. A strong argument can be made, however, for making greater use of workplace surveys. These can complement case studies and related methods by establishing wider generalizability and emphasizing the importance of *explanation* to comparative research.

The central objective of this chapter is to report on two approaches to the development of comparative international workplace survey data. These are secondary matching and primary collection. Both have their relative advantages—the former, that it provides size and scope; the latter, that it has the potential to ease many of the constraints under which the secondary analyst operates. The use of each of these approaches poses different questions for the researcher, although many of these stem from common underlying causes.

Workplace Surveys and Comparative Analysis

A great deal of comparative research is based on highly aggregated information. Much other work has used case studies.

Workplace surveys offer the advantage over other methods in which more aggregated information is collected of permitting a wider range of questions to be asked. Much comparative research using national-level data is simply concerned with how industrial relations systems differ. Many important questions, however, relate to *why* systems differ and the *effects* of these differences. For example, it is of interest to know why Australia has a less well-developed system of grievance procedures than, say, Britain and whether this has resulted in more turbulent industrial relations. If it is the case that the former system reflects the stultifying effect of compulsory arbitration and that its consequence is a poorer record of long-term dispute resolution, there is a *prima facie* case for changing the arbitral system in Australia. Workplace survey data provide a better source for examining such questions since it is at the workplace that many of these cross-national differences manifest themselves.

Relative to case studies, workplace surveys have the potential to be representative of the population from which they are drawn. In some cases they are nationally representative (e.g., the Australian Workplace Industrial Relations Survey and British Workplace Industrial Relations Surveys). On the one hand, this enables general inferences to be made as opposed to conclusions about a specific case. On the other hand, surveys are much blunter instruments than case studies and, in particular, are less useful for understanding processes and idiosyncratic relationships.

Workplace surveys are extremely useful for uncovering variations within countries. While international comparative analysis is based on the premise that significant differences exist between countries, differences within countries may be at least as substantial. Thus differences in the incidence of training may vary more across industries within a country than within an industry across countries. This would suggest that the determinants of such phenomena are industry-specific rather than country-specific, a finding of much importance, albeit negative, for comparative study.

At the very least, therefore, there are advantages in developing workplace survey material to complement more extensive aggregate and case study material. Moreover, there are areas of research for which workplace data offer the most productive research avenue, for example, when investigating characteristics that vary systematically by both industrial sector and establishment size, such as strike propensity.

Secondary Matching versus Primary Collection

As national-level workplace surveys become more common, there is growing interest in comparing their findings. *Secondary matching* involves comparing the results of two or more such surveys. To the extent that such surveys have common questions and comparable sample populations, such comparisons can result in informed international comparative analysis at the micro level. This opportunity will not be realized, however, without considerable forethought. Secondary matching is as hazardous as it is seductive, as will become apparent as we reflect upon the experiences of conducting secondary matching of the AWIRS and the third U.K. Workplace Industrial Relations Survey (WIRS3) and of a smaller-scale U.K./Norwegian study. (See chapter 9, "Large-Scale National Surveys for Mapping, Monitoring, and Theory Development," for a detailed discussion of the problems involved in undertaking workplace surveys.)

The AWIRS/WIRS3 research team chose to concentrate on the question of whether the differing regulatory systems in Australia and Britain produced distinctly different patterns of workplace industrial relations, both in institutional arrangement and economic/industrial relations outcome (Whitfield, Marginson, and Brown 1994). This placed the project within a comprehensive body of literature, including the debate on the relative merits of the Australian conciliation and arbitration system and overseas collective bargaining systems (for an overview, see Mulvey 1986). The approach was explicitly deductive in orientation, and the central aim was to develop a "like-with-like" data set that could be used to test a number of hypotheses in a more rigorous manner than had previously been possible.

In common with most other data sets, the two workplace surveys did not have robust variables for key institutional elements in the regulatory system. It was possible to approach the issue indirectly, however, via the development of hypotheses about the differential effects that the two regulatory systems might be expected to have on the workplace. This has been the most common technique used in empirical work in the area of regulation. A prime example in previous work is the hypothesis that centralized regulatory systems will have more rigid wage structures than those that are decentralized (e.g., Brown et al. 1980).

An analysis of the kind proposed requires the development of a substantial data set containing information on the main factors that might be expected to influence the institutional arrangements and economic/industrial relations outcome of concern (so as to control for the influence of factors other than the regulatory system). To obtain this information on a country-specific basis is far from easy; to do so on a cross-national basis, using secondary information, is harder still.

In contrast to secondary matching, *primary collection* involves the development and application of a comparative research method from inception. With this approach, comparative research is the purpose of the project from the outset. The International Motor Vehicle Project (IMVP), coordinated by researchers at the Massachusetts Institute of Technology, is perhaps the best-known example. During the late 1980s a team of researchers gathered data from car assembly plants throughout the world in an attempt to determine manufacturing performance and establish the management practices that best supported high performance (Womack, Jones, and Roos 1990). The researchers used questionnaires to gather data from management on factory practices, work systems, and human resource management practices and developed a methodology to compare plant performance (Krafcik 1988).

This approach offers certain advantages over secondary matching since the researchers themselves are able to make decisions concerning the method, sample, and application. Primary collection has a number of problems of its own, however, which are discussed here with respect to the IMVP and one of the authors' experiences in conducting the Worldwide Manufacturing Competitiveness Study (WMCS).

WMCS involved a comparative analysis of the manufacturing performance and management practices of seventy-one automotive components plants in France, Germany, Italy, Japan, Mexico, Spain, the United Kingdom, the United States, and Canada. A questionnaire methodology was developed by a research team from Cardiff Business School and Cambridge University; benchmarking principles were then applied to enable systematic comparisons to be made of core manufacturing processes and the practices utilized in their management (Delbridge, Lowe, and Oliver 1995).

An explicit intention of the research program was to test in a sector other than car assembly the hypothesis developed in the IMVP that lean production necessarily provides enhanced performance. To test this hypothesis, a questionnaire was developed that enabled the research team to establish manufacturing performance benchmarks and to profile management practices in the areas of factory practice, work organization, human resource management, and customer and supplier relations. The performance of plants was then compared, and the management characteristics of the top performers were contrasted with the lean production model (Oliver, Delbridge, and Lowe 1996).

Incompatibility Problems and Secondary Matching

Obtaining comparable data poses difficult challenges when the data come from existing survey material. Even when surveys are very similar, as was the case with AWIRS and WIRS3, the data will be far from identical. Comparative analysis can be a considerable problem, specifically, ensuring that only those variables for which there are actual or potentially compatible data are used. Incompatibility can take a variety of forms. The most important are sample incompatibility, question incompatibility, phenomenon incompatibility, and response incompatibility.

Sample Incompatibility

Sample incompatibility takes many forms. In its most extreme, it occurs when the sample populations for the two surveys are different. In AWIRS, the sample included all Australian workplaces with more than twenty workers, whereas the sample for WIRS3 included all British workplaces with more than twenty-five workers. Fortunately, this difference could be allowed for by eliminating all the workplaces from the AWIRS sample with twenty to twenty-four workers. If this had not proved so easy, there would have been significant incompatibility in the samples, which, given the importance of employment size as an explanatory variable in industrial relations, could have resulted in invalid inferences.

Sample incompatibility can also occur when there are guideposts or "go-to" statements that direct some respondents to skip several questions, thereby severely limiting the sample for those questions. A prime example is the guidepost in WIRS3 that instructs respondents to answer certain questions only if their workplace has a recognized union. The concept of recognized union has no meaning within the Australian system of conciliation and arbitration. Hence, AWIRS contains no similar restriction. The result is an inevitable and irretrievable sample incompatibility with respect to these questions.

Question Incompatibility

Even subtle differences between questions can evoke major differences in responses, especially to more qualitative questions. A prime example from AWIRS and WIRS3 is the question dealing with the frequency of union-management meetings. The AWIRS question asks, "How often, if at all, in the last year has this committee or any of its representatives met with management?" The WIRS3 question asks, "During the last year, apart from meetings of a formal negotiation or consultative committee, have you had contact with management here above supervisor level to discuss matters affecting the workers you represent?"

Although these questions may seem similar at first sight, the AWIRS question concerns meetings of the union committee or its representatives with management, whereas the WIRS question relates specifically to contact made by the union representative. Furthermore, the AWIRS question refers simply to "management," whereas that for WIRS specifies "management above supervisor level." The effect of these slight differences cannot be fully ascertained but could well be substantial. Such differences were less substantial in the AWIRS/WIRS3 comparison than in most other comparisons, because WIRS1 and WIRS2 were used as exemplars for AWIRS and there was close collaboration between the AWIRS and WIRS3 research teams. The differences were significant nonetheless.

One of the most common examples of question incompatibility occurs because the answer categories, such as "always; usually; sometimes; never," are different. In some cases this can be adjusted by recategorization to a common denominator. In other cases, however, exact compatibility cannot be achieved except by revising the answer scales to simple "yes/no" dichotomies to indicate whether an institution possesses a given characteristic or not. The result is the loss of potentially important detail.

Other question incompatibilities occur because of differences in the wording of questions so that different dimensions of a given phenomenon are being tapped. In AWIRS and WIRS3, the questions on the closed shop differ markedly, for example. The AWIRS question focuses on outcomes and asks whether at least one occupational group has 100 percent unionization. The WIRS3 question is more direct, focusing on procedures, and asks whether some or all workers have to be union members to keep their jobs. Some of the workplaces classed as closed shops in one survey may therefore not be classed as such in the other. Comparative analysis of such data must be undertaken with extreme care.

Phenomenon Incompatibility

Phenomenon incompatibility is much more subtle than the incompatibilities outlined above. It results because similar institutions and organizations in different countries tend to play different roles. For example, most countries have organizations concerned with arbitration processes, but the roles played by these bodies differ markedly. Identical questions may thereby evoke very different responses, and the researcher must be aware of this and its significance.

Another example, which inhibits the comparison of the results of British and Norwegian surveys, arises because establishments in Norway are substantially smaller than in Britain. Thus, many of the distinctive characteristics of industrial relations in large workplaces in Britain are not found in Norway because no workplaces where such characteristics might be found even exist. Phenomenon incompatibility is suggestive of the need for a broader approach than a strict like-for-like comparison.

Response Incompatibility

Even in situations in which the three incompatibilities outlined above are not problematic, response incompatibility may occur, making it impossible to make like-for-like comparisons. Response incompatibility is particularly likely if perceptions of given phenomena vary. Such incompatibility was uncovered in an analysis of the relative importance of internal labor markets in Japan and the United States (Cole 1979). A key question concerned the importance of mobility within the firm. Respondents were asked to indicate how often they made job changes. *A priori,* the expectation was that the figure would be much higher in Japan. The survey evidence, however, did not support this. Cole concluded that part of the reason for this disjunction was the lower occupational consciousness of Japanese workers, who were thereby less likely than their American counterparts to see a change in job duties as a job change. Although this incompatibility prevented the researchers from making a like-with-like comparison, closer inspection suggested an insight into workers' perceptions of their work situations.

Weinstein (1995a) reports a similar problem in using Likert-type agreement scales across cultures. In some cultures a high score on a given scale may suggest stronger agreement than in others. Similarly, a midpoint score might mean "no opinion" in some cultures and "mild agreement" in others. This represents a problem when combining data sets.

Implications

Incompatibilities create three main issues for the comparative researcher. The first is that, in practice, the data available for a like-with-like analysis are likely to be limited. The second is that like-sounding and like-looking institutions must be examined carefully for differences in the manner in which they operate in practice. The third is that phenomena are typically defined in reference to their overt structural characteristics, yet organizations differ because of interactions that are specific to the system in which they are located. Even the apparently neatest "matches" of questions rarely have more than proximal validity.

Problems Associated with Primary Collection

In primary collection, the researchers are responsible for both the research design and the data-collection process. At first this appears to offer a solution to the problems of incompatibility associated with secondary matching. Primary collection has other problems, however, to do with the *comparability* of the data across cases. These are closely related to the compatibility problems encountered in secondary matching. The main issues of concern when doing primary collection are sampling, ensuring a uniformity of approach, accounting for qualitative differences in systems, and issues surrounding language and "common understanding."

Sampling

The problem of sampling in primary collection is analogous to that of sample incompatibility in secondary matching. Obtaining comparable samples in two or more countries is far from straightforward. First, potential sampling frames may differ. At the very least, the dates of construction may be dissimilar. The collection of data for a large international sample takes time; the first IMVP, for example, ran for five years. Also, samples may exclude different types of organizations. Projects that are to include benchmark data on performance must ensure that accurate comparisons can be made on core process activities. Hence, these studies are typically based on one industry (Arthur 1992; MacDuffie 1995; Oliver, Delbridge, and Lowe 1996). A major question remains concerning the comparability of, say, the motor industry and other industry sectors (Bresnen 1996; Purcell 1996). Hence, the generalizability claimed for survey approaches may be contested.

Second, workplaces in different countries vary with respect to significant variables, such as size, market demand, and levels of technology. For example, the average size of establishments is known to vary markedly across countries. Researchers conducting comparative studies must therefore decide whether to compare similar-sized establishments in the same country or those at the same point in the size distribution of the sample. This choice depends crucially on whether size is seen to be exogenous or endogenous to the factors under investigation.

Similarly, levels of demand and capacity utilization will vary across countries and over time. Even studies in a single industry sector may reveal systematic national differences in such variables. The IMVP studies have been strongly criticized for attempting to standardize capacity utilization and adjust for its impact on productivity (Williams et al. 1994), whereas the WMCS reports that capacity utilization is a potential explanator for productivity differences.

Third, what is meant by the term "establishment" varies among countries, depending in part on the laws relating to the firm, and among different companies. For example, it is often difficult to disentangle activities and processes that are conducted simultaneously across different sites of multinational organizations. Both the IMVP and WMCS were conducted at the plant level, but this can create problems when individual plants are not responsible for, or have no autonomy over, certain functional management activities. A related problem is that of the location of individual establishments within a value chain and the relative level of value-added activities across individual cases in the sample.

Uniformity of Approach

Once the sample has been identified, a fundamental requirement of comparative workplace research is ensuring that *accurately comparable* data may be gathered. As with the secondary matching approach, there should be "question compatibility" across the cases and therefore a uniformity of approach. This need to standardize the approach typically mandates the use of a questionnaire. However, the use of questionnaires is necessarily restrictive in tracing systems differences and uncovering process details. As a consequence, comparative workplace surveys are typically positivist and deductive in approach. This represents a particular problem, since the questionnaire must ultimately prove effective in gathering data from respondents in markedly different institutional contexts and with very different cultures.

Qualitative Differences in Systems

A basic assumption of comparative analysis is that it is possible to compare like with like in different countries. However, countries may vary qualitatively. This is especially possible in the industrial relations area and where countries have evolved highly idiosyncratic mechanisms for handling industrial disputes. In secondary matching this difference may cause phenomenon incompatibility. Questions need to be formulated with care so as to avoid one system being distorted to match another. This is particularly problematic when utilizing questionnaires that are rigid and deductive in approach. As a consequence, surveys typically identify structures that may not represent common/uniform phenomena. For example, questionnaires may record the presence or absence of "teams" or "company councils," but these structures may differ dramatically in their functions from company to company and from country to country.

Collecting primary data in face-to-face interviews allows some of these problems to be highlighted. In this case the onus is often on the researchers to interpret whether and how these structures operate, which may require further clarification by means of open-ended questioning. For example, Japanese firms regularly report extraordinarily low levels of absenteeism (approaching zero) and that workers choose not to take all the holidays to which they are entitled. This finding should not be used as a proxy for "commitment," however, since Japanese workers often have to use accrued holiday time if they have long-term illnesses, which are not adequately covered in many companies' sickness plans.

Language and "Common Understanding"

Language difficulties can seriously affect the construction of survey questionnaires. This is most obviously the case when the surveys have to be conducted in several different languages, but problems can also arise when the languages are ostensibly the same. Subtle differences in meaning can have important effects on how a survey question is interpreted. This is particularly important with terms for which there are precise legal definitions in each country—such as participation, industrial democracy, and arbitration—and when the definitions used in one country differ from those used in other countries.

The WMCS project questionnaire was translated into a total of five languages, and, when necessary, members of the research team were supported in the field by translators. The difficulty in understanding foreign languages is compounded, however, when researchers seek to apply foreign concepts or ways of thinking. For example, Domsch and Lichtenberger report "a lack of correspondence between oriental and occidental understanding of research" in their study of German expatriate managers in China. Indeed, the authors reflect that differences in understanding may "render the results of cross-national research fairly meaningless" and cite the work of Hofstede and Bond (1988), who found that "items like 'truth' can and will be answered by Chinese managers, but, in fact, they are more or less irrelevant for them" (Domsch and Lichtenberger 1990: 83–84). Similarly, the WMCS research team found that many Japanese managers appeared to be unfamiliar with the concept of "throughput" time in measuring material flows in production.

These problems are similar to the problem of response incompatibility identified earlier and are a function of the ability of the respondents to answer the questions appropriately. The case of union density in Spain provides a further example. Managers in many plants are simply unaware of the level of unionization of their workforces since relatively few workers pay union dues directly through the company and union leaders keep membership levels secret. Consequently, any estimates Spanish managers make are likely to underestimate the *de facto* strength and influence of a union.

A research method that incorporates workplace visits and therefore face-to-face discussions can assist in identifying ambiguity and the failure to secure common understanding. Such visits represented a vital feature of the WMCS, in which managers were required to explain their responses to researchers during a second visit to the plant. Through this cross-checking process, unanticipated areas of uncertainty and ambiguity were identified and subsequently clarified. The quality of the data secured would have been dramatically reduced had the researchers been unable to make these visits.

Implications

As we have seen, the underlying causes of data incompatibility in secondary matching, such as qualitative differences in systems or a lack of common understanding, can also be problems in primary collection. The research method one employs and one's interpretation of the findings are important in overcoming these problems.

The aim of the questionnaire approach is to generate comparable data systematically across the sample. If the research plan also involves face-to-face interviews, the researchers will be able to obtain additional details about crucial aspects of the case and to extract important contextual information that will assist in the interpretation of the questionnaire data. In such circumstances, continuity in the research team will help to ensure uniformity of approach and that comparable qualitative data are gathered.

The research phase of the WMCS included two visits to each of the participating plants, and at least one of the three members of the core research team participated in every one of these visits. The first visit was used to introduce the project and explain its objectives, to tour the plant's manufacturing facilities to ensure that the plant was suitable for inclusion, and to explain key principles to the managers who were going to complete the questionnaire. Once managers at the plants had completed the survey, the research team returned to the plant and systematically reviewed each response, looking for evidence of ambiguities or mistakes.

In seeking a more sophisticated understanding of research sites, it is possible to develop questionnaires that can gather data that go beyond "yes/no" binary response modes. The Helper/Sako questionnaire, used to research buyer-supplier relations as part of the latest IMVP, incorporates "scenario" analysis, in which managers identify likely outcomes to hypothetical situations (Sako and Helper 1995). The WMCS questionnaire asks for the proportional responsibility for various tasks that is held by different groups of employees.

The research method also informs the likelihood of achieving uniform responses and gaining "common understanding." International workplace surveys that involve field visits require exceptional time and resource commitments, but significant doubts exist about the ability of mail questionnaires to elicit truly comparable data. The field visits conducted during WMCS were critical in clarifying something as fundamental as the manufacturing processes that were actually conducted in-house.

An alternative research approach, adopted in the Price Waterhouse/ Cranfield project, involves convening panels of academics and practitioners to design the questionnaire and interpret the results. The Price Waterhouse/Cranfield study, which involved identifying trends in human resource management in a number of European countries, was based on mailed questionnaires but also involved local business school researchers, panel meetings of human resource practitioners in the countries concerned, and symposia of academics and practitioners (Holden 1991).

Approaches to Data Analysis

The approach to data analysis adopted in a comparative project depends crucially on the data set that is developed. In particular, a like-with-like approach requires the development of closely comparable data. Where this is not possible, a more circumspect approach is required. While this requirement applies particularly strongly to the analysis of data obtained from secondary matching, it also applies to primary collection and analysis.

In the AWIRS/WIRS3 project, a wide range of variables proxying institutional arrangements and industrial relations/economic outcomes were constructed and analyzed using a range of multivariate statistical methods. These variables included proxies for union presence (density, presence, "active" presence), workplace size (number of employees in the establishment), company structure (independent entity or part of a multiestablishment organization), and the composition of the workforce (proportion of female and part-time employees). It should be noted, however, that the variables analyzed were a small subset of those available in either AWIRS or WIRS3, which in turn were a subset of those that would be ideal for a comprehensive comparative analysis. In short, the research project focuses on the data set that is most feasible, rather than the one that is most desirable, thereby providing a contrast between the rigor of the method used and the inexactitude of the data deployed.

Nonetheless, the available variables allowed a much more comprehensive test than had previously been possible of key hypotheses that have become common (either implicitly or explicitly) in the industrial relations literature. For example, it was possible to examine whether the existence of a centralized system of conciliation and arbitration has resulted in the Australian workplace having a less well-developed set of workplace dispute resolution procedures than a broadly comparable British workplace. This was a key issue in the arbitration/collective bargaining debate that took place in Australia in the 1970s and 1980s. Thus, despite inevitable concerns about the proximate nature of the match between the data used and the underlying factors that it was attempting to represent, it can be said that the AWIRS/WIRS3 project represented a substantial development of the preceding literature.

Any analysis that is based on a comparison of less closely comparable data must, by its very nature, be more circumspect. At the very least, however, such an analysis can offer broad indications of significant differences in workplace arrangements and outcomes in two countries. Additionally, it can suggest differences in the nature of these arrangements and outcomes and thereby provoke further research. For example, preliminary analysis of two data sets indicated that formal grievance procedures are more prevalent in Britain than in Australia. Although this in itself does not say a great deal about the relative importance of such institutional arrangements, it does suggest an avenue for further research. Does the greater prevalence of grievance procedures in Britain result from the greater development of collective voice arrangements in the more decentralized Britain or is it simply a passive response to legal requirements? Are grievance procedures used more fully in Britain than in Australia?

Regardless of the methodological stance taken, it is clear that any survey-based analysis will at most offer only a limited picture of the complex relationships that make up an industrial relations system. Surveys are blunt instruments, and compared with other research methods, such as case studies and ethnography, are typically less rich in institutional detail. Surveys tell us little about causal relationships and processes. Surveys do, however, offer the prospect of generalization and presentation of a broad picture. They should therefore be seen as a part of rather than the totality of the research process, building on studies using alternative methods and contributing to them. Used in conjunction with more intensive research methods, surveys can provide important information that these studies are unable to tap. For example, surveys can uncover valuable data about the differential impact of organizational scale on a given phenomenon. Methodologically, it is not a question of either/or but of getting the best of both worlds.

The Future

The increasing interest in comparing workplaces in different countries suggests that there will be continuing and possibly greater pressure to develop comparative workplace surveys. Furthermore, the development of industrial relations surveys in different countries offers the prospect of extending the range of comparative research. Such analyses require great care, however, particularly with regard to the derivation and use of data.

Given the different institutional environments in different countries and the differences in research agenda, data sets can differ markedly and thereby pose important methodological questions for researchers. Consequently, the impact of such research on comparative analysis may be limited unless conscious attempts are made to integrate the various national efforts. In drawing up new surveys, explicit attempts should be made to develop data sets that permit useful cross-country comparisons. This is not a trivial exercise; great care must be taken to eliminate the potential, often subtle, incompatibilities outlined above. Such an exercise requires that researchers maintain a dialogue with those undertaking national surveys and that the latter see the advantages of minimizing cross-national incompatibilities.

For those engaging in the primary collection of comparative workplace data, the challenges and opportunities are equally significant. The difficulties in securing comparable data are not insurmountable, and the influence of the IMVP findings is eloquent testament to the opportunities international workplace surveys offer. There are lessons to be learned and pitfalls to be avoided.

As with the problem of incompatibility in secondary matching, primary collection can be dogged by noncomparability. Researchers must address problems of sample design, uniformity of approach and response, and potential bias resulting from qualitative differences in systems and cultural misunderstanding. Equally, there are fundamental questions of research design and interpretation. For example, the research emanating from the IMVP has been widely criticized with regard to both how the data sets and variables were constructed and the authors' interpretations of the findings.

Nevertheless, the analysis of truly comparable workplace survey data drawn from different countries offers a powerful complement to other forms of comparative industrial relations research, particularly for researchers seeking generalizable explanations of workplace phenomena.

A consideration of both approaches—secondary matching and primary collection—underscores the fundamental significance attached to the *interpretation* of data. As with all research, the key to analyzing and presenting data drawn from international workplace surveys is to provide a convincing interpretation of what the data represent and what they in turn imply for our understanding of industrial relations.

Data obtained from comparative workplace surveys can greatly expand the scope of a research study. Used in conjunction with other research techniques, these data can contribute significantly to our knowledge of the world of work.

Part IV

Disciplinary Approaches

Disciplinary Approaches

A wide range of fields and disciplines examines the world of work and is relevant to industrial relations. Part IV deals with the strategies and methods used by three of these disciplines—history, law, and sociology.

These disciplines have been chosen because they offer something unique to the industrial relations debate. The contributions of other fields, such as economics, psychology, human resource management, and political science, which are more closely related to industrial relations, are not described here because the strategies and methods used by these fields are so closely aligned with those of industrial relations that there would be considerable overlap with the other chapters in this already long volume.

Except when they are engaged in purely theoretical work, economists use roughly the same quantitative techniques as researchers in other disciplines. True, economists generally use data gathered by others and, compared with psychologists, are more likely to employ regressions than factor analysis. Psychologists concerned with workplace issues use experiments and attitude surveys. These data-gathering methods are often also employed by sociologists and increasingly even by economists. At least in the United States, many scholars studying human resource management have been trained as psychologists, and they too utilize experiments and attitude surveys. In addition, they may use case studies and workplace surveys. The focus of political science is changing. Traditionally, research in that field was theoretical. Data-based studies tended to be inductive and to employ what might best be described as case studies. Today, however, political scientists are increasingly likely to employ attitude surveys and various forms of quantitative analysis of publicly available data.

Most of the data analyzed by researchers in the fields just discussed are contemporary or fairly recent. History is concerned with the past and so, for the most part, different data-gathering methods are employed. For example, rather than asking managers questions about current practices, the historian consults company archives. Opinions cannot be sampled on a scientific basis, so diaries, autobiographies, and newspaper articles must be examined for clues to what people were thinking during the period under investigation.

Most of the data in law books and legal analysis are very different from traditional social science data. As chapter 14 points out, however, there are those who would broaden the scope of legal scholarship to include various forms of empirical data. This suggests a potential synergy between law and industrial relations.

It is hard to make sharp distinctions between the methods sociologists use and those used by researchers in other disciplines. Sociologists sometimes ask different questions, however, than do most "mainstream" industrial relations researchers. In particular, sociologists are typically more likely to use a deductive approach that is grounded in testing propositions from a distinct theoretical framework.

CHAPTER THIRTEEN

Digging Up the Past: Historical Methods in Industrial Relations Research

Greg Patmore

S cholars interested in the world of work have used historical methods to explore a wide range of issues. This chapter aims to indicate why such methods are important. It also examines how historical methods developed. Historians have traditionally focused on the examination of documents, but since the 1960s historiographical debates have broadened the horizons of historians to include new methods such as oral history. Finally, this chapter evaluates the strength and weaknesses of some of these methods, such as documentary research, oral history, the study of visual history and material culture, and the use of quantitative material. The conclusion is that the preferable approach is to combine a variety of methods where possible.

Historical Methods and the World of Work

History helps academics understand why things happen. It enables theories to be generated and tested. For example, historians have tested and challenged Braverman's deskilling hypothesis (Knox 1986; Shields 1995).

History also provides researchers with a long-term perspective, enabling them to avoid the pitfalls of the snapshot.[1] Because the focus is on process, researchers can develop dynamic rather than static theoretical frameworks.

---

1. For example, Gospel's historical study of British employers established that firms gradually took direct control of labor management and grew less reliant on the external labor market (1992: 10, 171).

Theoretical perspectives that fail to take account of a changing economic, political, and social climate have limited explanatory power.[2]

Historical methods are useful not only in the formulation of theories. They can be helpful in understanding the present and can thereby contribute to contemporary public policy debates. The attacks on the Australian arbitration system by deregulationists during the 1980s provided the background for a reassessment of its genesis by industrial relations academics and others supportive of the system (Macintyre and Mitchell 1989). Sometimes there is public policy amnesia, in which industrial relations scholars who develop so-called new initiatives ignore similar innovations in the past. This has been particularly true of the industrial democracy debate. Ramsay (1980) in the United Kingdom and Wright (1995) in Australia have noted that employers have adopted a cyclical approach to worker participation driven by threats to management authority. Why did such schemes fail in earlier periods? Are the conditions for failure still present today? Historical research enables academics to explore these questions and provide another perspective for contemporary debates.

Sometimes contemporary research may not be possible on particular questions because of the implications for an individual's privacy and commercial considerations. Management may be reluctant to admit its role in provoking industrial disputes or to reveal divisions over important issues. The passage of time may make these issues less sensitive. For example, in 1912, managers at the Lithgow Small Arms Factory in Australia denied that they were involved in the formation of a new union at the plant, which was owned and operated by the federal government. Evidence available since the 1960s, however, indicates that not only did local managers lie but that they ignored a directive by a federal government Cabinet minister against forming a company union (Patmore 1994a: 48).

Mainstream industrial relations researchers generally ignore history. Lyddon and Smith (1996) argue that since 1979 historical articles have rarely been published in industrial relations journals in the United Kingdom or in the two main industrial relations journals in the United States. A review of the articles in the *Journal of Industrial Relations* (Australia), *Industrial and Labor Relations Review* (United States) and the *British Journal of*

---

2. Jacoby (1990: 319–20) makes a similar point in his discussion of the new institutional economics. He notes that orthodox theory is *synchronic:* an abstraction from reality that denies history or place. Institutionists, such as Commons and the Webbs, however, also insisted on a *diachronic* analysis, which explored how the economy acquired its features and how those features varied over time and space.

Industrial Relations (BJIR) for the period from 1990 to 1994 revealed that only 19 percent used historical data—defined here as predating 1980.

Those industrial relations scholars who do engage in historical research prefer to use quantitative methods, especially in the United States and the United Kingdom. Of the historical articles in the *Review* and the *BJIR,* the overwhelming majority employed quantitative data—90 percent and 62 percent, respectively. Examples include Boal's (1990) study of unionism and productivity in West Virginia coal mining during the 1920s and the study of British coal mining strikes by Church, Outram, and Smith (1990). These examples highlight the influence of labor economists in industrial relations research and reflect a general trend toward the use of quantitative methods.

British and U.S. industrial relations academics appear reluctant to draw on qualitative historical methods. Exceptions include Cobble's (1991) study of waitress unionism, which used both documentary and oral sources. By contrast, approximately 75 percent of the historical articles in the Australian *Journal of Industrial Relations* employed qualitative techniques. A notable example is Sheridan's (1994) study of waterside workers.

What Is Distinctive about Historical Methodology?

Historical methodology can be defined in two ways. First, it can be viewed temporally. Historical methodology is concerned with analyzing the "past" (Marshall and Rossman 1989: 95). It is not clear, however, when the "past" ends or the "present" begins. The past may terminate yesterday or at the beginning of the last decade. Evidence drawn from the past can also help us understand the present.

Researching the past has particular problems. People forget or die. Documents may be lost or deliberately destroyed. Consequently, the historical researcher has to weave together fragments of the past to achieve understanding. Researchers of the present have similar problems, however. People may lie and withhold documents because of their political or commercial sensitivity.

Second, historical methodology has been defined as a particular set of practices. The traditional image of the historian is of someone who visits archives and interviews elderly people. There are claims that historical research is a craft that involves skills such as the ability to weigh evidence, to compress a range of events into a single trend, to hold evidence up to "a dark Satanic light of evaluation," to fill in gaps with "innovative detective work," and to evaluate secondary sources critically (Markey 1987: 177). But these skills are not the exclusive domain of historians; they characterize all innovative research in the social sciences. Further, defining a distinctive historical methodology is a problem. For example, some researchers may view the survey as a contemporary research tool; however, one innovative English historian undertook a survey of Edwardian life by interviewing survivors of this period by means of a quota sample based on the 1911 U.K. census (Thompson 1975).

Although it may be difficult to distinguish between the skills and methods of the contemporary researcher and the historian, there are differences. Both researchers of the present and the past use documents. The written word is not constant over time, however. Some words disappear, words are invented, and other words change meaning. These problems are greater for a historian studying the late nineteenth century than for a researcher of current trade union amalgamations. The passage of time creates particular problems for the historical researcher.

Changes in Historiography
and the Historical Method

The research methods used by historians examining the world of work have reflected ideas of what history is and how historical research should be done. Prior to the 1960s the dominant perspective was that history was a positive science composed of facts. Once the historian had collected the empirically verifiable facts, it was his or her duty to judge them. The historian could not study class or modes of production since these concepts were not empirically verifiable. Some historians also adopted a "whig view" of history. They argued that the theories of humanity had to be drawn from great men.

The ideas of German historians, particularly Von Ranke, influenced historical methodology in this period. Empirical verification for these historians was possible only through the existence of written documents in archives and libraries—"no documents, no history." Archaeological evidence and verbal evidence were inferior. The expert handling of these documents distinguished historians from other researchers and amateurs. Historians could also claim objective neutrality by cutting themselves off from the outside world and spending their time in archives (Scott 1990: 10–11; Thompson 1988: 50–52).

The expansion of universities in the English-speaking world during the 1950s encouraged academic historians to specialize. They became economic historians, business historians, and military historians. Specialist historians still operated largely within a positivist paradigm, however, and claimed that their particular specialization was contributing to the construction of a broader picture of society (Merritt 1982: 117). By contrast, French historians showed an interest in "total history." From the 1920s, the Annales school emphasized history that focused more on analysis than on narrative. Dialogue developed between French historians, sociologists, anthropologists, and geographers. There was interest in quantitative methods as well (McLennan 1981: 129–44).

During the 1960s there was a major questioning of traditional historiography in the English-speaking world. The protests over the Vietnam War, the civil rights movement, and the growth of women's liberation provided the background for this discontent. The radical ideas of Althusser, Gramsci, and others influenced the dissidents. Four British historians were particularly important—Carr, Stedman Jones, Thompson, and Hobsbawm. Carr attacked the positivist methodology of British historiography. He argued that historians did not simply show "how it was," with facts providing the interpretation. Rather, he said, the political and cultural values of historians determine their choice of "significant" facts. Carr notes that the collection and analysis of data are generally simultaneous. Further, documentary sources, even if they survive fire, flood, and vermin, are the selective thoughts of their authors. Thompson challenged whig history by calling for a focus on the "culture of labouring people"—"history from below." He also criticized "one class" history, claiming that class arose from a historical relationship and was not distinct. The working class existed only if there was a ruling class, and vice versa. Hobsbawm supported social history—the history of society—and dismissed specializations, such as economic history. Social history involved the construction of theory in history and the borrowing of techniques from the social sciences. Feminist historians also criticized the traditional preoccupation of historians with "great men" and institutions dominated by men (Merritt 1982: 130–35).

The critiques of the 1960s also led historians to examine alternatives to documentary research. Two such approaches were oral history and quantitative methods. Thompson's call for "history from below" and the feminist critique invited the exploration of the experiences of women, working-class families, unorganized workers, and native peoples. Generally, these groups did not leave written records and researchers turned to oral history to capture their recollections. The availability of cheap cassette recorders also made this research method more accessible to both professional and amateur historians (Thompson 1988: 55–56).

In the United States, social historians applied quantitative methods to issues such as labor force composition and occupational mobility. Historians found quantitative techniques useful in dealing with the large amounts of data found in census manuscripts and city directories. The computer revolution also increased accessibility to quantitative methods (Brody 1980: 261–62).

These debates in mainstream historiography have influenced labor historians. Traditionally, they focused on trade unions, labor parties, and the legal regulation of industrial relations. In the United States prior to the 1960s, labor history was written by people who were closely identified with the fields of industrial relations and labor economics. Commons and the Wisconsin school pioneered both industrial relations and labor history in the United States. Similarly, the Webbs were the founders of both fields in the United Kingdom. In Australia, participants in the labor movement wrote celebratory histories of trade unions as early as 1888. In all three countries, there was little interest in the labor movement in university history departments until the 1950s. Under the influence of Thompson and others, labor historians shifted their focus away from labor institutions and their leaders to working-class communities and culture, the shop floor, women, immigrants, and ethnic minorities. Labor historians also adopted new historical research tools, such as oral history and quantitative methods. The rise of the "new labor history" in U.S. academic history departments coincided with the decline of traditional labor history in academic industrial relations courses in the United States, where there was increasing focus on labor economics and organizational behavior.

Both mainstream historiography and labor history continue to face challenges. Social history has merged into cultural history, which focuses on image, representations, and modes of narration. Cultural history involves exploring music, clothes, buildings, and celebrations such as Labor Day marches. Labor historians influenced by this approach continue to be interested in oral history and "history from below" (Curthoys 1994).

Business historians and labor process theorists have encouraged labor historians and others concerned with the world of work to examine management and explore company records. There have even been calls for "employer history," ignoring the critique of "one class" history by Thompson (Jacoby 1991: 14; Wright 1995).

Some labor historians have reemphasized the importance of institutions by embracing neoinstitutionalism or Zeitlinism (Montgomery 1991: 111–12; Patmore, 1994b: 164–66), which is related but not identical to institutionalism in organizational theory. Zeitlin (1987) argued that institutional forces rather than spontaneous economic and social processes or informal work groups were the crucial determinants of relationships between workers and employers in Britain. Zeitlin's rejection of history from below or of "rank and filism" was accompanied by a call for the replacement of labor history with industrial relations history, which is the study of the changing relationships between workers, unions, employers, employers associations, and the state.

More recently, Kimeldorf (1991) in *Labor History* reinforced Zeitlin's views by calling for the end of the "tyranny of culturalism" and for bringing back unions into labor history. These ideas would return labor historiography to the 1950s. Although neoinstitutionalists have little to say about the implications of their ideas for research methodology, there is no reason to assume that they would reject oral history and other historical methods embraced by the social or cultural historians.

Overall, the historiographical debates since the 1960s have broadened both the subject matter and the tools of historical research. The remainder of the chapter focuses in detail on the strengths and weaknesses of various methods of historical research.

Historical Documents

Documents remain the main focus of historical research. They are a written text and may be contained in a variety of physical forms—clay tablets, paper, and computer files (Scott 1990: 12–13). There are both primary and secondary documents. Primary documents are those that were written during the historical period under examination. Secondary documents are written after the event and include books, theses, and journal articles.

Primary documents may be either manuscripts or printed materials. The former include diaries, letters, minute books, memos, and company wage books. The latter include company annual reports, union journals, staff magazines, legislative papers, court transcripts, and newspapers. Manuscripts can be highly personal and written for a limited audience. At one extreme are diaries, usually kept only for the diarist. Likewise, within some organizations, memos may be restricted to senior personnel. Printed materials are intended for a larger audience. Metropolitan newspapers can be read by several hundred thousand readers. Generally, the restricted audience for manuscripts makes them more valuable than printed material, providing insights into organizations that would not be known to outsiders at the time. Manuscripts also provide a useful check on printed sources.

Regardless of what documents the historian uses, people have written them. Documents therefore contain their authors' interpretations of events and biases. This must be taken into account, as much as possible, in their interpretation. Some historians treat newspapers with enormous reverence as sources of information, ignoring the contemporary debate over the political bias in newspaper reporting. Newspaper reporters and editors, whether in the 1890s or the 1990s, are forced to make judgments about what events to report on, and the articles they produce incorporate their prejudices and beliefs.

Diaries incorporate an individual's perceptions of the world—what may be a "demonstration" to one diarist may be a "riot" to another. Minutes are generally brief summaries of meetings, which may not capture the mood and may downplay important issues. Even statistical data drawn from legislative reports, submissions in response to government inquiries, and censuses have to be handled with care. Social and economic statistics rely on interviews and forms submitted by organizations. Employers may provide inflated data on labor costs to further their case for tariff protection. Transcripts of wage hearings are not pure sources of information, either, since witnesses may be tutored by unions or employer organizations to present their respective cases in the most favorable light. Witnesses may also be intimidated by the courtroom proceedings (Thompson 1988: 101–6).

A historian also has to ask why some documents have survived and others haven't. Governments, trade unions, employers, and other agencies regularly cull records because they take up too much space. Culling involves making decisions about what is significant from the organization's point of view. Organizations may decide to preserve records that portray them favorably. Records that focus on decision making are sometimes seen as more important than financial records and therefore preserved. This may create problems for researchers who wish to construct employee or union membership profiles from wage books or union subscription lists respectively. Outgoing union executives may destroy records to ensure that rivals cannot obtain unfavorable information. Companies are not required to retain a large proportion of their records and may also destroy embarrassing records relating to, say, the recruitment of strikebreakers, antiunion strategies, or collusive trade practices. Some documents that survive may be fakes. In a classic case in the early 1980s, the infamous "Hitler diaries" were initially authenticated by a leading British historian but subsequently found to be modern forgeries through chemical testing of the paper and ink (Scott 1990: 175–76).

Another problem is that not all documents are made available to researchers. Restrictions are justified on a number of grounds, including national security, the need to ensure that information does not get in the hands of rival organizations, and individual privacy. In the case of personal collections, restrictions may be lifted only after the death of the depositor. In Australia and the United Kingdom, national government records are subject to a thirty-year restriction on their use.

Government security services are notorious for the restrictions they impose on their records. Where individuals obtain their personal files, large amounts of information may be blacked out. Some private organizations also have rules limiting access. BHP, Australia's largest public company, has a thirty-year rule.

Even if the researcher can obtain the necessary documents, they may be difficult to understand because words have disappeared from usage or have different meanings. Reference is made in nineteenth-century U.K. censuses to the occupation of "whitster." Not only is this term no longer used but it had two meanings in the nineteenth century. A whitster could be either a textile bleacher or a metal finisher (Scott 1990: 28–29).

Problems also arise if the writer was semiliterate. Some minute books of early trade unions are filled with poor spelling and grammar. The researcher has to decide from context and other evidence on the period whether there is a textual error.

In short, the historical researcher examining documents has to bring together fragments of the past and must be aware that they are products of human agency—the thoughts and actions of people. It is almost impossible for the researcher to consult all documents of interest because of selective survival and access restrictions. The historical researcher has to cross-check surviving documentary sources and be sensitive to the biases of the creators of the documents. He or she also has to be sensitive to the historical context of the document and changes in the meaning of written text over time.

Oral History

Oral history is an important source of information for the historian and provides a means of cross-checking documentary sources . A major feature of oral history is that the researcher is not a passive recipient of surviving documents but a creator of new historical sources (Portelli 1981: 104–5). Oral history is the process of gathering oral evidence, usually in a tape-recorded interview. Although historians prefer to tape-record their interviews, sometimes interviewees may be reluctant to speak in the presence of a tape recorder and the interviewer may be forced to take notes. Under these circumstances, the interviewer may have to submit the interview notes later on to the interviewee for verification. Typically, the interviewer has some knowledge of the subject under discussion, and the interviewee speaks from the perspective of personal participant or observer. Ethically, it is important that the interviewee know that he or she is being interviewed and that the information he or she provides will be used for research.

Researchers may employ unstructured interviews or design questionnaires for structured interviews. Many oral historians employ a life-cycle approach to interviewing, in which the individual talks about his or her parents, childhood, and finally adulthood.

Although interviews may be transcribed, original tapes are considered superior sources. Transcriptions do not capture all the meanings of interviews, since they cannot convey speakers' inflections, rhythms, and accents. Further, errors in comprehension and therefore transcription can occur in the process of preparing transcripts. Nonetheless, historians generally prefer the convenience and familiarity of written transcripts. They also highlight the overlap of documentary and oral sources. Historians also use the oral testimonies found in transcripts of court cases and public inquiries (Douglas, Roberts, and Thompson 1988: 2–7).

There are several problems with oral history. The historian may find that important informants have died. Further, in the 1990s the memories of the oldest interviewees generally stretch back to only World War I. Also, there is the question of the reliability of memory. Individuals can forget events completely or distort them. Some interviewees compress events in the 1920s, 1940s, and 1960s. There are even examples of collective amnesia, as arose among working-class militants in Turin over the period of fascist rule. Immediately after observing or participating in an event, individuals begin discarding information. The information that survives the discarding process tends to be retained until senility. Retention can be determined by the personal significance of the event or by whether there is a need to remember it. Memory can also be influenced by subsequent events and hindsight. Interviewees read, watch television, and listen to accounts of events by other participants. In other cases, interviewees may say little or lie because they dislike the interviewer. Overzealous interviewers may put words into an interviewee's mouth or ask leading questions that reflect their own biases (Douglas, Roberts, and Thompson 1988: 22–28).

Despite these problems, oral history can sometimes provide insights that documents cannot. While census data and industrial agreements list occupations, oral history enables the researcher to understand what jobs entailed. Interviews may uncover sensitive issues that are seldom acknowledged in written documents. In Australia, for example, surviving archives reveal little about the sectarian rivalry between Protestants and Catholics. But interviews with New South Wales Government Railways employees indicate that two rival unions—the Australian Railways Union, for Catholics, and the National Union of Railwaymen, for Protestants—capitalized on this rivalry in their organizing campaigns (Patmore 1988: 7).

Although oral history may not be particularly useful for collecting specific information on names and dates, it can capture information about the strength of particular attitudes and provide meaning for particular events. As Portelli noted, oral sources "tell us not just what people did, but what they wanted to do, what they believed they were doing, what they now think they did" (1981: 100–101). Oral history may provide little data on the economic costs of retrenchment, for example, but it offers important insights into the psychological impacts.

Oral testimonies and documents share similar problems of selectivity and bias. Where possible, several participants should be interviewed. Oral history should also be used in conjunction with surviving documentary sources. Documentary sources are useful not only in providing background information for the interviews but also in providing an important means for cross-checking.

Other Historical Methods

Visual History

Visual history includes sketches, photographs, videotapes, and film. These sources provide important information on issues such as working conditions and social status. It is very difficult to get an image of a workplace from either company or union documents, but a photograph can highlight plant layout and the level of technology. For example, photographs and films of worker protests can provide an indication of levels of participation and support.

People take photographs, however. One has to ask why particular pictures were taken. Companies may photograph their factories for publicity reasons. Management may remove safety hazards, such as the waste on the factory floor, to ensure the best possible image. Surviving visual material may represent only a small proportion of what was originally taken.

Care also has to be taken when there are captions accompanying pictures and film with sound. In the United Kingdom almost all the film sound during World War II was faked. As with documentary sources, it is important to understand the context in which pictures were taken and the biases of their creators (Horne 1988: 87–94; Thompson 1988: 107). One example of a researcher who used visual history is Larry Peterson (1992), who explored how the Pullman Company in the United States used photography to define its view of work and community and counteract alternative perspectives.

Material Culture

The term "material culture" refers to a wide range of objects and artifacts, including buildings, machinery, workers' tools, and union banners and badges. Tool kits for particular trades highlight their skills. Artifacts, such as banners and badges, convey workers' images of themselves.

Industrial archaeology plays a particularly important role in the study of material culture, highlighting the spatial dimensions of work. At a particular site the historical researcher can find out where particular work was performed and what level of interaction was possible between groups of workers. A toolroom may be housed within the same building as the production line or sited at a separate location. Status may also be reflected in the location of worker housing. The company may build a substantial house for a manager on an elevated lot but provide more temporary accommodations for laborers on a flood-prone river embankment. Again, the historical researcher has to ask why some artifacts have survived and others have vanished (Birmingham, Jack, and Jeans 1983: 9–10; Pickett 1988: 81–86).

An example of a researcher who made an important contribution by studying material culture is Grace Karskens (1986). She examined the stonework, built by convicts, of the Great North Road near Sydney, Australia, to challenge the traditional view that road gangs composed of convicts were inefficient and unproductive.

Quantitative Methods

Historians use quantitative methods when they cull information from databases provided by the state, companies, unions, universities, and other sources or they develop new databases.[3] Like social scientists, historians use quantitative methods in two ways. First, they use them to prepare formalized descriptions that include tables and graphs. Second, in a more sophisticated approach, they use statistical methods such as multiple regression to test hypotheses.

---

3. Michael Quinlan and Margaret Gardner (1994) are among the researchers who have developed their own databases. They have constructed an Australian Trade Union database for the period from 1825 to 1900 by scanning a variety of documentary sources, including newspapers, union records, and state archives.

Historians use quantitative methods to examine issues such as trade union growth, strikes, the economic impact of slavery, labor mobility, and living standards. The advantage of this method is that it allows greater precision in making statements.

There are problems, however, with developing historical databases. If the data are poor, then the outcomes of quantitative analysis will be useless. The definitions of variables such as trade union membership and strikes change over time. Data-collection procedures may also change. Trade unions could submit their own returns concerning membership or a central statistical agency may undertake a general survey of union membership.

Whether historical researchers rely on existing statistical data or construct their own, the problems of selectivity and bias still apply. Focusing on quantitative data also narrows our understanding of the past to the measurable and may result in the rich details of a particular period being ignored. There is also the problem of quantifying concepts such as class, power, and nationalism (Jarausch and Hardy 1991: 1–2).

George Bain and Faroukh Elsheikh (1976) are examples of historians who have used multiple regression in historical research. They tried to develop a model to explain the rise and fall of trade union density in Australia, Sweden, United States, and the United Kingdom. Their findings included a positive relationship between rises in prices and union density in all countries except Australia. Bain and Elsheikh argued that this arose because the Australian basic wage was linked to the price index and workers were less dependent on unions to defend them from declining real wages. Although Bain and Elsheikh used rigorous statistical methods to analyze their data, a major problem was that their data were weak. Ray Richardson (1977) noted that labor force data are crucial for estimating trade union density. For the years before 1945 in the United Kingdom, however, the only sources of this information are diennial censuses. Bain and Elsheikh constructed labor force data by a linear interpolation for the noncensus years, which led Richardson to conclude that their prewar density measure for the United Kingdom was wrong.

Conclusions

Historians use a variety of research methods. These methods allow researchers examining the world of work to develop more dynamic theoretical frameworks, to test established theories, and to enrich debates on current public policy issues. Despite this potential contribution, historical methodology remains marginal in important areas such as industrial relations. Further, industrial relations academics use only a small proportion of possible techniques. The focus on quantitative data restricts historical research to the measurable. Concepts such as class, culture, and community, which have become central to debates in labor historiography and which place industrial relations in a broader context, are rarely explored.

There are a variety of methods that academics and others can use to explore the "past." Traditionally, historical research involved the examination of documents. Historiographical debates during the 1960s and 1970s, however, broadened historical methodology to incorporate oral history, quantitative methods, visual history, and material culture.

No technique can be considered superior since all are the consequence of human agency. The best approach for historical research is to use a variety of sources for cross-checking.

CHAPTER FOURTEEN

Legal Methods:
Asking New Questions about
Law and the World of Work

Suzanne Hammond and Paul Ronfeldt

S ince the 1980s there has been considerable debate within academic labor law circles about the future direction of research in this area. Much of this debate has concerned how the field of labor law should be defined—that is, what legal issues should be included in discussions of the relationship between law and work relations. For many scholars, the recent dramatic changes in the nature of work, labor markets, and the law have challenged the tradition that made collective bargaining the central object of labor law scholarship (Weiler 1990; Collins 1991; Gottesman 1991). This chapter is, like this debate, motivated by a concern with ensuring that legal scholarship remains relevant to the world of work. But rather than considering the entire scope of the field of labor law, our discussion examines the application of legal research methods to research about the world of work. In this regard, our discussion follows the work of others who have critically considered the extent to which traditional forms of legal analysis can be relied on to develop our understanding of the politics of industrial relations and the impact of law on the interactions of workers and managers in industry (Bennett 1994; Klare 1990).

Our central contention is that traditional legal research methods are derived from the practices and reasoning of the legal system and are incommensurable with the objectives of systematic empirical social science. We also contend, however, that an understanding of legal practices and reasoning is a necessary component of research about the social character and social impact of the law. As such, we conclude that an appreciation of the practices and reasoning used by professional lawyers and the research methods used by social science researchers is necessary to develop a more sophisticated understanding of the interaction of legal and behavioral norms in the world of work.

Our chapter is divided into three parts. First, we examine the traditional mode of legal analysis. Second, we critically assess the application of traditional legal methods and examine several approaches that have gone beyond these methods. Third, we examine strategies that have aimed to broaden legal research methods by embracing approaches more akin to the empirical social sciences.

Traditional Legal Methods

Reflecting on how lawyers approach their craft helps illustrate the difference between their frame of reference and that of social scientists. The object of legal training is to teach people how to interpret legal doctrine. To serve this end, lawyers are trained to perform two related functions. First, they are trained to find the law. This involves learning to navigate through a law library and find primary (case law, legislation, regulations, and so on) and secondary (texts, articles, legal encyclopedias, and so forth) legal sources relevant to particular legal issues. Second, lawyers are taught how to digest and apply legal doctrine to hypothetical and "real" legal disputes. This involves learning the "canons" of legal interpretation, such as the doctrine of precedent, the distinction between ratio decidendi and obiter dicta, and various rules relating to statutory interpretation (Williams 1982). Both tasks involve a good deal of technical training, if not much imagination. By spending years of countless frustrations searching through legal textbooks, periodicals, case citators, law reports, statutes, and Hansard and through the application of formal rules of interpretation, lawyers perform the much-needed task of reducing complex and obscure legal sources in a manner that enables them to advise clients, governments, and the community about the legal rules that affect them.

For example, in studying how antidiscrimination laws can be used to redress inequality in the workplace, the following traditional legal method is likely to be used. The researcher will commence by reading legal commentaries in textbooks and articles by specialists in this area that describe the operation and requirements of antidiscrimination law. The researcher will then consult relevant statutes and case law to gain an even more detailed understanding of the legal rules governing the area. As the researcher becomes more familiar with the minutiae of antidiscrimination law, he or she is likely to begin to see ways in which these laws might be applied to provide more extensive protections and remedies against discrimination. This might include more expansive readings of statutory expressions, reformulating statutory law, or borrowing concepts from other areas of law, such as torts. In this way, specialist academic labor lawyers and researchers both describe how legal rules have been applied in the past and suggest strategies through which existing rules could be reformulated to address the problem of discrimination in the workplace.

It must be recognized, however, that the legal method involves a particularly circumscribed form of research concentrated on the analysis of legal sources and devoted to the exegesis of legal doctrine. As such, legal research begins and ends at the door of the law library. Nonetheless, legal research of this kind serves invaluable functions for those interested in the world of work. First, it explains how law can be used in practical situations. Second, it can be used to help explain the development of legal norms. Third, it can serve to inform debates about law reform. The first two functions involve a positivist approach, which asks, "What is the law?" The third function involves using doctrinal analysis normatively, by critically considering the limits of current legal doctrine and suggesting how law could be changed to better reflect "important" values and social concerns.

The obscurity of many legal sources, the technical form of much legal language, and the specialized modes of legal reasoning require the assistance of those trained in "the legal method." As such, a major role of specialist labor lawyers in the operation and study of industrial relations systems has been to research, analyze, and synthesize doctrine with a view to providing expositions and criticisms of legal rules for others.

Beyond Legal Formalism: Evaluative Research

In addition to providing exposition and translation of legal doctrine, academic labor lawyers have a long tradition of conducting what Hepple and Brown (1981) refer to as *evaluative* research. Research of this kind endeavors to move beyond the formalist paradigm with respect to the questions asked, the analytical framework used, and the methods employed. The intention of evaluative research is to consider the relationship between labor law and what we might describe as the "real world" of industrial relations—that is, the exchanges and interactions that constitute day-to-day industrial relations.

The evaluation of the relationship between legal rules and the world of work involves two broad questions, the first concerning the *politics* of law and the second relating to the *impact* of legal norms on work. Investigating the first question involves examining the influence of social relations on the creation of legal norms, including debates concerning why governments intervene in private industrial exchanges through legislation, why governments choose particular forms of legal regulation, and the influence of political, economic, and social conditions on the judiciary and quasijudicial standard-setting agencies. The second question, which addresses the impact of legal norms, involves a range of concerns, including compliance with statutory employment conditions, the operation of enforcement and administrative agencies, and the influence of law in shaping the strategies of trade unions, employers, and governments.

The Politics of Labor Law

Traditionally, labor law has tended to take a relatively unsophisticated approach to the politics of the law. This is partly because of the narrow ideal of political processes associated with formalist legal reasoning. According to the tacit political theory of legal formalism, changes in legal doctrine come about through the operation of liberal democratic practices. Statutory law is seen as the expression of the democratic will. Traditional legal method suggests that democratic processes determine the composition of legislatures and of ruling political parties and, through such processes of democratic political choice, statutory laws are fashioned in a manner that advances the public interest.

Similarly, formalists view the courts as advancing liberal democratic ideals. In applying laws, courts interpret legal concepts through the use of a series of rules. Briefly, the courts in the common law system, including those in Great Britain, the United States, Canada, and the British Commonwealth, are expected to interpret legislation according to interpretative conventions that seek, above all, to give paramountcy to the legislatures' will (Williams 1982: 97–111).

Formalist reasoning assumes that courts apply common law rules according to the doctrine of *stare decisis* (the doctrine of precedence). This doctrine requires courts to determine legal disputes consistent with previous decisions. Formally, this doctrine does not allow courts to create new rules. In practice, however, judicial innovation is common and is executed under the veil of devising new ways of restating established legal rules. Occasionally this process of restatement leads courts to *uncover* new rights and obligations. For instance, in the case of *Donaghue v Stevenson* (1932), which established the modern law of negligence, Lord Atken found that the existence of duties of care in a number of disparate circumstances implied a general duty to take reasonable care for the safety and welfare of others.

Legal formalism, however, does not view this process as judges making the law. Rather, formalist theory considers that judges act as ciphers through which the innate potential of common law doctrine becomes manifest. As with the canons of statutory interpretation, formalists view the role of judges in the common law tradition as that of unbiased interpreters of extant doctrine upholding the "rule of law."

The formalist approach to legal analysis thus suggests that doctrine is *autonomous* from social and political controversy and *determinate* in the sense that judges only look inward toward extant legal sources to explain how the law is to be interpreted. As such, formalism eschews analysis of the influence of broader political and social forces on the construction of legal doctrine and views legal analysis by judges, academic writers, and legal practitioners as objective and value free.

The first break from this tradition involves those labor lawyers who have sought to analyze the distinctiveness of labor law doctrine (Wedderburn 1986). This approach involves interpreting the development of labor law doctrine in a manner that takes account of its particular industrial context. Among Australian and British labor lawyers, recurring themes have been to identify the distinctively collectivist character of industrial exchanges (Kahn-Freund 1954 and 1965) and the capitalist imperatives of maintaining industrial peace and hierarchical control (Sorrell 1979; Collins 1982; Wedderburn 1986). These writers seek to identify the values and assumptions of democratic capitalist society that underpin labor law systems.

In North America, such analysis has its foundations in the legal realist movement of the first half of the twentieth century and is more recently manifest in the critical legal studies and feminist jurisprudence movements. Leaders among the critical legal studies movement include Klare (1990) and Van Wezel Stone (1981). Critical legal writers attack formalist assumptions regarding the determinancy and autonomy of law and seek to demonstrate how ideological choices inform legal development. In the main, however, their approach remains bound to the traditions of doctrinal analysis. Albeit in a more critical vein, this research continues to begin and end largely at the door of the law library.

Similarly, feminist jurisprudence writers criticize legal formalism for separating legal issues from related political and moral questions (Mossman 1986). Smart argues, for instance, that legal formalism is blind to issues relating to gender. She also suggests that formalism possesses significant ideological power because it promotes legal discourse as a unified field of knowledge, thereby allowing nonlegal discourses to be discounted on the grounds that they were unable to "speak the truth" (1989: 4).

The aim of feminist analysis is therefore to challenge the truth value of formalist jurisprudence by exposing its claims to neutrality. Thus, feminist writers have sought to demonstrate that labor law has been constructed around a conception of the worker as a male breadwinner. As a consequence, labor laws have not responded to the needs of women workers and many areas of women's work have been excluded from regulation (Conaghan 1986; Owens 1993). Like critical legal studies, such analysis provides a critique of the invisibility of society within formalist method. As with other "critical" jurisprudence, however, the analysis remains doctrinally based and tends to rely on a raft of untested theoretical and historical assumptions pertaining to the relationship between law and society.

Beyond this, other researchers have tied their accounts of the development of labor law to detailed histories of labor relations (Tomlins 1995; Forbath 1991; Bennett 1994). This approach tends to be more satisfactory than critical theory as it evinces a genuine desire to explore the historical record to demonstrate how the instrumental, structural, and ideological dimensions of politics explain specific developments in judicial decision making and legislative enactment. In this manner, such work also demonstrates a growing interdisciplinarity in labor law research by combining legal and historical techniques. The integration of detailed doctrinal analysis with the approach of political historians and sociologists leads to a more sophisticated understanding of political *and* legal processes. Interdisciplinary research of this kind is vital if labor law research is to move beyond the confines of doctrinal methods and the limitations of both traditional and critical legal theory (Trubeck 1984).

Impact of Law on the World of Work

As noted above, the second type of evaluative research examines how labor law shapes exchanges between industrial relations actors at the workplace and in collective bargaining. This question has long been a concern for labor lawyers and industrial relations writers. For instance, Dunlop saw labor law as being a major part of the "Power Context" within which the processes of collective and individual job regulation take place (1958: 94–128). Similarly, Kahn-Freund (1954) sought to describe how a series of relatively disparate laws served to provide a framework for collective bargaining. More recently, Collins (1991) has argued that labor law researchers should explore how law affects power relations between employees and employers. However, attempts by lawyers to account for the influence of law on society, by relying on traditional legal research methods, tend largely to ignore significant methodological and theoretical problems.

To illustrate this crucial point, it is worth returning to Kahn-Freund's seminal 1954 essay in which he describes how the law shapes the system of industrial relations in Britain. He begins his analysis by positing that the function of British labor law was as a support to a system of voluntarist collective bargaining; this assertion underlies his thesis that the state had largely abstained from directly regulating collective bargaining in Britain. He also argues that the law serves only as a secondary constraint on the activities of unions and employers, as opposed to industrial sanctions, which exert a coercive effect.

Kahn-Freund continues by describing the many laws that play a role in supporting collective bargaining. The essence of the discussion remains an exposition of legal rules that directly regulate terms and conditions of employment, that constrain the ability of the parties to use industrial sanctions, or that establish regulatory institutions. That is, Kahn-Freund's approach is to *describe* the complex tapestry of laws relating to employment as behavioral constraints within which market and other social exchanges take place.

Kahn-Freund's work involves an important departure from the preoccupations and approach of purely doctrinal legal exposition. In particular, his work begins by evaluating the social function and impact of the law. It does so by isolating a particular social phenomenon, in this case collective bargaining, and then identifying law that a priori can be seen to have a possible role in shaping that phenomenon. The force of Kahn-Freund's analysis, however, owes more to his comprehensive survey of law and his rhetorical elegance than to the weight of what social scientists would describe as systematic evidence. For instance, there is no evidence as to the enforcement or the level of compliance with minimum conditions laws; nor is there any attempt to assess the extent to which the strategies of employers and trade unions have in practice been constrained by legal sanctions or to discuss the operation of particular regulatory institutions.

The type of analysis undertaken by Kahn-Freund has been followed by a number of others. Indeed, when most labor law scholars sit down to plan general labor law texts and case books, their selection of writings is informed by their understanding of which laws are most significant in the real world. Furthermore, it is not uncommon for labor law writers to slip into impressionistic evaluations of the impact of law when developing interpretive expositions or for labor lawyers to direct their analyses explicitly toward evaluating the *impact* of law. Like Kahn-Freund's work, however, such evaluations tend to be based on untested behavioral assumptions and are more or less *fact-free*. As Schuck has noted, lawyers are not taught how to handle, find, interpret, prove, and rebut facts (1989: 334). Although courtroom argumentation relies on facts, the focus of legal contests and the conventions (known as the rules of evidence) that govern the presentation of such facts involve questions concerning the veracity and relevance of testimony when formulating accounts of single instances of behavior. The training lawyers receive does not extend to the critical use of more systematic empirical sources, such as surveys or archives. Again, labor law research and writing is constrained by the legal method—the method used by lawyers to interpret the law rather than to determine its role in mediating work relationships.

In the same respect, when assessing the role or impact of law, much legal sociology, including the writings of the critical legal studies and feminist scholars discussed above, has ignored the need to support claims with non-doctrinal empirical evidence (Schuck 1989: 329). Clearly, if one wishes to argue that developments in labor law have been affected by nonlegal discourses or that the law itself has helped construct the ideology of industrial actors, it is both possible and necessary to support such claims using research methods beyond the law library catalogue (Forbath 1991; Trubeck 1984). Along these lines, Bennett has criticized the lack of empirical research in textual approaches such as feminist jurisprudence. She suggests that

> whilst a textualist analysis can reveal much about the gendered nature of decision-making within the law it can say nothing about the impact of those decisions on women. It is quite possible for negative gender assumptions to have positive effects on particular groups of women (as with some forms of protective legislation) while supposedly gender positive measures (such as the current push for flexibility) may have massive negative effects. The only way to resolve the issue of how laws based on particular assumptions about gender impact on women is to undertake empirical analysis (1995: 142).

An example of this problem can be found in Owens's theoretical critique of the Australian labor law regime, which suggests that the common law of employment is free of many of the masculinist assumptions underpinning arbitral legislation and that a shift toward a greater emphasis on the contract of employment could benefit women (1995: 17–21). Although her arguments regarding the gender bias of Australia's conciliation and arbitration system can be sustained historically, Owens provides no empirical support for the contention that women will benefit from a more contractual approach.

By contrast, Hammond and Harbridge's work (1993) on the abolition of arbitration and the move to the Employment Contracts Act of 1991 in New Zealand provides evidence relating to wages and conditions that *demonstrates* that the movement toward a contractualist framework has significantly disadvantaged women workers. To summarize, labor law research and writing have been constrained by traditional methods and have resisted embracing different approaches.

Embracing Different Approaches

As with research relating to the politics of labor law, evaluations of the impact of law on labor relations must involve empirical methods. Obviously, concern must also be shown for epistemological and theoretical matters. Since there is no general theory (or generally accepted) theory of the relationship between law and behavior, however, it is necessary to build our understandings on the basis of detailed and systematic empirical inquiry. In this respect, labor law can learn a great deal from the interdisciplinary tradition of industrial relations. As the other chapters in this volume demonstrate, the interdisciplinary approach embraced by industrial relations has created a huge body of research relating to processes and outcomes in industrial relationships that draws on a variety of theoretical perspectives and research methods.

Labor law teaching and research methodologies must move away from the library and its client problem-solving focus to encompass social sciences methods. This is not to argue that labor law research has been completely devoid of contact with other disciplines and methodologies. As we have already mentioned, the critical legal studies movement and feminist legal scholarship writers have given labor law research a much more vibrant texture; however, the prevailing view still remains that law is found in "formal" institutions and processes.

Industrial relations writers have for some time acknowledged that workplace relations are regulated by both formal and informal practices (Flanders 1965). Just as courts and parliaments are sites of regulatory activity, so are workplaces, company boardrooms, and union offices. The challenge for labor lawyers then is to combine with historians, sociologists, and others to explore the interaction of various forms and levels of regulatory activity. Such inquiry would of course involve building upon the formal legal record by collecting and analyzing a variety of other forms of qualitative and quantitative data using ethnographic and survey techniques (Johnstone and Mckenzie 1995). Many of these techniques are described elsewhere in this volume.

By combining traditional legal methods with those used by social scientists, researchers will develop new understandings of the questions that legal researchers have been exploring for some time. To return to our earlier example, researchers interested in the use of antidiscrimination laws could move beyond the examination of doctrine by researching the activities of antidiscrimination agencies or by examining the impact of antidiscrimination law in the workplace. For instance, they might examine evidence of employment practices to determine whether, or under what conditions, employers have responded to new laws prohibiting discrimination by instituting controls against discriminatory hiring, sexual harassment, and other proscribed practices. Such workplace-based research may well conclude that dramatic changes in the requirements of antidiscrimination law over recent times have had little impact on the working lives of women, people from ethnic minorities, and other groups for whose benefit these laws were designed. The systematic empirical exploration of the operation of legal controls will ultimately yield far more important insights about how law is affecting workplace practices than will formal legal research techniques.

There are, of course, many fine examples of interdisciplinary labor law research. More recent examples include Dannin's study on changes to the legal regime governing industrial relations in New Zealand. Dannin's work (1995) relies on various methodologies such as qualitative and quantitative data, case studies, and traditional legal research methods. Her work provides a good example of how researchers can study the impact of law on industrial relations. Her work also contributes to our understanding of the effects of national legal regimes by adopting an international comparative dimension. A collection edited by Tomlin and King (1992) illustrates the range of nonformalist approaches to labor law research encompassing issues relating to both the construction of legal norms and the impact of doctrine and legal institutions on the emergence of the American system of industrial relations.

There are, however, major obstacles to the development of interdisciplinary research of this kind. In particular, it is potentially hazardous for legal researchers to adopt methods from other disciplines without having been formally trained. For instance, Getman, Goldberg, and Herman's (1976) survey of representation elections in the United States was widely criticized on methodological grounds (Dickens 1983). Although lawyers should be encouraged to make use of data from other fields, they need to ensure that they do so in accordance with the standards of empirical rigor demanded by social science disciplines.

Another more practical obstacle is that there are few incentives for lawyers working in most law faculties to undertake empirical work. By and large, academic prestige continues to go to those researchers whose work concentrates on doctrinal exegesis. Interdisciplinary work involving both doctrinal and empirical research tends to be more expensive and time-consuming than traditional doctrinal approaches. As such, the additional resources, time, and training required to undertake such work impose significant disincentives on career-conscious legal academics who can succeed in law faculties without bothering with nondoctrinal methods (Schuck 1989).

While a broader approach to legal research will enhance our understanding of law and work, we must also be cautious not to allow labor law to be subsumed by other disciplines by replacing one mode of thinking and research with another. One branch of sociolegal work that is often mistaken as interdisciplinary is the law and economics tradition. Because labor law can be seen as a device of labor market regulation, it has become fashionable in recent times to suggest that labor law debates should be led by economic theory and analysis. Not surprisingly, most applications of economics (particularly from the neoclassical school) involve a considerable antagonism toward labor market regulation (Epstein 1983; Brook 1990), even though economic analysis can equally be used to contradict such arguments (Gahan and Mitchell 1995).

Clearly, where issues concerning the distributive effects of law are at stake, the application of economic theory and econometrics will be of benefit. The questions we should be asking about the relationship between labor law and society cannot be reduced, however, to the concerns of labor market analysis alone. Also, even if our concern is for the relationship between legal regulation and allocative outcomes, traditional economic theory is inadequate. Economic analysis, like legal formalism, is constrained by the ideology that imbues the discourse. It rests on the assumption that individual behavior is the product of utility-maximizing decisions made by free-thinking rational actors. This tends to reduce all interactions between legal controls and behavior to a form of cost-benefit analysis. But, as a number of legal theorists suggest, notably critical legal studies scholars, the law operates on a symbolic level, constructing our preferences, our ideologies, that is, our "rationality" (Klare 1990). This would tend to imply that economic analysis of labor law, particularly where it involves slavish applications of neoclassical assumptions, will seldom improve our understanding of the relationship of law and society (Schuck 1989: 327–28).

Interdisciplinarity should involve a conversation and interchange, rather than colonization, between fields of knowledge. If approached properly, interdisciplinarity requires social scientists to recognize the knowledge of labor lawyers regarding the themes and history of law as much as it requires traditionally trained lawyers to adopt methods used by social scientists.

Conclusion

Our principal aim in this chapter has been to consider how legal research can contribute to our understanding of the world of work. We have examined the nature of traditional legal research methods and argued that the traditional approach to legal research derives from the concerns of professional lawyers, whose role is to interpret legal doctrine for others. We then argued that doctrinal analysis, whether conducted in a formalist or a critical manner, is an incomplete means for understanding the relationship between law, legal systems, and the interactions and exchanges that constitute the world of work.

In our view, however, this observation does not mean that legal analysis is worthless to an understanding of the real world of industrial relations interactions and exchanges. The practices of industrial relations actors are, in all developed societies, subject to forms of legal regulation, and it is of vital importance that we understand the impact of formal legal norms on the behavior of industrial relations actors. This is especially the case because industrial relations inquiry is often geared toward explaining the efficacy of state policy in reorganizing work to enhance equity and efficiency.

To improve labor regulation, we must first understand the relationship between law and behavior in the work world. Traditional methods of legal analysis, particularly those that seek to incorporate some understanding of the ideology of labor law, are a necessary *starting point* for such research. Together with critical doctrinal analysis, labor law should then build upon the interdisciplinarity of empirically based industrial relations scholarship. Thus, labor lawyers must begin to reconceptualize both labor law and labor law research, thereby fusing an understanding of the nature of law and legal doctrine with the questions asked by other industrial relations scholars.

CHAPTER FIFTEEN

Sociological Approaches to Employment Research

Daniel B. Cornfield and Melinda D. Kane

C hanges in the content and outcomes of the employment relationship constitute an enduring sociological issue. Research in the contemporary sociological subfields of industrial and labor sociology, the sociology of work, and the sociology of labor markets continues to resonate with such classical themes as Weber's bureaucratization of economic institutions and the development of rule-bound organizational careers; Durkheim's social solidarity-enhancing functions of occupational associations; and Marx's sharpening income inequalities that accompanied capital concentration and technological change (Kalleberg and Berg 1987; Wipper 1994). In this chapter we discuss the major conceptual tools used by sociologists in research on the dynamics of the employment relationship, a branch of sociology that, for the sake of brevity, we refer to as industrial sociology.

Industrial sociology and industrial relations differ more in the conceptual tools they use than in their data-collection and analytical methods. Research in industrial sociology, like that in industrial relations, continues to be based on a wide range of qualitative and quantitative data and methods. The industrial sociology of the 1950s was based largely on qualitative methods, including fieldwork and interviews, participant observation, ethnography, and archival data. Beginning in the 1960s and with the advent of computers, industrial sociologists added many multivariate statistical techniques to their arsenal of methods, including those for continuous dependent variables[1] (e.g., ordinary least squares regression), categorical dependent variables

---

1. A dependent variable is a variable whose variation is hypothesized to depend on, or to be predicted from, the variation in the independent variable. In statistical analysis, independent variables are used to calculate or predict the dependent variable. For example,

(e.g., logistic regression), counts (e.g., Poisson), and rates (e.g., event history analysis). During the 1980s, comparative historical methods became increasingly common in industrial sociology. Industrial sociologists use these qualitative and quantitative methods to analyze data from organizational, occupational, industrial, and community case studies and from national and international labor force and questionnaire survey data sets.

Since industrial relations and industrial sociology use roughly the same methods of data gathering and processing, this chapter focuses not on methodology but on the conceptual tools of sociology. Whereas industrial relations research has emphasized the functioning of the formal features of employment, labor relations, and collective bargaining, industrial sociology uses conceptual tools that emphasize the interrelationships among individuals and the formal and informal features of workplace organization so as to research a range of social processes that often unfold in workplaces.

After comparing briefly the disciplines of industrial sociology and industrial relations, we present the conceptual tools that are used in industrial sociological research. These tools derive from a sociological conception of the workplace and have been developed largely in the context of enduring sociological research questions about the determinants of inequalities in life chances. We conclude with a discussion of the unique ways in which industrial sociology enhances our understanding of the dynamics of the employment relationship.

We do not review the related and large "labor sociology" research literature on labor unions and labor movements per se. This body of research has addressed such issues as cross-national, comparative labor movement structure, function, and membership growth trends; temporal variations in strikes and labor unrest; the role of labor movements in the shaping of national welfare states; the impact of organized labor on the degree of inequality in income and, generally, in life chances; and the determinants of union democracy and oligarchy (for reviews of the issues researched by labor sociologists, see Delarbre 1989 and Stern and Cornfield 1996).

Industrial Sociology and Industrial Relations

Industrial relations scholars have long acknowledged an overlap in substantive mission and approach between the disciplines of industrial sociology

---

if education is hypothesized to predict an individual's rate of career mobility, education is the independent variable and career mobility, which is dependent on education, is the dependent variable.

and industrial relations. In his *Industrial Relations Systems,* Dunlop explicitly derived his theory from the structural-functionalism of Harvard sociologist Talcott Parsons. For Dunlop, the industrial relations system was a subsystem of industrial society, the subsystem with its web of workplace rules being the province of industrial relations and "the social system as a whole" being "the province of sociology" (1958: 4–5, 13).

Kaufman, in contrast, considers industrial sociology to be a member of the IR family of disciplines. In arguing for a broader IR mission than did Dunlop, Kaufman advocates "the study of all aspects of the employment relationship" (1993: 158). He distinguishes this mission from the narrower "study of trade unionism and collective bargaining," which, Kaufman argues (102, 158), has become the chief substantive emphasis of IR since Dunlop.

The missions of the two fields overlap. The emphasis on workplace rules in Dunlop and the Wisconsin school of IR is shared by industrial sociologists. In their synthesis of industrial sociology, Kalleberg and Berg emphasize "work structures" (1987: 2) as the chief object of industrial sociological research and define them as follows:

> [Work structures are] the rules on which many people have agreed and thus legitimated, for longer or shorter periods, as effective means of solving the economic and political problems of production and distribution. Work structures also represent the hierarchical orderings of persons and clusters of interests, configurations of norms, and the rights and obligations that characterize the relations among different types of actors in the economy. These structures describe the ways in which labor is divided, tasks allocated, and authority distributed (Kalleberg and Berg 1987: 2).

Work structures include firms and labor unions and range between occupations and nation-states (Kalleberg and Berg 1987: 2).

Despite their common interest in work structures, IR scholars and industrial sociologists study them for different reasons. For IR scholars, work structures themselves are the object of analysis (Dunlop 1958: viii–ix). For industrial sociologists, in contrast, work structures house and partly shape social processes—for example, the development of group identities and group inequalities in power, social status, and life chances—of longstanding sociological interest. Therefore, sociological concepts differ from IR concepts in their emphasis on the interrelationships between individuals, groups, and workplace organization; on the development of informal workplace organization (e.g., gender and race-ethnic relations) that derives from the wider social and cultural normative context of workplaces; and on the interrelationships between the formal and informal features of workplaces.

Conceptual Tools of Industrial Sociology

Industrial sociologists have developed a unique set of concepts for analyzing social processes that occur inside large bureaucratic work organizations. Embedded in a web of laws, formal agreements, and culturally defined societal norms about informal intergroup relations (e.g., race-ethnic and gender relations), these bureaucracies constitute the arenas for the unfolding of processes of social mobility and status attainment that interest industrial sociologists (Bridges and Villemez 1994; Ministerio de Trabajo y Seguridad Social 1994; Wipper 1994).

The convergence of two intellectual trends around 1980 led sociologists to develop a "new structuralism" focused on the structure and functioning of the bureaucratic corporation in segmented labor markets. First, the legacy of Weber's essay on "bureaucracy" as the site of power and status in industrial society had been passed on in such works as Mills's *White Collar* (1953), Bendix's *Work and Authority in Industry* (1956), Gouldner's *Patterns of Industrial Bureaucracy* (1954a), Chinoy's *Automobile Workers and the American Dream* (1955), and, later, Kanter's *Men and Women of the Corporation* (1977). Second, as sociologists developed a demand-side orientation to the study of career mobility, they became increasingly enamored of the reviving institutional labor economics, especially the dual economy, dual labor market, and internal labor market theories. This demand-side orientation derived from what was seen critically as the omission of institutional factors in the more individualistic status attainment and human capital theories.

Consequently, industrial sociology rests on three concepts. The first concept is that of *bureaucracy*—a model of a formal organization that characterizes many workplaces and consists of written rules, a pyramidal authority structure, a detailed departmental and occupational division of labor, and a graduated occupational or job status hierarchy. The second is *career mobility*—intragenerational social mobility in which individual workers attain more or less social status by changing (or remaining in) jobs in bureaucratic job sequences or career ladders, such as those found within internal labor markets and between bureaucracies. The third concept is *embeddedness*—the infusion of societal intergroup relations, such as gender and race relations, inside the bureaucracy. These relations often generate informal organization (e.g., cliques, factions) that exists within and cuts across the formal structure of a bureaucracy (on the development of these concepts, see Acker 1990; Cornfield 1993; Kalleberg and Berg 1987: chap. 4; Rosenfeld 1992; and the October 1994 special issue of *Acta Sociologica* on "studying employers and their employees").

These three concepts form the image of the workplace that underlies much industrial sociological research and from which the conceptual tools of industrial sociology derive. Bureaucracy is a sociological conception of formal workplace organization; embeddedness allows conceptually for the infusion of societal cultural norms into the bureaucracy, which, in turn, generates informal group relations and organization within the bureaucracy; and career mobility is the multifarious process by which individual life chances result from the interrelationships among individuals and the formal and informal features of the workplace.

Not all sociologists share this bureaucratic image of the workplace, however. "Postmodern" organizational perspectives, for example, differ in two important ways from the bureaucratic image. First, the structure of a postmodern organization is conceived to be less hierarchical and less functionally differentiated than that of the conventionally depicted bureaucracy and consists of such "post-Fordist" arrangements as flexible specialization, multiskilling, and a niche-based marketing strategy. Second, organizational power is conceived not as a property of individual actors or of organizational structure but as a fluid, ongoing process of interaction between interdependent actors (on postmodern organizational theory, see Hassard 1993: chap. 6).

In addition to the dominant bureaucratic image of the workplace, industrial sociologists have developed a set of conceptual tools in the context of two large research traditions. The first line of research focuses on trends and patterns in job content and skills and addresses the impact of technological and organizational change and embeddedness on the content, skill level, and, hence, social status of jobs. The second line of research focuses on labor market outcomes, such as inequalities in individual earnings and in rates of promotions and layoffs.

Concepts in Research on Job Content and Skills

The research on job content and skills has attempted to assess and analyze the direction of occupational skill levels. The labor process research tradition centers on a debate about the impact of capital accumulation and technological change on the direction of change in occupational skill levels. In this tradition, *deskilling* refers to a decline in the level of skill required to perform a job; *enskilling* refers to the opposite trend (see, for example, the

November 1990 special issue of *Work and Occupations*, "The Meaning and Measurement of Skill"; the Winter 1994–95 special issue of *Sociología del Trabajo*, "Human Resources, Technology, and Participation"; Bills 1995; Penn, Scattergood, and Sewel 1992; Smith 1994; and Vallas 1993). Multiple research methods, including organizational case studies based on archival and interview data (Vallas 1993), contemporary and historical industry case studies (Cornfield 1987b and 1992), community surveys (Penn, Scattergood, and Sewel 1992), and multivariate statistical analyses of large-scale national surveys of hundreds of detailed occupations over time (Bills 1995), have been used in analyses of skill distributions and job content and show patterns of skill upgrading, downgrading, polarization, and stability.

Industrial sociologists have developed multidimensional frameworks for gauging and analyzing job content and skill changes. According to Robert Szafran (1996), five commonly used *job task characteristics* are substantive complexity (referring to numerical and verbal aptitude, abstract thinking, training length, etc.); gross motor skills; fine motor skills; climatic conditions; and social interaction (i.e., dealing with coworkers, superiors, subordinates, and customers, what Kilbourne et al. [1994] refer to as "nurturant skill").

Each job task characteristic is quantified in a multi-item scale derived from a factor analysis of some five hundred detailed occupations from the U.S. Census occupational classification scheme.[2] The factor analysis compares the occupations in terms of some forty detailed job traits derived from the *Dictionary of Occupational Titles* of the U.S. Bureau of Labor Statistics. Each occupation is assigned a factor score for each of the five job task characteristics. Occupations can then be compared to one another in terms of their factor scores on the five job task characteristics cross-sectionally and longitudinally (Kilbourne et al. 1994; Szafran 1996). Furthermore, survey sample respondents can be assigned the factor scores of their occupations so as to analyze the impact of occupational characteristics on individual differences in a variety of labor market outcomes, including earnings.

The growing employment in service occupations has increased the sociological study of *emotion work* as a job skill. Emotion work is the expression of appropriate emotion(s) in particular settings and is a formal requirement of some jobs, especially service occupations that involve worker-customer interactions (Hochschild 1983). Just as filling a prescription is part of the

---

2. Factor analysis is a statistical technique used to identify statistical relationships between variables. A fuller description can be found in chapter 4, "Quantitative Methods."

job of being a pharmacist, friendliness is a formal task requirement for the job of flight attendant.

Sociologists are continuing to redefine and operationalize emotion work; however, most definitions stem from Hochschild's *The Managed Heart* (1983). She argues that emotion work can be detected in paid labor through three characteristics: face-to-face interaction with the public, the creation or maintenance of an emotion in another person, and employer control over the emotional activities of the worker. Emotion work is usually studied through qualitative, occupational case studies, and only recently have researchers begun to operationalize emotion work quantitatively (for a review of research on emotion work, see Wharton 1993).

Much industrial sociological research has implicitly adopted a deterministic view of the development of life chances. The view is deterministic in its assumption that, more than individuals, institutional and cultural forces, such as bureaucratization, technological change, and the reproduction of embeddedness, shape inequalities in life chances. To overcome this determinism in much of the research on job content and skills, sociologists have developed the concept of *agency*—that is, individual and collective purposive action typically exercised by workers to resist managerial control and improve their livelihoods (Smith 1994). To operationalize "agency" for research, Hodson (1995a and 1995b) has developed a comprehensive typology of on-the-job worker behaviors classified simultaneously by the individual, work group, and organizational goals to which they are directed. The behaviors range from sabotage to being a "company man."

Concepts in Research on Labor Market Outcomes

To explain individual differences in labor market outcomes, sociologists have generated a vast corpus of multivariate statistical analyses of national labor force and firm workforce data sets. This research tradition has addressed a wide variety of labor market outcomes, including earnings (Kilbourne et al. 1994) and the rates and probabilities of promotions (Brüderl, Preisendörfer, and Ziegler 1993), layoffs (Cornfield 1987a), turnover (Mueller et al. 1994), and job mobility (Mach, Mayer, and Pohoski 1994).

Sociologists have developed features of the formal and informal structure of workplaces in order to analyze the impact of workplace structure on individual differences in labor market outcomes. Regarding formal workplace structure, sociologists have developed and operationalized characteristics of industries, labor and economic segments, occupations, organizations, internal labor markets, and production technology, all of which can be utilized as predictor variables in individual, firm, and multi-level analyses of labor market outcomes (see Farkas and England 1988 for comprehensive overviews). For example, the widely used Tolbert-Horan-Beck typology of economic segmentation was derived from a factor analysis of fifty-five U.S. Census-derived industries by seventeen industry character-istics, including concentration, profits, union density, quit rates, and wages. Each industry is assigned a factor score indicating its degree of institutional approximation to an industry in the "core" or "periphery" economic sector of the dual economy. The factor scores can serve as dependent or predictor variables by assigning them to individuals and firms on the basis of the products and services made in their workplaces (Tolbert, Horan, and Beck 1980; Farkas and England 1988: chap. 3).

Recently, sociologists have developed techniques for collecting *matched samples* of employees and their employers in order to improve the quality of organizational variables and their link with individual respondents in na-tional and metropolitan labor force surveys (on these recent developments and matched sampling procedures, see Bridges and Villemez 1994: chap. 2 and appendices and the October 1994 special issue of *Acta Sociologica* on "studying employers and their employees"). According to Kalleberg (1994), higher-quality organizational data, such as firm size, authority structure, and product market share, can be obtained from managers and company documents than from worker respondents. Matched sampling techniques match individual employees with employer-derived organizational data about their employers. These samples are built either by sampling individu-als first and obtaining contact information from respondents about their employers, from whom the researcher subsequently obtains organizational data, as in the U.S. National Organizations Study, the Chicago Metropoli-tan Employer Worker Survey, and the Swedish employee-employer survey, or by sampling organizations first and then their workforces, as in the Aus-tralian Workplace Industrial Relations Survey and the Norwegian Study of Organizations and Employees (see chapter 9, "Large-Scale National Sur-veys for Mapping, Monitoring, and Theory Development").

The *social network*, a web of interpersonal relationships, is a sociological concept for gauging and analyzing the impact of informal workplace struc-ture on labor market outcomes. Sociologists have developed a complex, multidimensional framework for describing *social network characteristics*. Whole social networks are distinguished, for example, by their size, density, hierarchy, competitiveness, strength of interpersonal ties, connections with other networks, homophily (i.e., degree of sociodemographic similarity among network members), and so on. Individual positions within networks vary, for example, by their centrality, control over resources, and hierarchical position.

Social network data are collected in several ways, including from social surveys of respondents' number, type, frequency of interactions in, strength of feelings about, and overlaps with others in their interpersonal relations and institutional memberships and from organizational archival data on, for example, overlapping corporate board memberships (for reviews of the literature on social networks and labor markets, see Campbell 1988; the December 1994 special issue of *Acta Sociologica* on social networks; and the journal *Social Networks*).

Occupational segregation by sex and/or race, the separation of men and women or races at work, is an important conceptual tool in research on the impact of embedded gender and race relations on labor market outcomes in bureaucratic workplaces. Occupational segregation occurs in one of two ways: (1) through the physical separation of the genders or races performing similar job tasks or (2) through the concentration of different demographic groups into different occupations.

Occupational sex type, although often measured by the percentage female of an occupational labor force, refers to the culturally normative, gender image of an occupation. Occupational segregation has been shown to have a strong influence on several labor market outcomes and inequalities, including gender and race gaps in earnings and career advancement (Hakim 1992; Reskin and Padavic 1994; Tomaskovic-Devey 1993). Given that sex segregation is more prevalent and studied more often than race segregation, we will limit our discussion to sex segregation.

There are two types of sex segregation research. The first examines variations in the level of segregation. Using national samples, such as the U.S. Census and the European Community Labor Force Survey, researchers use the *index of segregation,* or a similar statistic, to measure the extent of gender segregation in occupations, jobs, or firms within a particular country or between nations (Charles 1992; Hakim 1992; Jacobs 1989). The index is an index of dissimilarity that indicates the percentage of women (or men) that would have to be redistributed across occupations or jobs to achieve full occupational sex integration. The index is often a dependent variable, but it can also be used as an independent variable in regression equations examining other forms of inequality (for a recent example of this type of research, see Sorensen and Trappe 1995). To study the determinants of occupational sex *desegregation,* Baron, Mittman, and Newman (1991) estimated a discrete-time linear, partial-adjustment model of annual change in the index of segregation among ninety state government agencies over the period from 1979 to 1985.

The second body of research on occupational sex segregation examines changes in the sex composition of jobs. Most of this research consists of studies on the *feminization* of industries or occupations (on occupational *masculinization*, see Penn, Martin, and Scattergood 1991). This research tends to be based on qualitative case studies of why specific occupations or industries that were primarily male later became dominated by women (Crompton and Sanderson 1990; Reskin and Roos 1990).

Occupational segregation research focuses on segregation within occupations or industries rather than on the more detailed job-level segregation (for an exception, see Baron, Mittman, and Newman 1991). Studying segregation at highly aggregated levels, such as the occupational level, actually captures less segregation than investigating the phenomenon at the detailed job or organizational level (Reskin and Roos 1990), suggesting that most segregation research underestimates the prevalence of segregation. Segregation data, however, are more available for industries and occupations.

Another important sociological field that investigates embedded gender relations at work is *comparable worth* and *pay inequity* research. According to theories of comparable worth, sexist societal norms lead to the devaluing of jobs and occupations that are sex-typed female but otherwise comparable in skill level and worth to male-dominated occupations, contributing to pay inequity between women and men (England 1992). This theory calls for a reevaluation of organizational job analysis and pay systems so that the work done primarily by women that is comparable but not necessarily the same as work done primarily by men is paid the same. Researchers are often asked by companies or governments to evaluate and revise existing pay systems (for an example of applied work becoming a study, see Acker 1989).

Pay equity research addresses the gender gap in pay. One line of pay equity research attempts to examine comparable worth theory empirically. Using qualitative and quantitative methods, sociologists have studied the extent to which jobs held predominantly by females are devalued and how policies based on comparable worth are implemented (Acker 1989; England 1992). To test the theory of comparable worth on a national or firm labor force data set, sociologists calculate from U.S. Census data the national percentage female of an occupation as an indicator of occupational sex type and composition; assign to each respondent the percentage that corresponds to the respondent's occupation; and regress an indicator of earnings or income on the national percentage female and on multiple indicators of individual and job task characteristics to assess the relative importance of occupational sex composition as an earnings or income determinant (for a review of the research on pay inequity in the United States, see Marini 1989).

To analyze how the interrelationships among individual characteristics and formal and informal workplace structure affect labor market outcomes, sociologists have researched the interactive or multiplicative effects among these determinants of labor market outcomes. Interactive analyses are performed by either including a multiplicative interaction term[3] between two or more determinants in a multivariate estimation of a labor market outcome or by estimating identical equations on two or more subsamples of the same survey data set. For example, in her study of individual differences in income in a sample of Swedish business executives, Meyerson (1994) estimated the effect of the interaction between human capital (education) and social capital (a measure of the respondents' ties to external social networks) with a multiplicative term between human and social capital in a multiple regression equation of income; and Cornfield (1987a) examined the interaction effect of unionization and ethnicity-race on individual differences in the odds of being laid off from a telecommunications carrier by estimating separate logistic regression equations for the odds of layoff for the unionized and nonunion subsamples.[4] Cross-national comparative analyses of regression estimations of labor market outcomes are used to analyze variations across types of *national political economies* (e.g., corporatist, capitalist, socialist) in the signs and strengths of individual and workplace structural, labor market outcome determinants (e.g., Mach, Mayer, and Pohoski 1994 and Rosenfeld and Kalleberg 1990).

Sociological research has also addressed temporal variations in the effects of labor market outcome determinants. For example, in their study of the chances of promotion in a West German mechanical engineering company, Brüderl, Preisendörfer, and Ziegler (1993) estimated the effects of age, ethnicity, and gender on the likelihood of promotion in separate proportional hazards log-logistic models for subperiods of business expansion and contraction.

3. An interaction term is the statistical coefficient that describes the effect of one independent variable on the magnitude and sign of the *effect* of another independent variable on a dependent variable.

4. Logistic regression is a maximum-likelihood technique used to predict dichotomous dependent variables. Each regression coefficient is an estimate of the change in the logarithm of the odds of the dependent variable that is associated with a unit change in the independent variable.

With recent corporate downsizings, restructurings, workforce reductions, and the growing employment of part-time and temporary workers, sociologists have begun to address the implications of the decline of internal labor markets on orderly organizational careers and the shape of career mobility. Furthermore, sociologists are developing concepts for modeling the impact of organizational change on individual differences in labor market outcomes. Schellenberg (1996), for example, in her study of the impact of organizational change on individual differences in the odds of quitting a high-tech firm, has developed three measures of individual experiences of organizational change that she uses as predictor variables in a multivariate logistic regression of the odds of quitting: the total number of organizational department changes experienced by an employee; a dummy variable indicating whether or not the employee was assigned to another organizational department during the previous time interval; and the percentage of employees who experienced an organizational department change during the previous time interval.

Conclusion

As a discipline, sociology provides a unique view of the dynamics of the employment relationship. The enduring research questions about the evolution and impact of a culturally embedded bureaucracy on inequality in life chances inspire contemporary industrial sociology. By weaving together informal race, ethnic, and gender relations with the formal institutional structure of workplaces, sociologists have developed a compelling approach to the study of inequality in a wide range of processes involving career mobility.

Sociological concepts can enrich IR research on collective bargaining outcomes and unionization. The cultural embeddedness of bureaucracy and the employment relationship suggests that collective bargaining outcomes partly result from the interests of worker groups defined by their positions not only in the formal structure of the workplace but in informal workplace structures. Collective bargaining outcomes, such as occupational pay differentials and wage–fringe benefit tradeoffs, may reflect the interests of workers whose formal positions (e.g., department, job classification) differ and workers who belong to different informally defined gender, ethnic-racial, and other culturally determined groups. Similarly, variation among nonunion workers in their desire to unionize, and in the issues that motivate them to unionize, may reflect differences in career mobility prospects. The most pro-union, nonunion worker groups tend to be those whose career mobility prospects are limited by their disadvantageous position in the formal occupational hierarchy and by discriminatory and disrespectful management by managers whose ethnic-racial and gender characteristics differ from those of these employees. In sum, incorporating sociological concepts into IR research can broaden the analysis of how the structure and functioning of the contemporary corporation influence industrial relations systems and the demand for unionization among nonunion workers.

Part V

Public Policy

Public Policy

R esearch in a field close to public policy formation, such as industrial relations, raises many questions regarding ethics and the relationship between researchers and their "subjects." The two chapters in part V focus on two aspects of the problems raised by such questions.

Jay Siegel discusses the appropriateness of some industrial relations research for use in policy making. His main concern is that the move toward quantification has resulted in the development of models that lack a basis in real-world behavioral knowledge. He suggests that researchers should be more multidisciplinary and multimethodological in approach. Siegel also bemoans the growth of policy guidance based on research from special interest groups. These cannot be seen as "independent."

William Brown examines the potential for researchers to be perceived as partisan. Industrial relations is concerned with power relationships and can therefore readily become enmeshed in political controversy. Unless they recognize this potential and guard against its attendant difficulties, researchers could suffer from accusations of bias. In short, they must be seen to be objective in their endeavors.

CHAPTER SIXTEEN

Industrial Relations Research and the American Policy-Making Process

Jay S. Siegel

*I*ndustrial relations research continues to play a vital role in the formulation of labor policy in the United States, but its value in providing adequate guidance for policy makers deserves reexamination.[1] Despite early warning signals from respected academicians, a disturbing pattern over the past three decades calls into question the direction and validity of policy-oriented industrial relations research.

Kerr observed in "A Perspective on Industrial Relations Research" (1983b) that industrial relations is an applied field and that, although it may be connected with theory, it has a special obligation to be based on facts. It is thus disquieting to find that over the years such research has been subject to two disabling trends. First, in constructing models to test industrial relations hypotheses, researchers unfamiliar with the real world have been either disregarding or omitting relevant factors, thus producing distorted outcomes. Second, studies have become dominated by researchers who tend to dismiss qualitative behavioral observations as unreliable. Instead, they attempt to define all workplace interests in quantifiable analysis terms, which invites outcomes that are at variance with what is actually occurring in the workplace.

The risk, as Eberstadt has pointed out, is that "when a problem-solving government uses inaccurate data, selects accurate but inappropriate statistical indicators or misanalyzes available facts and figures, the consequences are typically direct and injurious" (1995: 15–16).

---

1. For definitional purposes in this chapter, I have adopted the scope of the discipline as defined by Dunlop (1993).

The problem in the United States, as the examples in this chapter illustrate, arises primarily from dubious assumptions, the improper choice of data, and, most important, because the researchers are unfamiliar with the synergy of industrial relations or lack adequate knowledge of the subject under consideration. Each of these factors can distort the validity of the outcome of a study. This disturbing trend has not received sufficient attention, which is most unfortunate because industrial relations research has a legitimate role to play in the guidance of policy makers who are struggling to deal with workplace areas in which they have little or no expertise.

My examination of industrial relations research leads me to question the abuse of the quantitative analysis methodology, which researchers have misguidedly attempted to use to explain all aspects of industrial relations behavior, particularly those that do not readily lend themselves to mathematical measurement.

Their experiences in serving the U.S. government during World War II taught Dunlop, Kerr, and Ross, three early industrial relations research pioneers, "the limitations of classical economic theory in explaining institutional reality" and led to their developing a realistic balance between theory and practice based on the traditional methodology of documentary research and the analysis of historical events (Strauss and Feuille 1981: 80). It is a lesson that has not been learned by many of today's researchers, who risk having their suspect conclusions relied on by policy makers, leading to misguided policy decisions.

This chapter will briefly review the nexus between American policy making and industrial relations research. It will then examine several examples of research efforts that possess negative characteristics that make them inappropriate for policy guidance purposes.

Policy-Oriented Industrial Relations Research

The political and administrative process that produces U.S. policy makers, either on an elective or an appointive basis, does not insure that they will have the expertise in all the areas with which they will be required to deal in carrying out their responsibilities. Although policy makers may be well versed in the macro parameters of key issues, they wisely look to others for guidance and recommendations in micromanaging specific components. It is in this latter mode that well-grounded industrial relations research has played a significant role in guiding the nation's policy makers over the years.

The tendency since the post–World War II years has been for the U.S. government to turn to the academic community to prepare studies on issues that are under consideration by policy makers. In 1968, George Shultz, the newly appointed Secretary of Labor, proclaimed that "industrial relations has come of age" and that it produced research that "increasingly contributed to the discussion and formulation of private and public policies" (1968: 1).

Nonetheless, in the 1970s, a spirited debate broke out in the field over the direction of policy-oriented research. Much of the work was characterized as being ineffective because it was too parochial and failed to take into account relevant historical and institutional factors that provided the necessary environmental framework to give validity to the conclusions reached (Dunlop 1977). Some of the American scholars who welcomed the introduction of the precise methodological approach argued that the researchers were not primarily to blame and that the problem was really one of a shift in emphasis because many issues involving labor markets and wage curves were more closely related to elements of classical economics than to industrial relations. One labor economist, however, conceded an element of validity to the criticism, noting that some researchers had utilized quantification to the point where they had "perhaps gone too far, at the expense of a proper grounding in history and institutions" (Rees 1977: 3–4).

As with most academic debates, the basic issues were thoroughly explored but never resolved. Yet, despite these cautionary signs, current industrial relations research has moved in a direction *away from* the integration of theory and practice. This has been the major factor in undermining its validity for policy guidance purposes.

Flawed Research and Its Impact on Policy

Three examples illustrate that this trend is a continuing one in the United States.

Research on Preelection Campaigning

In 1976, a highly controversial study was published that purported to dissect the synergy involved in union representation secret-ballot elections conducted by the National Labor Relations Board (NLRB), which regulates the establishment and conduct of collective bargaining relationships in the United States (Getman and Goldberg 1976). One of the key elements the study examined was the effect of campaign efforts by employers to convince workers to reject unionization. A major conclusion was that these employers' preelection activities had little or no impact on the outcome of the election.

This finding astounded many practitioners who had extensive experience in such matters. On the one hand, they knew that management always sought the maximum time between the union's filing of a petition for an election with the Board and the eventual date of the vote. This allowed management time to put the case to the workers for rejecting unionization. Unions, on the other hand, sought to have the election held as soon as possible to limit employers' activity, since they knew it had a substantial negative effect on the outcome.

This study, which was at variance with real-world conditions, went wrong because the researchers (two nonpracticing lawyers and a psychologist) were unfamiliar with the dynamics of NLRB election campaigns and had inappropriately made an analogy to studies of voters in political elections. One major difference is that union representation elections have a much greater immediate impact on the voters than do ordinary political elections, in which there is an element of remoteness in time between the outcome and its ultimate effects on voters in personal terms under legislation that may take several years to enact. In view of the heavy criticism of the Getman and Goldberg study, a "reconciliation" attempt was made through a "reanalysis" of the data by another researcher (Dickens 1983) who took into account the extensive objections raised and the response of the original researchers. This second effort only proved the point, for the new model incorporated many of the factors omitted in the original version, thus producing a result more in tune with the real world.

Further, every experienced labor practitioner knows that union representation elections have special characteristics all their own involving the geographical location of the workplace and activities by unions at other employers in the community, to which the employer usually refers during preelection campaigning. Such factors play a vital role in influencing workers in their decision to accept or reject union representation.

The flawed study had a direct policy impact in that a majority of NLRB members specifically relied on it when they voted to overturn the Board's fifteen-year-old preelection campaign policy. Thus, in the 1977 case of *Shopping Kart, Inc.*, the Board abandoned its policy, adopted in 1962, of closely monitoring such elections. It announced that it was no longer going to review the parties' campaign statements that were alleged to be misrepresentations of the facts because the Getman-Goldberg study had convinced the Board that such conduct had no impact on election results. In spite of this conclusion, dissenting Board members John Fanning and Howard Jenkins vigorously attacked the study as being unrealistic.

Research on First-Contract Bargaining Results

In 1985, a study was published that endeavored to explain why American unions were sometimes unsuccessful in obtaining an initial collective bargaining agreement after winning an NLRB election and being certified as the bargaining agent. The study claimed that employer resistance to unions was at the heart of this frustration, which occurred about 30 percent of the time after successful elections and certification. The researchers reached this result by constructing an elaborate model that ostensibly accounted for all the factors involved in such negotiations. A close analysis of the model reveals, however, that the researchers failed to ascribe any significance to a factor that veteran negotiators know is a major impediment to a successful outcome, particularly in attempting to reach a first contract.

Specifically, when a labor union approaches the bargaining table, one of its major concerns is the existence of other agreements between the union and the employer's competitors or elsewhere in the industry. Where these have resulted from long-standing bargaining relationships, there is serious concern on the union's part that if it is too concessionary in its attempt to work out a first contract with newly organized employers, the outcome could be harmful to workers operating under other agreements. Thus, to maintain the integrity of these existing contracts, the union is sometimes forced into a "take it or leave it" negotiating strategy. Of course, it is not couched in those terms, since doing so would be an unfair labor practice. Rather, the union indicates that it wishes to obtain contracts equivalent to those enjoyed by its members in other companies in the same or related industries with mature labor-management relationships.

The employer's objective is to negotiate an agreement that reflects conditions within its own organization with little regard for agreements elsewhere. The union caught in a bargaining stance more tied to union institutional and political considerations is reluctant to move away from the standard industry framework. One of the best examples of this quandary is the demand by U.S. Teamster union locals for inclusion of its existing area health and welfare benefit plan at the contributory rate paid by employers who have been under contract for many years. This is a strike issue in some of the joint councils and helps set the tone for the entire negotiations. Where the nature of the union's hard and fast first-contract demands threatens the economic survival of the enterprise, the employer has no choice but to resist. The result is endless rounds of negotiation meetings and in some cases eventually a strike and no agreement during the certification year.

One searches in vain for the inclusion of such a factor in Cooke's first-contract bargaining model (1985). He does make a passing reference to other union forces exerting control but concludes that the existence of such outside contracts *increases* the probability of a first-contract settlement, allegedly because it gives the newly organized employer an advantage over his nonunion competitors, which many employers would challenge as being true.

The Cooke study was cited in the 1994 *Fact-Finding Report* of the distinguished Dunlop Commission as a "representative sample" of studies on first contract situations. The commission, which ascribed the failure in such situations solely to employer bargaining conduct (Commission on the Future of Worker Management Relations 1994a: 74 n.15), relied on the study in developing its recommendations for changes in procedures involving first-contract bargaining remedies and did not mention the intransigent negotiating behavior used by unions as a factor that prevents agreement from being reached in a first contract environment.

Research on NLRB Decision-Making Patterns

One ambitious attempt at model building is a recent study involving the decisions of the National Labor Relations Board. According to the authors, it draws upon "decision science theory and notions of rational economic decision-making" as the basis for their analysis of a sample of 527 decisions in the period from 1957 to 1986 (Cooke et al. 1995). Claiming to have developed a "unique theoretical model of NLRB member decision making," they assert that only 20 percent of the Board's important or complex cases were decided based on such factors as personal preferences or the preference of the U.S. president who appointed them. In the other 80 percent, the study claims, the Board members merely rubber-stamped either the positions taken by the regional offices that processed the cases or the recommendations of administrative law judges.

As an active and seasoned Board watcher during the period of this study, I suggest the researchers have been led astray by their attempt to construct a "model" to explain the behavior of the close to fifty presidential appointees who sat as Board members during this time under the statutory five-year term scheme. One major problem with the study's alleged findings is John Fanning, who served during the entire study period and was appointed in 1953 by President Eisenhower, a Republican. Fanning did not present the views of his appointer, as suggested by the study, and usually sided with the union position. Although Fanning's political acumen enabled him to obtain continual reappointment until 1990 under a succession of presidents, both

Democratic and Republican, he maintained highly consistent views that on many occasions plainly were at variance with the views of all of his Republican appointers.

Other relevant factors not assessed by the study include the instinct for political survival that at times has led some NLRB members, particularly in the final year of their appointment and desirous of reappointment, to join in decisions that were at variance with their own prior rulings. Further, although the study refers to the Board's unique panel system for deciding cases, it omits the critical element that the panels are carefully structured by the Office of the Executive Secretary. For years when the Board was split three to two in favor of deferral to arbitration under *Collyer Insulated Wire Co.* (1971), the executive secretary's office *never* named both Fanning and Jenkins to a case in which deferral was an issue since both members opposed it and could have issued a two-to-one decision seriously undermining the overall position of the Board's majority. Although the authors should not be faulted for being unaware of these details, this example points up the shortcomings when researchers rely too much on statistical analysis where sophisticated patterns of behavior are involved in an area outside their expertise.

Finally, the authors attempt to explain Board decisions by correlating them to labor market conditions. They outline elaborate calculations based on unemployment figures. Never in my thirty years of being directly involved with both Board members and their staff personnel have I seen any evidence to suggest that such a factor was even remotely a consideration in a decision by the agency. This "finding" is a prime example of the ultimate fantasy that results when proponents of a methodology believe that all behavior can be explained by distilling it through the chemistry of statistical analysis.

Conclusion

The studies touched on here are examples of the misguided direction that some U.S. policy-oriented research has taken since the pioneers' warnings went unheeded. This trend, if maintained, will further reduce the value of industrial relations research to policy makers as they become more astute in recognizing the limitations of such studies for their purposes. It is also incumbent upon many researchers to reassess candidly the direction they have been taking in the past thirty years.

The heart of the matter is that model-building researchers lacking real-world behavioral knowledge are attempting to reduce the unmeasurable factors involved in industrial relations to a statistical format so they can be manipulated in the abstract. The problem is not so much with modeling "errors" as with the use of the modeling approach, which leads researchers to produce questionable findings and distorted outcomes. As seen in the examples discussed earlier, in developing a hypothesis and then attempting to construct a model to demonstrate its validity, researchers run the risk of either ignoring factors unknown to them or basing their research on assumptions that are designed to produce a result in conformity with the theory being tested.

Using economic theory as a "starting point" for industrial relations research is proper, but, as Kochan has cautioned, "Used alone, however, economic models lose much of their predictive power at the micro level" (1976: 241). He suggests an integrative approach that combines economic, institutional, and behavioral methods; this approach deserves more serious consideration.

Shultz observed that "in the area of industrial relations, policymakers and researchers have a demonstrated community of interest" (1968: 13). Independent, well-documented, and carefully prepared studies that mirror the real-world environment of the industrial relations arena are valuable tools for reaching informed and valid conclusions leading to appropriate policy guidance.

The recent two-part study by Freeman and Rogers (1994–95) of the attitudes of American workers toward greater empowerment in the workplace is an example of research based on a approach that more accurately mirrors industrial relations behavior. In not using the modeling approach but instead turning to detailed surveys and follow-up interviews of workers, the researchers avoided the dangers of trying to prove a predetermined hypothesis.[2] It is still to be seen how policy makers will put such research to use, but at the least there is an assurance that it rests on a solid foundation of industrial relations realism.

Can policy makers develop adequate safeguards against the problems discussed here when they rely on outside research assistance for making policy decisions? Lacking the expertise of those who prepared the research, is there a "due diligence" test that could be applied that would alert policy makers to serious shortcomings in research tendered to them for guidance purposes? An imperfect answer may lie in having the research results reviewed by an independent authority known for his or her intellectual in-

---

2. That the results contained a great number of surprises, even to seasoned labor-management observers, provides an additional note of value to this approach.

tegrity in the field and unconnected with either the study, the researchers, or their sponsors and home organizations. Clearly, these are matters deserving of further study.

This brings us to another aspect of industrial relations research that deserves consideration—the use of "policy guidance" studies from centers established by labor or management interest groups. As opposed to independent research efforts, in which the outcomes may be disappointing to the sponsors, results-driven research emanating from interest-oriented "think tanks" becomes merely another vehicle for the furtherance of the research institution's policy goals. These centers came of age in the 1980s and 1990s. They not only analyze policy issues but participate in the formulation of legislative initiatives, thus becoming ancillary "players" in the policy process itself.

As to the fate of industrial relations research in the United States and the ever-widening gulf between those who insist on quantitative analysis as the ultimate methodology for measuring industrial relations factors and the silenced current generation of institutionalists and behavioralists, one can only hope that focusing the spotlight on the inadequacies of the former will serve as an invitation for renewal of the academic debate that was so vigorous in the 1960s and 1970s but that has lost its voice for the past twenty years. Unfortunately, the "Renaissance" longed for by Strauss and Feuille in 1981 has never materialized, and the ensuing period may more appropriately be looked upon as one of decline than of regeneration.

CHAPTER SEVENTEEN

Funders and Research: The Vulnerability of the Subject

William Brown

A nyone bold enough to conduct academic research on live power relationships soon learns that it is a hazardous activity. The research is close to foolhardy if, in addition, those power relationships are the subject of wider political controversy. By the nature of their subject, industrial relations researchers are usually concerned with power and often cannot avoid the politics. It is therefore important for them to acquire an early respect for these hazards. All too often they are stumbled into too late, when permission to conduct fieldwork has been withdrawn, publication rights have been blocked, or research funding has been aborted.

This chapter discusses the challenge of defending the academic integrity of industrial relations research. The focus is not on the micropolitics of fieldwork, which, though fascinating in its own right, is common to much social science and has received substantial attention. Rather, the focus is the very particular risk that faces those who explore current collective employment relationships. The risk is that the researchers come to be perceived as partisan, as so biased in their sympathies toward either the employer or the union that their judgment is believed to be corrupted and their findings, thereby, are thought to be invalid. Such a perception is damaging enough when it is that of those being studied. The damage is far greater when it is

The author is much indebted to George Bain, Fred Bayliss, Kenneth Berrill, Chris Caswill, Glyn Davies, Linda Dickens, Paul Edwards, Bob Hepple, Roy Lewis, Bill McCarthy, Michael Posner, Keith Sisson, Mike Terry, David Williams, and the editors of this volume for many helpful comments; none can be held responsible for any errors of fact or judgment that remain.

held by the wider constituency of practitioners, policy makers, social scientists, and those in control of research funding.

Much of the material for this discussion is drawn from a series of critical events in the history of British industrial relations research in which that subject became the test case in a wider political questioning of the social sciences. The focus of attention was the Industrial Relations Research Unit (IRRU) at the University of Warwick. The unit had been established there in 1970 as an outstation of the semiautonomous government organization the Social Science Research Council (SSRC). The focus here is on the period before 1985, when a renamed Economic and Social Research Council, while continuing to fund the unit, decided to hand it over to the university. During these years labor legislation, wage policies, and increasingly bitter strikes had persistently forced their way onto the center of the British political stage. This public preoccupation with industrial relations issues had made research in the subject particularly newsworthy and controversial.

In pursuing what was then the largest industrial relations research program in Britain, the IRRU was constantly kept aware of the need to maintain both the reality and the appearance of objectivity. The SSRC's awareness of the political sensitivity of much of the work carried out in its research units was reflected in the conditions of service that had been devised especially for their staff. These required them to "ensure that the Unit's and the Council's impartiality and objectivity [were] not jeopardised in any way," but added that "the Council recognise[d] that a Unit member's research may attract public controversy even though he has acted with the care and discretion expected of him." Five yearly external review procedures had been devised that focused particularly on this aspect of research standards, which the unit's staff in any case knew was the sine qua non for research access. These procedures contributed to the unit's achieving, among employers, trade unions, and civil servants, a strong reputation for objectivity in its research, a reputation it has maintained to the present.

Careful procedures, however, did not prevent the occurrence, in 1982, of what the *Financial Times* described as "a small but stirring chapter in the history of government-academic relations" (20 May 1983). It was this incident that caused the government to make the IRRU the subject of a unique official inquiry into allegations of academic bias.

This chapter provides an account of these events as both warning and guidance for future researchers whose work may become politically inconvenient. It starts with a review of the development of "government-academic relations" in the subject and concludes with a more general discussion of the issues at stake.

Who Pays the Piper?

Nikita Khruschev once observed that, although there may be neutral nations, there are no neutral men. In social science, the conduct of research has to be neutral to have any validity, even if the researchers, as individuals, are far from neutral. Whether political bias is an issue thus depends on the validity of the research methods used. Quite separate from this is whether the choice of the subject of the research and the methods used are influenced, let alone corrupted, by the researcher's personal political beliefs. Thus, the critical first question is not who is doing the research but how it is being done.

The second question concerns the choice of the subject. Insofar as individual researchers have discretion in this regard, they are likely to have a diversity of motivations, many of which will be politically sensitive. These include whether the work is likely to yield publishable and career-enhancing results and whether it may shed light on what the researchers feel to be politically important issues. Social science would not have advanced far if the private passions of individual researchers had not caused them to forage ahead. Whatever the motivation for the choice of subject, the validity of research ultimately depends on the methods used.

The integrity of the research process also depends on ensuring that researchers have the opportunity to explore what they consider to be important issues and the means available to challenge received beliefs. Since empirical research is often expensive, obtaining funding becomes a critical issue. This is a common concern across the whole range of academic research. Medicine, for example, has been accused of neglecting the ailments of the poor, and the relative neglect of the predominantly black disease of sickle-cell anemia is given as a standard example. The funding available for British social science research has been a source of public concern for at least fifty years.

Since World War II, the British government has initiated a series of independent inquiries into the funding of social science research. As early as 1946, the Clapham Committee considered the funding of social science research to be "lamentably inadequate" and advocated an increase in university teaching posts as a means of encouraging "routine research." In 1965, the Heyworth Committee successfully advocated the creation of the Social Science Research Council, with the observation that "social science research done on contract is not filling the gaps in present knowledge, nor would a haphazard expansion, however large, through contract funds do so" (46). Reports on the funding of government research were produced in

1971 by Lord Rothschild and in 1981 by Sir Fred Dainton. These reports shared Heyworth's skepticism of arguments that placed faith in what he had called "the force of the market" (46) with respect to academic science in general and social science in particular. Much socially desirable research would not be carried out without government support.

Nonetheless, beginning in the early 1980s, considerable official pressure was placed on British social scientists to develop commercial, "customer-contractor" relationships with the "users" of research wherever possible. There were four Social Science Research Council–owned research units by this time, based at different universities and dedicated respectively to ethnic relations, demography, and sociolegal studies, as well as industrial relations. Growing pressure to win external funds had encouraged them to take on projects funded by a variety of relatively small paid commissions.

Their research was conducted in keeping with five jointly agreed guidelines that the IRRU had developed earlier on the basis of hard practical experience. These reflected the IRRU's need to ensure that the members of its staff were not perceived as "servants of power," so that pressure to undertake commissioned research would not compromise their research access for wider noncommissioned work. The guidelines, which are applicable to much empirical social science, were as follows:

1. The work must possess substantial academic interest, likely to lead to the production of new research results, and should be related to other work which is being done in the unit.
2. Regardless of who is paying for the research, all organisations whose interests are affected by it must agree that the research should be undertaken.
3. A unit must be able to decide how the research is to be carried out and to control the day-to-day management of the project. This does not preclude the formation of a "steering committee," composed of representatives of those organisations with a vested interest in the research, meeting periodically to determine the general course of the research and to review its progress.
4. Data gathered under guarantee of anonymity will be made available to the customer in such a way that these guarantees are respected. Similarly, unpublished material obtained from the customer's official sources will not be made available, without its permission, to any other organisation or person.
5. So long as all guarantees of confidentiality and anonymity are respected, a unit must be free to publish any work, other than reports to the customer, which derives directly or indirectly from the basic data. A unit must be prepared, however, to delay publication until such a time as it has submitted the final report to the customer. Work will

generally be shown to the customer and to any other interested parties
prior to publication, and it will generally carry a statement acknowl-
edging their help but absolving them from all views expressed.

These guidelines were to prove both useful and robust for a wide variety
of commissioned research studies. The IRRU developed fruitful contractual
relationships with both public- and private-sector organizations to carry out
substantial research on, for example, employee directors (Batstone, Ferner,
and Terry 1983), trade union reorganization (England 1979; Hyman, Price,
and Terry 1988), and the extension of collective agreements (Jones 1980).
Such work always required careful management, not least because of the
contractors' often mixed desires for publicity, anonymity, credits, and dis-
claimers. For the IRRU, however, relationships between the funder and the
unit did not prove to be a substantial source of embarrassment. That was to
come from a different quarter.

The Government as Paymaster

For more than one hundred years, the British government has been a major
benefactor of industrial relations research. From the Royal Commissions of
1867 and 1894 onward, there had been a flurry of government-inspired research activity whenever industrial relations problems created political
problems. Wartime work by Clay (1929) on wages and by Florence (1924)
on industrial fatigue are early examples. The Royal Commission of
1965–68 provided a major stimulus by commissioning its own research activity in the 1960s, as did its contemporary, the National Board for Prices
and Incomes, and its offspring, the Commission on Industrial Relations. Although the government cut back sharply on conducting its own industrial
relations research in the 1970s, its indirect support, largely through the
agency of the SSRC, rose substantially (Brown and Wright 1994).

The loss of direct control over research did not appear to bother either
the Labour or the Conservative governments of the 1970s, despite their
preoccupation with industrial relations problems. Research studies critical
of aspects of recent legislation were published without incurring official
disapproval (e.g., Mellish and Dickens 1972; Weekes et al. 1975; Dickens
1978). Perhaps this was because these governments broadly upheld the traditional stance of their twentieth-century predecessors in supporting the
principle of collective bargaining, differing mainly over the manner and extent of its reform. Research on the status quo is usually valued by those trying to achieve incremental reform, in whatever direction.

The Conservative election victory of 1979 was to lead, within a couple of years, to a sea change in government views on industrial relations. A Conservative minister for employment, Gillian Shephard, was later to say that "there was a war against trade unions" in the 1980s (*Financial Times,* 16 July 1992). A succession of laws were enacted that weakened both collective bargaining and the organizational capacity of trade unions. The government unequivocally took the employers' side in a series of bitter and conspicuous industrial disputes. So radical was the shift in policy that those developing it sought little guidance from industrial relations research. At best, its findings were too detailed to guide broad strategy; at worst, it was a source of political embarrassment.

Monitoring Labor Legislation

That industrial relations research was becoming a source of embarrassment first became evident with regard to research on labor legislation. In the mid-1970s, an SSRC committee with responsibility for encouraging sociolegal research decided that progress could be made by initiating projects concerned with evaluating the behavioral impact of legislation. Experience suggested that employment legislation would be a fruitful place to start. This view was reinforced at a conference in late 1977 that brought together researchers who had previously done work on the Health and Safety at Work Act, the Equal Pay Act, and the Industrial Relations Act.

Thus encouraged, the conference organizers were ready when the first Queen's Speech of the 1979 Government set forth the measures to be included in the 1980 Employment Act. Two topics that were covered by the proposed legislation and that had been relatively neglected in postwar research were picketing in industrial disputes and balloting in trade unions. In June 1979, the SSRC approved the allocation of funds and the establishment of the Panel on the Monitoring of Labour Legislation to initiate research on these issues. As a fuller account of the panel's work describes, the SSRC "deliberately chose these two politically contentious topics in preference to two others"—health and safety and termination of employment—because of "the considerable pressure current in the late 1970s to produce 'policy-relevant' research findings" (Brown and Hepple 1985: 11).

The panel invited research teams to submit proposals for projects to explore the empirical status of picketing and balloting and to monitor the impact on them of the legislative innovation under consideration. From several applications, one research team was chosen for each topic. There was no problem with the choice for the balloting study, and in due course the completed research resulted in an influential book (Undy and Martin 1984).

The choice of the team for the picketing study, however, was challenged by the Department of Employment on the grounds that one of its members had recently coauthored a Fabian Society pamphlet (Lewis, Davies, and Wedderburn 1979) that was critical of the legislation and had thereby, it was suggested, demonstrated prejudicial bias. The SSRC responded by providing the panel with additional funds with which to support a second team for the project. The justification given was that two teams would ensure a balanced approach. Paradoxically, the publication record of the members of the second team suggested that they were probably more critical of the legislation than the members of the first team. But the fact that a second team had been chosen succeeded in silencing the objections from the Department of Employment.

In both cases the teams made solid contributions to our knowledge of the role and conduct of picketing (Evans 1985; Kahn et al. 1983). The panel went on to initiate projects on well-established legislation on health and safety and on short-time working arrangements, and in due course these studies also bore fruit (Dawson et al. 1988; Szyszczak 1990).

Further difficulties with the Department of Employment arose, however, when the Panel on the Monitoring of Labour Legislation proposed to monitor what was to become the 1982 Employment Act. After initially encouraging the panel to study the impact of the forthcoming act on strike behavior, the Department of Employment became uncompromisingly hostile. The panel rejected the department's advice to desist, but, before any research could be commissioned, Lord Rothschild wrote a report on the SSRC that was published in May 1982 and that led to the panel being suspended, for reasons we shall turn to. By the end of the one-year suspension, the opportunity to conduct the research as it had been conceived had been lost. No further monitoring work was commissioned, and shortly afterward the panel was dissolved.

Many fascinating research questions remain to be explored about whether, how, and why legal intervention influences the conduct of the employment relationship. What are politicians' motives and assumptions? How are these modified by drafting and debate? How are laws interpreted by those who have to administer and obey them? How far are they allowed to influence the, in many ways, very private relationship between employer and employee? The methodology of "running alongside" the legislative process has proved to have considerable research potential. But those who seek to do so should be aware of the political sensitivities involved.

The Problem of Bias

Antipathy between government and social science has a long history. Those grappling with the prejudices of the electorate and the immediacy of events rarely find social scientists' analyses to be readily applicable or their criticisms helpful. Social science researchers particularly irritated Mrs. Thatcher's first administration, whose many academic critics included 364 economists who published a petition against its economic policy. Her Secretary of State for Education and Science, Sir Keith Joseph, authorized an investigation into alleged "left-wing bias" in courses run by the Open University (*Times* Higher Education Supplement, 15 October 1982). Believing that the term "social science" was philosophically a contradiction in terms, Joseph would have summarily abolished the Social Science Research Council late in 1981 had his junior minister (and fellow ex-Oxford academic) William Waldegrave not prevailed upon him to ask Lord Rothschild to carry out a public review of the SSRC before abolishing it (*Times,* 20 May 1983).

This review saved the SSRC. Lord Rothschild, a biological scientist for part of his distinguished career, produced a rapid and highly personal report, drawing on both solicited and unsolicited written evidence (1982). The report amounted to a powerful defense of social science and of the need for something like the SSRC:

> The need for independence from government departments is particularly important because so much social science research is the stuff of political debate. All such research might prove subversive of government policies because it attempts to submit such policies to empirical trial, with the risk that the judgement may be adverse. It would be too much to expect Ministers to show enthusiasm for research designed to show that their policies were misconceived. But it seems obvious that in many cases the public interest will be served by such research being undertaken (para. 3.12).

A serious problem remained for the SSRC, however. Contrasting sharply with the other generally palatable recommendations was one for "the Chairman of the SSRC to have investigated the accusation that the SSRC's Industrial Relations Research Unit at Warwick, or (sic) the Panel for the Monitoring of Labour Legislation, are unfairly biased in favour of the unions" (R.21).

There is authoritative evidence that this recommendation was added after Rothschild sent his draft report to the Secretary of State. As it happened, the main text contained two sympathetic references to the IRRU.

The unit was used to illustrate the circumstances under which the "customer-contractor" principle was inappropriate: "The TUC [Trade Union Congress] and CBI [Confederation of British Industry] could not be expected to fund research which might undermine their respective interests, while the nature of the research commissioned by government departments in this field is likely to be influenced by the politics of the government" (para. 3.11). Similarly, Rothschild quoted the written opinion offered by the Confederation of British Industry that "the SSRC's Industrial Relations Research Unit at Warwick is important to us and the fact that its work, of necessity, takes it into politically sensitive areas underlines the need for some independent source of funds" (para. 9.51).

The source of the allegation of bias had been a brief letter of evidence from Lord Beloff, a retired Oxford historian and an active Conservative peer. In a broad attack on the SSRC, he had included, among a number of assertions, that "there has been so much dissatisfaction with the strong pro-TUC bias" of the IRRU that "a new Institute of Labour Affairs is being founded by a group of businessmen and academics" (para. 9.16).

Nothing was ever heard again of the proposed institute, but Beloff's passing reference was picked up by Rothschild: "As the SSRC's Industrial Relations Unit at Warwick has been accused of being unfairly biased in favour of the unions, the Chairman of the SSRC should set up an impartial examination, in depth, of this accusation and ventilate the results. The Council should then take such action on the findings as appropriate" (para. 11.10). To this was added a footnote: "The examination should of course include that of the SSRC Panel for the Monitoring of Labour Legislation." Nowhere in Rothschild's report was there any reference to any allegations or evidence about the panel, which had no direct connection with the IRRU except that the present author was a member of both.

Disproving Academic Bias

If the overall verdict of Rothschild's report was a matter for celebration for the chairman of the SSRC, Michael Posner, the obligation to hold an inquiry into the IRRU was not. He was acutely aware of the unpredictability of the outcome of any such inquiry, especially one into such vague charges. An adverse or uncertain verdict could, in the hands of the SSRC's detractors, have broad repercussions. Posner selected a former Cambridge academic, Sir Kenneth Berrill, as chairman. Although now chairman of a stockbroking firm, Berrill had (like Rothschild) earlier run the Downing Street "think tank" and was thus tuned into Whitehall. The other two members were Sir Henry Phelps Brown, then the most distinguished living British labor economist, and David Williams (later knighted), an administrative lawyer who was soon to become a professor and subsequently the first full-time vice chancellor of Cambridge University. By any standards, it was a strong and shrewdly chosen committee.

The Berrill Report (Berrill 1983) was finally published a year to the day after Rothschild had published his report containing the initial allegations about the IRRU. As was noted in the foreword, "The task of reducing the allegations from the level of generalisations to specific charges was a lengthy one but produced only the relatively meagre list of instances which are discussed in the report."

This problem had become evident at the first hearing of the committee, when, to discuss procedure, the members separately cross-examined Beloff and the present author, who had been director of the IRRU since 1981 and a member of its staff since 1970. Beloff, they reported, "told us that he had no expert knowledge of industrial relations and was not familiar with the Unit's output" (para. 4.12). At the same hearing, the IRRU's director was faced with a diversity of questions that starkly revealed the impossibility of refuting so broad an allegation as the committee had to explore.

From this point on, the director, his IRRU colleagues, and the two previous directors, Hugh Clegg and George Bain, were to be greatly helped by the guidance of a sympathetic solicitor with expertise in civil procedure and liberties. His key strategic advice was, first, strictly to avoid the temptation to enter into any sort of debate with the committee members about such issues as the meaning of bias, the nature of academic freedom, or the motives of the accusers. Second, he advised that the committee should be forced to specify all its charges precisely and in writing, so that a formal written response could be made. A letter making this second point was dispatched to the committee.

The committee then set out to trawl for evidence: "We approached those who seemed most likely to be able to provide informed opinions on the work of the Unit. In particular we asked if they would wish to give specific examples from the work of the Unit which might illustrate the presence or absence of bias" (para. 1.5). Hearings were held for oral evidence from civil servants, academics, employer representatives, and Rothschild himself. Written evidence was gathered, notably from overseas academics. Some of those approached refused to give evidence. There were also 189 listed unit publications to be considered. Eventually a thousand-word long "Statement of the Complaints of Bias" was compiled and sent to the IRRU's director with an invitation to submit his observations.

The statement marshaled three kinds of "complaint." The first was that the concentration of resources in one unit inevitably led to one research outlook being unduly favored. The second was that the IRRU was dominated by a particular philosophy of collective bargaining, favored by the 1968 Royal Commission, which played down the potential use of legal regulation and led to undue emphasis on trade unions. The third kind of complaint related to three particular publications in which, it had been alleged, "the argument has always gone to show that what the trade unions objected to was wrong and that what they desired was right." The receipt of the "Statement" at last gave the unit something tangible to sink its teeth into and led in due course to a painstakingly drafted thirty-page response plus numerous appendixes.

"I am glad that the evidence has led us to firm conclusions in this difficult and unprecedented inquiry," wrote Berrill, when he eventually presented his committee's report. It first dismissed complaints against the Monitoring of Labor Legislation Panel: "None of our witnesses made any complaints of bias against the Panel or could offer any explanation for its inclusion in our terms of reference. Lord Rothschild agrees that he was under a misapprehension in linking the Panel and the IRRU and that there was no ground for including the Panel in our terms of reference" (para. 5(I)).

The report then analyzed the evidence on the IRRU in terms of three different senses of bias: bias in the choice of subjects for research, in the use of evidence, and in presentation. The report found no evidence of bias in any of these three areas. At the end of a long and careful discussion, the strongest comment concerned a unit discussion paper (Dickens and Lewis 1981) that had been a response to a government consultative paper (for what was to become the 1982 Employment Act); this "attributed motives to the Government in its approach to the trade union movement. . . . To those readers who were sensitive to the passages attributing motives to the Government the effect may have been to identify the IRRU with a partisan approach to industrial relations" (para. 4.20).

Looking back from the 1990s, the motives attributed in the offending passages, which suggested that government policy might in part be directed at weakening trade union organization, appear wholly uncontroversial. They are fully endorsed in the subsequent memoirs of contemporary Cabinet ministers (e.g., Tebbit 1988) and far milder than those implied in Shephard's reference to "a war against trade unions" ten years later.

"Industrial relations is an area of research of great political sensitivity," concluded the report. "Those in charge of the work of the IRRU need to be constantly aware of the need for all members of the Unit not to act in a way which would 'jeopardise the impartiality and objectivity of the Unit' and that any document associated with the Unit carries such a danger. It is our view that in one or two instances insufficient attention was paid to this." The report went on to say, however, that "in our judgement the accusation of bias in the published research work of the Industrial Relations Research Unit at Warwick University has not been substantiated" (para. 5).

Aftermath

The vindication of the Industrial Relations Research Unit was celebrated in some unexpected places. The *Times,* for example, in its leading editorial comment, entitled "Rout of the Rotarians," described Berrill's completion of Rothschild's task as "a timely antidote to the conventional wisdom that, since the 1960s, university life, not to mention social science research has been poisoned by people with a political axe to grind" (20 May 1983).

A cooler assessment came in the *Times* Higher Education Supplement, whose correspondent, Paul Flather, had kept a close and careful eye on the affair from the start:

> Uneasy questions remain. Why were the charges taken so seriously in the first place and why was the trial not called off once the charge sheet was found so empty? The probable answer is that Lord Rothschild needed some palliative to help the Government to swallow his whole report reprieving the SSRC, and that the air can only be cleared if "serious charges" are investigated away. The assumption was that the unit could stand up well to scrutiny. On the second [question], expediency dictated. Once the ball had been thrown into play, those on the pitch had to play to the finish even if the owner of the ball had gone off home (27 May 1983).

Victories are never total, and the fact that both the SSRC and the IRRU had avoided abolition did not mean they were unharmed. Staff at both were acutely aware that had the committee of inquiry been less subtle or had there been a few more "injudicious" words in the, perhaps, three million words in the unit's publications, the verdict could have been disastrously different. In any case, the Social Science Research Council found it expedient to bow to the Secretary of State's idiosyncratic views on the philosophy of science by changing its name to the Economic and Social Research Council.

There were substantial financial reasons for the council to turn over its four research units (including the IRRU) to their host universities over the following year, but at least a contributory consideration was the desire to keep potential political embarrassment at a disclaimable distance. Nor did official interest in the IRRU die with the report. When, in 1985, the director resigned to accept another position, the usual competitive procedure for finding his replacement was subject to unusual delay in official confirmation.

Despite the unit's exoneration, it is likely that industrial relations research in Britain suffered lasting damage. The year-long period of uncertainty during the investigation, and continuing official hostility to industrial relations research, branded the subject politically risky in the thinking of both funding bodies and universities long after the episode had, for all but the few people immediately involved, been completely forgotten.

The Wider Lessons

It is the essence of power relationships that they involve the manipulation of uncertainty, as each party to the relationship seeks both to minimize the uncertainty confronting itself and to gain control over the uncertainty confronting its opponent. But research is also concerned with the management of uncertainty. It is its essence that it aims to generate reliable information and to improve public understanding of the natural and human world. Consequently, the findings of research into live power relationships may have implications for the conduct of the very relationships being studied.

Managing this delicate relationship between the researcher and the researched is not helped by the truism that research findings are unpredictable. What makes management of this relationship particularly difficult in industrial relations is the fact that any impact that the research may have on the parties being studied is likely to be asymmetric. However impartial the researcher may strive to be, there can be no guarantees of impartiality in any subsequent application of the results.

An example is provided in a recurring debate during the 1970s among industrial relations researchers as to how far an improved understanding of shop steward organizations might enhance their effectiveness, as opposed to how far it would facilitate management countermeasures. Some of the issues in this debate are reflected in the criticisms John Goldthorpe leveled at the research agenda with which Hugh Clegg launched the Warwick IRRU (Goldthorpe 1974; Brown 1990).

Given the inherent sensitivity of bargaining relationships to research scrutiny, it is perhaps surprising that any such research is possible at all. But, in practice, the representatives of the competing interests have allowed researchers access to study a remarkably wide range of aspects of employment-related power relationships. This may sometimes have been because they considered the issues to be uncontroversial (e.g., the impact of some legal changes) or the findings likely to be remote (e.g., retrospective studies of disputes) or because they welcomed independent evaluation (e.g., the introduction of employee directors). But there is always a risk of unwelcome side effects for the interested parties, and it was partly to deal with this problem that the five guidelines described earlier were developed for the IRRU's commissioned research.

The guidelines had two other functions. One was to protect the academic quality and independence of the research and the right to publish the results. No less important was the need to protect researchers from inadvertently polluting each other's data sources. Anyone who has negotiated research access is aware that the chances of success are heavily influenced not only by one's own reputation and that of one's own institution but by the experiences of those with whom one is negotiating with other researchers. If a firm that has been studied feels itself to have been unfairly or clumsily treated, it will be wary of future approaches from researchers. The British Sociological Association has for many years maintained a code of professional ethics, one of the functions of which is to help researchers fulfill their implicit obligations to each other by leaving good fieldwork relations in their wake.

Perhaps the hardest lesson for social scientists to appreciate in dealing with controversial issues concerns the importance of preserving the *appearance* of objectivity. One aspect of this concerns the separation of valid research from valid polemic. Fellow social scientists will generally take a research paper on its merits, allowing its author to indulge in less rigorous debate through other channels. But politicians and the public are less discriminating.

Indeed, politicians and the public may impute political bias even if the researcher remains scrupulously aloof from popular debate. In making this point, Rothschild observed: "Home truths are often unpalatable, but that does not mean that their proponents are allowing their personal political views to influence the objectivity of their studies" (para. 11.10). As a test for such influence, Berrill and his colleagues devised their threefold distinction between bias in choice of subjects, bias in choice of evidence, and bias in presentation. In so doing, they carefully set the political views of the researcher apart from the validity of the research.

This chapter has described the fickle and sometimes clumsy way in which politicians may react to research that they perceive to be politically unhelpful. It has illustrated, with similarly uncomfortable implications for the democratic process, how social scientists may be restrained by legislators from evaluating the consequences of their legislation. It may have shown that it is possible for industrial relations researchers successfully to defend their cause against hostile political scrutiny. But it should also have made clear their need to be aware of its dangers. As a senior civil servant dryly commented after the Berrill inquiry, "The word at the top is that research inhibits policy options."

Part VI

Conclusion

Conclusion

*T*he aim of Part VI is to bring together the key points made by the contributors and to speculate on how industrial relations might develop a distinct approach to research design that would continue to distinguish it from other fields and disciplines examining the world of work.

CHAPTER EIGHTEEN

Retrospect and Prospect

Keith Whitfield and George Strauss

A cademic industrial relations is at a crossroads. There is uncertainty as to its subject matter, its conceptual makeup, its relations to other scholarly fields, and the approach its researchers are taking. This volume has been primarily concerned with the last of these issues, though there is inevitable resonance with the first three; the methods that industrial relations researchers use are linked to the subjects they investigate, the analytical concepts they employ, and the division of labor among academic fields.

As the previous chapters illustrate, industrial relations researchers are making use of an increasingly broad range of methods. Further, changes have occurred in research strategy and design, the relative importance of policy-based and theoretical research, the interaction between qualitative and quantitative methods, and the techniques used to validate research findings. The aim of this conclusion is to discuss these changes and to speculate on their significance in shaping the future direction of industrial relations research.

Changing Strategies and Methods

Many of the contributors to this volume believe that industrial relations research has changed markedly of late. This has involved, inter alia, a move away from a policy orientation to theory development, a shift from an inductive to a deductive approach to research, a greater incidence of quantitative analysis of secondary data as opposed to the collection of various forms of primary data (such as case studies), and increased interest in individual employees and employers as well in comparative international research.

In short, the nature of industrial relations research has changed markedly since the days of its pioneers. Moreover, rather than employing distinct strategies and methods, industrial relations is increasingly mirroring those of related fields of study. This is not necessarily bad, but combined with the fact that the field's conceptual apparatus is becoming less distinct, industrial relations may lose its claim to being distinct from other fields that study the world of work.

Kochan deals with this issue directly when he argues that, to be accepted as a paradigm, the field of industrial relations must show that it can conceptualize, explain, or solve some set of questions or problems better than alternative approaches. With respect to research methods, he suggests that the key issue is whether a distinct multimethod approach can evolve. The case for moving beyond the single-method approach is clear, but developing a strong multimethodological approach is fraught with severe problems. Kochan suggests that the solution lies in training industrial relations students more broadly than their counterparts in related fields, such as economics and psychology: "This places a greater methodological burden on students of industrial relations . . . but perhaps this is the price of admission to the field."

Cornfield and Kane agree. The approach used in industrial relations, they say, should be differentiated from that of other fields. Their concern, however, is with the conceptual apparatus rather than with the research methodology. It is their contention that industrial sociology and industrial relations use many of the same methods but that the former has a more distinct conceptual apparatus. They suggest that industrial relations researchers should put more effort into developing their own conceptual apparatus rather than borrowing from other fields.

Hammond and Ronfeldt argue for an alternative perspective. They focus on the development of research on labor law and bemoan that this has not moved beyond legal formalism. Consequently, much of the apparatus of the modern social sciences is ignored, including its rich battery of research methods. They argue that labor law should "build upon the interdisciplinarity of empirically based industrial relations scholarship." This, of course, requires that industrial relations has something distinctive on which to build.

The Move away from Policy-Based Research

A notable change in industrial relations has been the decreased emphasis on the policy issues that so marked early industrial relations research. To some extent this change can be seen to reflect change in academia and to some extent change in the world at large.

In academia a culture has gradually developed that values purely scholarly publication over teaching and various forms of service, publication, and consulting (even for the government). The most glaring example is the British Research Assessment Exercise, which has elevated publication in a narrow range of academic journals to prime importance in the ranking (and therefore funding) of academic research. Similar criteria are used in other parts of the academic world, including, for example, the U.S. tenure system. The consequence is that the incentives for ambitious academics are increasingly narrow. Applied, policy-based research is less highly rewarded than theoretically based research.

A related development has been the growing use by government agencies of full-time consultants rather than academics to provide the research support for policy formulation. Consultants tend to act in a much more directed fashion, closely following the guidelines laid down by the consulting organization, and are therefore typically less innovative than academic researchers. Brown explains part of the reason for this change in his chapter. He quotes a senior public official as warning that "the word at the top is that research closes policy options," thereby reducing policy makers' freedom to maneuver.

Part of the reluctance of policy formulators to fund academic research could stem from its inadequacies. Siegel argues that much industrial relations research fails to provide adequate guidance for policy formulation. He suggests that this results primarily from the adoption of dubious assumptions, the improper choice of data, and inadequate knowledge of the subject under study. He objects particularly to the abuse of quantitative methods.

In sharp contrast to the prevailing tendency to separate research from policy has been the development of participatory action research—a form of research that merges research and consultancy. Its main advantage, suggests Whyte, is that it yields "creative surprises," which jar the researcher out of conventional ways of interpreting the research world. He warns that by treating informants as passive subjects, social researchers are simply manipulating and distorting reality. Thus, good policy-based research requires that researchers minimize the distance between themselves and those they study. As Brown notes, however, this has attendant dangers.

Qualitative and Quantitative Methods

Industrial relations research has become increasingly quantitative. This has provoked a hostile response from some commentators and has occasioned a heated debate on whether the use of these techniques adds to or subtracts from the field. As noted, Siegel is skeptical of their contribution to policy formulation. Other contributors are less negative, and some suggest that qualitative and quantitative methods are often strong complements that can produce better research when used in tandem.

Whitfield argues that one of the main advantages of quantitative techniques is that they make research more formally rigorous but that, in practice, this rigor can sometimes be bought at too high a price in terms of the distortions that are consequently introduced. He outlines the main issues that quantitative researchers (and those using their work) need to address to reduce this price to an acceptable level.

Whipp suggests that, in practice, the divide between qualitative and quantitative research is less stark than some methodologists imply. Used together, qualitative and quantitative techniques can complement each other. Qualitative methods can be used to probe beyond the formal and, in particular, to expose contradictions between the official line and actual practice. Quantitative methods can be used to yield insights in areas in which such contradictions are not prevalent. Combined appropriately, they can be used to expand our knowledge beyond what can be gleaned from the use of one or the other.

A good example of an area in which qualitative and quantitative methods show considerable overlap is the analysis of employee attitudes. Traditionally this has been the domain of interviews and the qualitative researcher, but Hartley and Barling note the increasing use of attitude surveys that are susceptible to quantitative analysis. The use of these surveys has considerably expanded the scope of such research and has enabled researchers to analyze more precisely how attitudes change over time.

Improving Validity

An issue that is increasingly gaining prominence in industrial relations research is the relative validity of the conclusions reached using alternative methods. Validity is a multifaceted phenomenon, and researchers focus on different aspects of it, in part depending on their disciplinary backgrounds.

This is particularly a problem in industrial relations, which is at the meeting point of several disciplines with varying approaches to validity.

Some researchers focus on construct validity and are wary of using data that are collected for any reason other than the project in question. Others emphasize external validity and use only samples that are fully representative of the population to which their conclusions and policy recommendations relate. Still others emphasize internal validity and the need to use data (typically longitudinal) that match the causal processes of the underlying theoretical model.

The issue of validity is most directly addressed by Bruins in his contrast between laboratory and field experiments. The former yield high internal but low external validity, and the latter yield the reverse. Neither is therefore superior. Used in conjunction and with other methods, however, they can help build a more robust set of research findings. Whitfield notes that field experiments have sometimes been used to check the accuracy of differing statistical models and suggests that the judicious use of this technique can potentially promote the better use of quantitative analysis.

Validity is a fundamental issue in comparative international research. There are two key questions: first, whether the variables used to proxy the factors under investigation are accurate, and second, whether a given variable has the same significance in every country. According to Whitfield, Delbridge, and Brown, this is difficult to determine even when the researcher has the freedom to collect new information in different countries. It is even harder when a project is based on the secondary analysis of existing material.

Strauss makes similar points regarding the quantitative analysis of cross-national differences. A major problem, he suggests, is that such analysis tends to ignore key, perhaps difficult-to-quantify, variables. To obtain greater construct validity in such studies, he suggests that cross-national teams be used.

Patmore notes that researchers are often less wary of the validity of historical data than of its contemporary equivalent. For example, he suggests that "some historians treat newspapers with enormous reverence . . . ignoring the contemporary debate over the political bias in newspaper reporting." As researchers in other disciplines do, the historical researcher needs to cross-check information and be sensitive to who created a given document.

It is much easier to check the validity of quantitative than qualitative information. Thus, Friedman notes that "it is up to the individual ethnographer to convince the reader that the research was done properly, that the insights generated are accurate, and that they truly do understand the phenomenon under study. . . . We are left, then, with the individual ethnographer as the primary source of credibility."

Kitay and Callus raise similar caveats about case studies and add that it is difficult to subject their findings to rigorous external scrutiny. Even if it is possible to replicate a case study, this is often not done because of the time and effort that would be required. Whipp suggests that the qualitative researcher should respond to potential skepticism on the part of readers by "recording all the key choices and assumptions made throughout the framing of questions, data collection, and the generation of organizing ideas or frameworks."

By contrast, large-scale surveys, such as the Australian and British Workplace Industrial Relations Surveys, have a high degree of transparency. Millward, Marginson, and Callus also note that, because they are publicly available, they can be checked and replicated. They are, however, blunt instruments, and many of their variables may not be precise proxies for the underlying factors they are meant to represent. As a consequence, they could underrepresent key differences between settings and therefore have low construct validity.

Multimethod Research

The case for multimethod research is strong. The advantages of using more than one method include triangulation (it enables a question to be examined from different perspectives) and fine-tuning (using several methods improves the efficacy of other methods). There is, however, a tendency in parts of industrial relations and much of the social sciences to be more unidisciplinary and to focus on perfecting one method rather than linking it to others.

An ideal research project might start with a case study designed to raise hypotheses in an inductive manner, followed perhaps by several other case studies to reduce the chance that the original study site was completely atypical. The next step might be a survey to determine the extent to which the original hypotheses hold true. Other hypotheses derived from the literature generally might also be tested. Some hypotheses may apply to some parts of the overall population and not to others. To explain differences, further research might be appropriate utilizing either case studies or surveys or perhaps both. And so the research cycle continues.

Adler's study of high-commitment systems in the automotive assembly industry (1992) is illustrative of how original and inductive research can be linked with available theory. Adler began his research with an ethnographic study, observing and interviewing workers at NUMMI, a unionized plant jointly owned by General Motors and Toyota. Once he acquired a basic knowledge of how the NUMMI system worked, he and his colleagues then observed how the plant made a model change and the resulting high incidence of ergonomic problems (Adler, Goldoftas, and Levine 1997). This was essentially a case study. He then compared NUMMI with Georgetown, a nonunion plant wholly owned by Toyota (Adler, Goldoftas, and Levine 1995). His emphasis this time was on voice mechanisms.

Following this, Adler turned to theory. His next article sought to resolve the apparent conflict between research that shows that bureaucracy and rules reduce role stress ("enabling bureaucracy") and that finds that they stifle autonomy and creativity while fostering alienation ("coercive bureaucracy") (Adler and Borys 1996). In this article he linked his findings with a mass of earlier research and theory. He also postulated the conditions that are necessary for enabling bureaucracy to be successful. The next step (not taken yet) presumably would be to test these hypotheses in a much larger sample, perhaps using both attitude and workplace surveys. This would move him from qualitative to quantitative research. Adler is one of the relatively few industrial relations scholars who is comfortable conducting both types of research.

Back to the Future or Forward to the Past?

There is a strong possibility that, if current trends continue, industrial relations as a distinct research field will be subsumed within other disciplines related to the world of work. To avoid this, those who feel that the field and its researchers have something significant to offer need to identify what this is, distinguish it from what is offered elsewhere, develop it, and convince the research community that the product is good.

The main aim of this final section is to suggest that industrial relations can become more distinctive and well respected if it builds on two elements of its traditional approach to research. The first is its emphasis on policy, and the second is its attention to research design.

The pioneers of the field were famous for their concern with policy. They were not in the game of testing hypotheses for their own sake or of building elegant but impractical models. Their successors focus much less on policy, mainly in response to the incentives they have been given. Such incentives are powerful and cannot be easily overturned, but it is possible that the balance can be shifted back toward policy. It is likely that many editors and members of editorial boards of journals bearing the words "industrial relations" in their titles will read this. Our main question for them is: To what extent does your journal either encourage or discourage the sort of policy-based study that typified the research that originally made our field distinctive and well respected? A subsidiary question might be: Do you believe you do enough/anything to help encourage this tradition?

One of the hallmarks of this volume is the attention its authors pay to the design of their research projects/programs. We believe that this is typical of researchers in industrial relations. Great care is typically taken to avoid the superficiality most of us perceive in related areas of research (and unfortunately sometimes in our own). This tradition can be built upon. In particular, an explicit attempt can be made to get away from the single-method and single-validity approach that is becoming more common in some areas of scholarly activity. The need to triangulate and sharpen research tools by calibration and the use of a mixture of methods should be emphasized. The key lies in the training of postgraduate students. Programs currently offering advanced training in industrial relations should emphasize research design and break away from conventional subdivisions (quantitative/qualitative, case study/survey, and so on). The starting point must be the research process itself, however. Research design should not be something that is relegated to a footnote or an appendix but should be up front in the text. Once again, journal editors take note.

We accept that the tide engulfing industrial relations is strong, and we have no intention of being latter-day research method Canutes. But we feel that allied to changes in conceptual tools, a broadening of scope, and possibly a modification of the field's title, the development of a distinctive and powerful approach to research design can contribute to a renaissance in a field that has had a large impact on the research and policy process over the years but has recently fallen on lean times.

References

Acker, Joan. 1989. *Doing Comparable Worth: Gender, Class, and Pay Equity.* Philadelphia: Temple University Press.

———. 1990. "Hierarchies, Jobs, Bodies: A Theory of Gendered Organizations." *Gender and Society* 4 (June): 139–58.

Adams, Roy J., and Noah Meltz. 1993. *Industrial Relations Theory: Its Nature, Scope, and Pedagogy.* Metuchen, N.J.: Scarecrow Press.

Adler, Paul. 1992. "The 'Learning Bureaucracy': New United Motor Manufacturing, Inc." *Research in Organizational Behavior* 15: 111–94.

Adler, Paul, and Bryan Borys. 1996. "Two Kinds of Bureaucracy: Enabling and Coercive." *Administrative Science Quarterly* 41: 61-89.

Adler, Paul, Barbara Goldoftas, and David I. Levine. 1995. "Voice in Union and Nonunion High-Performance Workplaces." Paper given at the Annual Meeting of the Industrial Relations Research Association, January.

———. 1997. "Ergonomics, Employee Involvement, and the Toyota Production System: A Case Study of NUMMI's 1993 Model Introduction." *Industrial and Labor Relations Review* 50: 416-37.

Agar, Michael H. 1986. *Speaking of Ethnography.* Beverly Hills, Calif.: Sage.

Argyris, Chris. 1972. *The Applicability of Organizational Sociology.* London: Cambridge University Press.

Arthur, Jeffrey. 1992. "The Link between Business Strategy and Industrial Relations Systems in American Steel Minimills." *Industrial and Labor Relations Review* 45: 488–506.

Arvey, Richard, Gary Carter, and Deborah Buerkley. 1991. "Job Satisfaction: Dispositional and Situational Determinants." In *International Review of Industrial and Organizational Psychology,* vol. 6, edited by Cary L. Cooper and Ivan T. Robertson. Chichester: Wiley.

Asch, Solomon. 1946. "Forming Impressions of Personalities." *Journal of Abnormal and Social Psychology* 41: 258–90.

Bacharach, Samuel, Peter Bamberger, and Sharon Conley. 1990. "Professionals and Workplace Control: Organizational and Demographic Models of Teacher Militancy." *Industrial and Labor Relations Review* 43: 570–86.

Bain, George S., and Faroukh Elsheikh. 1976. *Union Growth and the Business Cycle.* Oxford: Basil Blackwell.

——. 1979. "An Inter-Industry Analysis of Unionisation in Britain." *British Journal of Industrial Relations* 17: 137–57.

Bamber, Greg S., and Russell Lansbury. 1993. *International and Comparative Industrial Relations.* 2d ed. London: Allen & Unwin.

Barbash, Jack. 1984. *The Elements of Industrial Relations.* Madison: University of Wisconsin Press.

Barker, Kathleen. 1995. "Contingent Work: Research Issues and the Lens of Moral Exclusion." In *Changing Employment Relations: Behavioral and Social Perspectives,* edited by Lois Tetrick and Julian Barling.Washington, D.C.: American Psychological Association.

Barling, Julian. 1979. "Verbal Proficiency: A Confounding Variable in the Reliability of Children's Attitude Scales?" *Child Development* 50: 1254–56.

——. 1988. "IRRA 'Blind Spot' in the Teaching, Research and Practice of Industrial/ Organizational Psychology." *Canadian Psychology* 29: 103–8.

Barling, Julian, Clive Fullagar, and Kevin Kelloway. 1992. *The Union and Its Members: A Psychological Approach.* New York: Oxford University Press.

Barling Julian, and Daniel Gallagher. 1996. "Part-Time Employment." In *International Review of Industrial and Organizational Psychology,* vol. 11, edited by Cary L. Cooper and Ivan T. Robertson. Chichester: Wiley.

Barling, Julian, E. Kevin Kelloway, and Eric H. Bremermann. 1991. "Pre-employment Predictors of Union Attitudes: The Role of Family Socialization and Work Beliefs." *Journal of Applied Psychology* 76: 725-31.

Baron, James N., Brian S. Mittman, and Andrew E. Newman. 1991. "Targets of Opportunity: Organizational and Environmental Determinants of Gender Integration within the California Civil Service, 1979–1985." *American Journal of Sociology* 96: 1362–1401.

Batstone, Eric, Ian Boraston, and Stephen Frenkel. 1977. *Shop Stewards in Action.* Oxford: Basil Blackwell.

——. 1978. *The Social Organization of Strikes.* Oxford: Basil Blackwell

Batstone, Eric, Anthony Ferner, and Michael Terry. 1983. *Unions on the Board: An Experiment in Industrial Democracy.* Oxford: Basil Blackwell.

Bean, Ron. 1994. *Comparative Industrial Relations: An Introduction to a Cross-National Perspective.* 2d ed. London: Croom Helm.

Beardon, William O., Richard Netemeyer, and Mary Mobley. 1993. *Handbook on Marketing Scales.* Newbury Park, Calif.: Sage.

Bélanger, Jacques, P. K. Edwards, and Larry Haiven, eds. 1994. *Workplace Industrial Relations and the Global Challenge.* Ithaca, N.Y.: ILR Press.

Bemmels, Brian. 1991. "Attribution Theory and Discipline Arbitration." *Industrial and Labor Relations Review* 44: 548–62.

Bennett, Laura. 1994. *Making Labor Law in Australia: Industrial Relations, Politics, and Law.* Sydney: Law Book Co.

——. 1995. "Rethinking Labor Law: Methodological Issues." In *Redefining Labor Law: New Perspectives on the Future of Teaching and Research,* edited by Richard Mitchell. Occasional Monograph Series no.3. Melbourne: Centre for Employment and Labor Relations Law.

Berggren, Christian. 1992. *Alternatives to Lean Production.* Ithaca, N.Y.: ILR Press.

Berrill, Kenneth. 1983. *The Berrill Report: Report of an Investigation into Certain Matters Arising from the Rothschild Report on the Social Science Research Council.* London: Social Science Research Council.

Beynon, Huw. 1984. *Working for Ford.* Harmondsworth: Penguin

Biggart, Nicole, and Richard P. Castonias. 1996. "Collateralized Social Relations, Social Calculus, and Economic Organisation." University of California, Davis. Typescript.

Bills, David, ed. 1995. *The New Modern Times: Factors Reshaping the World of Work.* Albany: State University of New York Press.

Birmingham, Judy, Ian Jack, and Dennis Jeans. 1983. *Industrial Archaeology in Australia.* Richmond, Victoria: Heinemann.

Blanchflower, David G., and Richard B. Freeman. 1992. "Going Different Ways: Unionism in the U.S. and Other Advanced OECD Countries." *Industrial Relations* 31: 56–79.

Bluen, Steve, and Julian Barling. 1988. "Psychological Stressors Associated with Industrial Relations." In. *Causes, Coping, and Consequences of Stress at Work,* edited by Cary L. Cooper and Roy Payne. Chichester: Wiley:

Boal, William M. 1990. "Unionism and Productivity in West Virginia Coal Mining." *Industrial and Labor Relations Review* 43: 390–405.

Bogdan, Robert, and Steven Taylor. 1975. *Introduction to Quantitative Research Methods: A Phenomenological Approach to the Social Sciences.* London: Sage.

Bramble, Tom. 1988. "The Flexibility Debate: Industrial Relations and New Management Production Practices." *Labour and Industry* 1: 187–209.

Bray, Mark, and Pat Walsh. 1993. "Unions and Economic Restructuring in Australia and New Zealand." In *Economic Restructuring and Industrial Relations in Australia and New Zealand,* edited by Mark Bray and Nigel Haworth. ACIRRT Monograph no. 8. Sydney: University of Sydney.

Bresnen, Michael. 1996. "An Organizational Perspective on Changing Buyer-Supplier Relations: A Critical Review of the Evidence." *Organization* 3: 121–46.

Brewster, Chris, and Ariane Hegewisch. 1994. *Policy and Practice of European Human Resource Management.* London: Routledge.

Brewster, Chris, et al. 1996. "Comparative Research in Human Resources Management: A Review and an Example." *International Journal of Human Resource Management* 7: 585–604.

Bridges, William, and Wayne Villemez. 1994. *The Employment Relationship: Causes and Consequences of Modern Personnel Administration.* New York: Plenum Press.

Brody, David. 1980. "Labor History in the 1980s: Toward a History of the American Worker." In *The Past before Us: Contemporary Historical Writing in the United States,* edited by Michael Kammen. Ithaca, N.Y.: Cornell University Press.

Brook, Penelope. 1990. *Freedom at Work: The Case for Reforming Labor Law in New Zealand.* Auckland: Oxford University Press.

Brown, Clair, ed. 1996. *The Competitive Semiconductor Manufacturing Human Resources Project: Second Interim Report.* CSM-32. Berkeley: Institute of Industrial Relations, University of California.

Brown, Henry Phelps. 1977. *The Inequality of Pay.* Oxford: Oxford University Press.

———. 1983. *The Origins of Trade Union Power.* Oxford: Clarendon Press.

Brown, William A. 1990. "Class and Industrial Relations: Sociological Bricks without Institutional Straw." In *John H. Goldthorpe: Consensus and Controversy,* edited by Jon Clark, Celia Modgil, and Solan Modgil. London: Falmer Press.

Brown, William A., and Bob A. Hepple. 1985. "The Monitoring of Labour Legislation." In *Industrial Relations and the Law in the 1980s*, edited by Patricia Fosh and Craig G. Littler. Aldershot: Gower.

Brown, William A., Paul Marginson, and Janet Walsh. 1995. "Management: Pay Determination and Collective Bargaining." In *Industrial Relations: Theory and Practice in Britain*, edited by Paul K Edwards. Cambridge, Mass.: Blackwell Business.

Brown, William A., and Martyn Wright. 1994. "The Empirical Tradition in Workplace Bargaining Research." *British Journal of Industrial Relations* 32: 154–64.

Brown, William A., et al. 1980. "Occupational Wage Structures under Different Wage-Fixing Systems." *British Journal of Industrial Relations* 18: 217–30.

Brüderl, Josef, Peter Preisendörfer, and Rolf Ziegler 1993. "Upward Mobility in Organizations: The Effects of Hierarchy and Opportunity Structure." *European Sociological Review* 9 (Sept.): 173-88.

Bruno, Michael, and Jeffrey Sachs. 1985. *Economics of Worldwide Stagnation*. Oxford: Basil Blackwell.

Bryman, Alan. 1988. *Quantity and Quality in Social Research*. London: Unwin Hyman.

——, ed. 1988. *Doing Research in Organizations*. London: Routledge.

Bryman, Alan, and Duncan Cramer. 1990. *Quantitative Data Analysis for Social Scientists*. London: Routledge.

Buchele, Robert. 1983. "Economic Dualism and Employment Stability." *Industrial Relations* 22: 410-18.

Burawoy, Michael. 1979. *Manufacturing Consent*. Chicago: University of Chicago Press.

——. 1985. *The Politics of Production*. London: Verso.

Burawoy, Michael, and Janos Lukacs. 1985. "Mythologies of Work." *American Sociological Review* 50: 723–37.

Burke, Warner, Celeste Coruzzi, and Allan Church. 1996. "The Organizational Survey as Intervention for Change." In *Organizational Surveys: Tools for Assessment and Change*, edited by Allen Kraut. San Francisco: Jossey Bass.

Burling, Temple, Edith Lenz, and Robert Wilson. 1956. *The Give and Take in Hospitals: A Study of Human Organization in Hospitals*. New York: Putnam.

Callus, Ron, et al. 1991. *Industrial Relations at Work: The Australian Workplace Industrial Relations Survey*. Canberra: Australian Government Publishing Service.

Calmfors, Lars, and John Drifill. 1988. "Bargaining Structure, Corporatism and Macroeconomic Performance." *Economic Policy* 3: 13–61.

Cameron, David R. 1984. "Social Democracy, Corporatism, Labour Quiescence, and the Representation of Economic Interest in Advanced Capitalist Society." In *Order and Conflict in Contemporary Capitalism*, edited by John H. Goldthorpe. New York: Oxford University Press.

Campbell, Karen. 1988. "Gender Differences in Job-Related Networks." *Work and Occupations* 15: 179–200.

Cappelli, Peter. 1985a. "Competitive Pressures and Labor Relations in the Airline Industry." *Industrial Relations* 24: 316–38.

——. 1985b. "Theory Construction in IR and Some Implications for Research." *Industrial Relations* 24: 90–112.

Carey, Alex. 1967. "The Hawthorne Studies: A Radical Criticism." *American Sociological Review* 32: 403–16.

Carnevale, Peter, and Patricia Keenan. 1992. "The Resolution of Conflict: Negotiation and Third Party Intervention." In *Employment Relations: The Psychology of Influ-*

ence and Control at Work, edited by Jean F. Hartley and Geoffrey M. Stephenson. Chichester: Wiley.

Cassell, Catherine, and Gillian Symon. 1994. "Qualitative Research in Work Contexts." In *Qualitative Methods in Organizational Research,* edited by Catherine Cassell and Gillian Symon. London: Sage.

Cassels, Michael. 1995. "Service with a Grimace: Using Theories of Emotions and Psychoanalysis to Shed Light on the Relationship between Bank Staff and Customers." Master's thesis, Birkbeck College, University of London.

Catano, Victor, Greg Cole, and Norman Hebert. 1995. "Can Union Commitment Be Developed? A Quasi-experimental Method." In *Changing Employment Relations: Behavioral and Social Perspectives,* edited by Lois Tetrick and Julian Barling. Washington, D.C.: American Psychological Association.

Chaison, Gary, and Joseph Rose. 1991a. "Continental Divide: The Direction and Fate of North American Unions." In *Advances in Industrial and Labor Relations 5,* edited by Donna Sockell, David Lewin, and David Lipsky. Greenwich, Conn.: JAI Press.

——. 1991b. "The Macrodeterminants of Union Growth and Decline." In *The State of the Unions,* edited by George Strauss, Daniel Gallagher, and Jack Fiorito. Madison, Wisc.: Industrial Relations Research Association.

Charles, Maria. 1992. "Cross-National Variation in Occupational Sex Segregation." *American Sociological Review* 57: 483–502.

Church, Roy, Quentin Outram, and David M. Smith. 1990. "British Coal Mining Strikes, 1893–1940: Dimensions, Distribution and Persistence." *British Journal of Industrial Relations* 28: 329–49.

Clapham Committee. 1946. *Report of the Committee on the Provision for Social and Economic Research.* Cmnd 6868. London: HMSO.

Clay, Henry. 1929. *The Problem of Industrial Relations.* London: Macmillan.

Clegg, Hugh A. 1975. "Pluralism in Industrial Relations." *British Journal of Industrial Relations.* 13: 309–16.

——. 1976. *Trade Unionism under Collective Bargaining: A Theory Based on a Comparison of Six Countries.* Oxford: Basil Blackwell.

Cobble, Dorothy S. 1991. "Organizing the Postindustrial Work Force: Lessons from the History of Waitress Unionism." *Industrial and Labor Relations Review.* 44: 419–436.

Coch, Lester, and John R. P. French, Jr. 1948. "Overcoming Resistance to Change." *Human Relations* 11: 512–32.

Cohen, Isaac. 1990. *American Management and British Labor: A Comparative Study of the Cotton Spinning Industry.* New York: Greenwood Press.

Cole, Robert E. 1979. *Work, Mobility, and Participation.* Berkeley. University of California Press.

Collier, David. 1991. "The Comparative Method: Two Decades of Change." In *Comparative Political Dynamics: Global Research Perspectives,* edited by Dankwart A. Rustow and Kenneth P. Erickson. New York: HarperCollins.

Collier, Ruth, and David Collier. 1991. *Shaping the Political Arena: Critical Junctures, the Labor Movement, and Regime Dynamics in Latin America.* Princeton, N.J.: Princeton University Press.

Collins, Hugh. 1982. "Capitalist Discipline and Corporatist Law." *Industrial Law Journal* 11: 78-91.

——. 1991. "Labor Law as Vocation." *Law Quarterly Review* 105: 468-84.

Collinson, Margaret, and David Collinson. 1996. " 'It's Only a Dick': The Sexual Harassment of Women Managers in Insurance Sales." *Work, Employment and Society* 10 (1): 29–56.

Commission on the Future of Worker Management Relations. 1994a. *Fact Finding Report.* Washington, D.C.: Departments of Commerce and Labor.

———.1994b. *Final Report and Recommendations.* Washington, D.C.: Departments of Commerce and Labor.

Commons, John. 1909. "American Shoemakers, 1648–1895." *Quarterly Journal of Economics* 24: 39–98.

Conklin, Harold. 1968. "Ethnography." In *International Encyclopedia of the Social Sciences,* vol. 5, edited by David L. Sills. New York: Free Press.

Conoghan, Janet. 1986. "The Invisibility of Women in Labor Law: Gender-Neutrality in Model-Building." *International Journal of the Sociology of Law* 14: 377-92.

Cook, John, and Toby D. Wall. 1980. "New Work, Measures of Trust, Organizational Commitment and Personal Need Fulfilment." *Journal of Occupational Psychology* 53: 39-52.

Cook, John, et al. 1981. *The Experience of Work.* London: Academic Press.

Cook, Thomas D., and Donald T. Campbell. 1979. *Quasi-experimentation: Design and Analysis Issues for Field Settings.* Boston: Houghton Mifflin.

Cooke, William N. 1985. *Union Organizing and Public Policy (Failure to Secure First Contracts).* Kalamazoo, Mich.: W. E. Upjohn Institute for Employment Research.

Cooke, William N., et al. 1995. "The Determinants of NLRB Decision-Making Revisited." *Industrial and Labor Relations Review* 48: 237–57.

Cornfield, Daniel. 1987. "Ethnic Inequality in Layoff Chances: The Impact of Unionisation on Layoff Procedure." In *Redundancy, Layoffs, and Plant Closures: Their Character, Causes, and Consequences,* edited by Raymond M. Lee. London: Croom Helm.

———. 1992. "Technological Change and Labour Relations in the United States." In *Technological Change and Labour Relations,* edited by Muneto Ozaki et al. Geneva: International Labour Office.

———. 1993. "Integrating U.S. Labor Leadership: Union Democracy and the Ascent of Ethnic and Racial Minorities and Women into National Union Offices." In *Research in the Sociology of Organizations,* vol. 12, edited by Samuel Bacharach, Ronald Seeber, and David Walsh. Greenwich, Conn.: JAI Press.

———, ed. 1987. *Workers, Managers, and Technological Change.* New York: Plenum Press.

Craig, Alton. 1990. *The System of Industrial Relations in Canada.* 3d ed. Scarborough, Ont.: Prentice Hall.

Crompton, Rosemary, and Kay Sanderson. 1990. *Gendered Jobs and Social Change.* London: Unwin Hyman.

Cully, Mark, and Paul Marginson. 1995. "The Workplace Industrial Relations Surveys: Donovan and the Burden of Continuity." Warwick Papers in Industrial Relations 55. Industrial Relations Research Unit, University of Warwick.

Curthoys, Anne. 1994. "Labour History and Cultural Studies." *Labour History* 67: 12–22.

Cutcher-Gershenfeld, Joel. 1991. "The Impact on Economic Performance of a Transformation in Workplace Practices." *Industrial and Labor Relations Review* 44: 241–60.

Dabscheck, Braham. 1989. *Australian Industrial Relations in the 1980s.* New York: Oxford University Press.

Dainton, Fred. 1981. *Report of a Joint Working Party on the Support of University Scientific Research.* Cmnd 8567. London: HMSO.

d'Alpuget, Blanche. 1977. *Mediator: A Biography of Sir Richard Kirby.* Melbourne: Melbourne University Press.

Dalton, Melville. 1959. *Men Who Manage.* New York: Wiley.

Daniel, William W. 1987. *Workplace Industrial Relations and Technical Change.* London: Francis Pinter.

Daniel, William W., and Neil Millward. 1983. *Workplace Industrial Relations in Britain: The DE/PSI/ESRC Survey.* London: Heinemann Education Books.

Dannin, Ellen J. 1995. "We Can't Overcome? A Case Study of Freedom of Contract and Labor Law Reform." *Berkeley Journal of Employment and Labor Law* 16: 1-168.

Dawson, Sandra, et al. 1988. *Safety at Work: The Limits of Self-Regulation.* Cambridge: Cambridge University Press.

Dean, Lois. 1958. "Interaction, Reported and Observed: The Case of One Local Union." *Human Organization* 18 (Fall): 36–44.

Delarbre, Raúl. 1989. "El Mundo del Trabajo en la *Revista Mexicana de Sociología:* Un Recuento: 1938–1988." *Revista Mexicana de Sociología* 51: 211–55.

Delbridge, Rick, Jim Lowe, and Nick Oliver. 1995. "The Process of Benchmarking: A Study from the Automotive Industry." *International Journal of Operations and Production Management* 15: 50–62.

Dickens, Linda. 1978. "Unfair Dismissal Applications and the Industrial Tribunal System." *Industrial Relations Journal* 9: 4-18.

Dickens, Linda, and Roy Lewis. 1981. "A Response to the Government Proposals for Industrial Relations Legislation 1981." Typescript.

Dickens, William T. 1983. "The Effect of Company Campaigns on Certification Elections: *Law and Reality* Once Again." *Industrial and Labor Relations Review* 36: 560–75.

Dilman, Don. 1978. *Mail and Telephone Surveys: The Total Design Method.* New York: Wiley-Interscience.

Domsch, Michel, and Bianka Lichtenberger. 1990. "In Search of Management Transfer: Leadership Style of West German Expatriate Managers in the People's Republic of China." *International Journal of Human Resource Management* 1: 73–86.

Dore, Ronald. 1973. *British Factory-Japanese Factory: The Origins of National Diversity in Industrial Relations.* Berkeley: University of California Press.

——. 1989. "Where Are We Now: Musings of an Evolutionist." *Work, Employment and Society* 3: 425–46.

Douglas, Ann. 1962. *Industrial Peacemaking.* New York: Columbia University Press.

Douglas, Louise, Alan Roberts, and Ruth Thompson. 1988. *Oral History. A Handbook.* Sydney: Allen and Unwin.

Dunlop, John T. 1958. *Industrial Relations Systems.* New York: Holt.

——. 1977. "Policy Decisions and Research in Economics and Industrial Relations." *Industrial and Labor Relations Review* 30: 275–82.

——. 1993. *Industrial Relations Systems.* Rev. ed. Cambridge: Harvard Business School Press.

Easterby-Smith, Mark, Richard Thorpe, and Andy Lowe. 1991. *Management Research: An Introduction.* London: Sage.

Eberstadt, Nicholas. 1995. *The Tyranny of Numbers-Measurement and Misrule.* Washington, D.C.: AEI Press.

Eckstein, Harry. 1975. "Case Study and Theory in Political Science." In *Handbook of Political Science: Strategies of Inquiry,* edited by Fred Greenstein and Nelson Polsby. Reading, Mass.: Addison-Wesley.

Edgeworth, Francis Y. 1881. *Mathematical Psychics.* London: Paul.

Edwards, Christine, and Edmund Heery. 1989. *Management Control and Union Power.* Oxford: Clarendon Press.

Edwards, P. K., Jacques Bélanger, and Larry Haiven. 1994. "Introduction: The Workplace and Labor Regulation in Comparative Perspective." In *Workplace Industrial Relations and the Global Challenge,* edited by Jacques Bélanger, P. K. Edwards, and Larry Haiven. Ithaca, N.Y.: ILR Press.

Edwards, Paul, ed. 1995. *Industrial Relations: Theory and Practice in Britain.* Cambridge, Mass.: Blackwell Business.

Edwards, Paul, and Richard Hyman. 1994. "Strikes and Industrial Conflict: Peace in Europe?" In *New Frontiers in European Industrial Relations,* edited by Richard Hyman and Anthony Ferner. Cambridge, Mass.: Blackwell Business.

Edwards, Paul, David Collinson, and Giuseppe Dell Rocca. 1995. "Workplace Resistance in Western Europe: A Preliminary Overview and Research Agenda." *European Journal of Industrial Relations* 1: 283–316.

Edwards, Paul K., and Hugh Scullion. 1982. *The Social Organization of Industrial Conflict.* Cambridge, Mass.: Blackwell Business.

Edwards, Paul K., and Colin Whitston. 1993. *Attending to Work: The Management of Attendance and Shopfloor Order.* Cambridge, Mass.: Blackwell Business.

Eisenhardt, Katherine M.. 1989. "Building Theories from Case Study Research." *Academy of Management Review* 14: 532–50.

England, Joseph W. 1979. "How UCATT Changed Its Rules: An Anatomy of Organisational Change." *British Journal of Industrial Relations* 17: 1-18.

England, Paula. 1992. *Comparable Worth: Theories and Evidence.* New York: de Gruyter.

Epstein, Richard. 1983. "A Common Law for Labor Relations: A Critique of the New Deal Labor Legislation." *Yale Law Journal* 92: 1357-408.

Evans, Stephen. 1985. "Picketing under the Employment Acts." In *Industrial Relations and the Law in the 1980s,* edited by Patricia Fosh and Craig G. Littler. Aldershot: Gower.

Fantasia, Rick. 1988. *Cultures of Solidarity: Consciousness, Action, and Contemporary American Workers.* Berkeley: University of California Press.

Farber, Henry, and Alan Krueger. 1993. "Union Membership in the United States: The Decline Continues." In *Employee Representation: Alternatives and Future Directions,* edited by Bruce Kaufman and Morris Kleiner. Madison, Wisc.: Industrial Relations Research Association.

Farkas, George, and Paula England, eds. 1988. *Industries, Firms, and Jobs: Sociological and Economic Approaches.* New York: Plenum.

Faucheux, C., and Jacques Rojot. 1979. "Social Psychology and Industrial Relations: A Cross-Cultural Perspective." In *Industrial Relations: A Social Psychological Approach,* edited by Geoffrey Stephenson and C. J. Brotherton. London: Wiley.

Ferner, Anthony, and Richard Hyman, eds. 1992. *Industrial Relations in the New Europe.* Cambridge, Mass.: Blackwell Business.

Fernie, Sue, David Metcalf, and Stephen Woodland. 1994. "Does HRM Boost Management-Employee Relations?" Working Paper no. 546, London School of Economics, Centre for Economic Performance.

Fetterman, David M. 1989. *Ethnography: Step by Step.* Newbury Park, Calif.: Sage.

Fink, Arlene. 1995. *The Survey Handbook.* Thousand Oaks, Calif.: Sage.

Flanders, Allan. 1964. *The Fawley Productivity Agreements.* London: Faber and Faber.

———. 1965. "Industrial Relations: What's Wrong with the System?" In *Management and Unions,* edited by Allan Flanders. London: Faber and Faber.

Flanders, Allan, and Hugh Clegg. 1954. *The System of Industrial Relations: Its History, Law, and Institutions.* London: Faber and Faber.

Florence, P. Sargant. 1924. *Economics of Fatigue and Unrest.* London: Allen and Unwin.

Forbath, William E. 1991. *Law and the Shaping of the American Labor Movement.* Cambridge: Harvard University Press.

Franke, Richard H., and James D. Kaul. 1978. "The Hawthorne Experiments: First Statistical Interpretation." *American Sociological Review* 43: 623–43.

Freeman, Richard B. 1994. *Working under Different Rules.* New York: Russell Sage Foundation.

Freeman, Richard B., and James L. Medoff. 1984. *What Do Unions Do?* New York: Basic Books.

Freeman, Richard B., and Joel Rogers. 1994–95. "Worker Representation and Participants Survey." Typescript.

French, John R. P., Jr., Joachim Israel, and Dagfinn Ås. 1960. "An Experiment in Participation in a Norwegian Factory." *Human Relations* 13: 3–19.

French, Wendell, and Cecil Bell. 1990. *Organization Development: Behavioral Science Interventions for Organization Improvement.* 4th ed. Englewood Cliffs, N.J.: Prentice Hall.

Frenkel, Stephen. 1994. "Patterns of Workplace Relations in the Global Corporation: Toward Convergence?" in *Workplace Industrial Relations and the Global Challenge,* edited by Jacques Bélanger, P. K. Edwards, and Larry Haiven. Ithaca, N.Y.: ILR Press.

Frenkel, Stephen, and Alice Coolican. 1985. *Unions against Capitalism?: A Sociological Comparison of the Australian Building and Metal Workers Union.* New York: Routledge.

Frenkel, Stephen, and Jeffrey Harrod, eds. 1995. *Industrialization and Labor Relations: Contemporary Research in Seven Countries.* Ithaca, N.Y.: ILR Press.

Friedman, Jonathan. 1996. "Post-modernism." In *The Social Science Encyclopaedia,* 2d ed., edited by Adam Kuper and Jessica Kuper. London: Routledge.

Friedman, Ray. 1994. *Front Stage, Backstage: The Dramatic Structure of Labor Negotiations.* Cambridge: MIT Press.

Fullagar, Clive, and Julian Barling. 1989. "A Longitudinal Test of a Model of the Antecedents and Consequences of Union Loyalty." *Journal of Applied Psychology* 74: 213–27.

———. 1991. "Predictors and Outcomes of Different Patterns of Organizational and Union Loyalty." *Journal of Occupational Psychology* 64: 129–43.

Fullagar, Clive, Don McCoy, and Carla Shull. 1992. "The Socialization of Union Loyalty." *Journal of Organizational Behavior* 13: 13–26.

Gahan, Peter, and Richard Mitchell. 1995. "The Limits of Labor Law and the Necessity of Interdisciplinary Analysis." In *Redefining Labor Law: New Perspectives on the Future of Teaching and Research,* edited by Richard Mitchell. Occasional Monograph Series no. 3. Melbourne: Centre for Employment and Labor Relations Law.

Gallie, Duncan. 1978. *In Search of the New Working Class.* Cambridge: Cambridge University Press.

———. 1983. *Social Inequality and Class Radicalism in France and Britain.* Cambridge: Cambridge University Press.

Garfinkel, Harold. 1967. *Studies in Ethnomethodology.* Englewood Cliffs, N.J.: Prentice Hall.

Gavin, James F. 1984. "Survey Feedback: The Perspectives of Science and Practice." *Group and Organization Studies* 9 (March): 29-70.

Gerhart, Paul. 1995. "Employee Privacy Rights: A Comparative Overview." *Comparative Labor Law Journal* 17: 1-12.

Getman, Julius G., and Stephen B. Goldberg. 1986. "The Behavioral Assumptions Underlying NLRB Regulation of Campaign Misrepresentations:An Empirical Evaluation." *Stanford Law Review* 28: 263-84.

Getman, Julius G., Stephen B. Goldberg, and Jeanne B. Herman. 1976. *Union Representation Elections: Law and Reality.* New York: Russell Sage Foundation.

Glaser, Barney G., and Anselm L. Strauss. 1967. *The Discovery of Grounded Theory.* New York: Aldine.

Glass, Gene V., Barry McGaw, and Mary Lee Smith. 1981. *Meta-analysis in Social Research.* Beverly Hills, Calif.: Sage.

Godard, John. 1993. "Theory and Method in Industrial Relations: Modernist and Postmodernist Alternatives." In *Industrial Relations Theory: Its Nature, Scope, and Pedagogy,* edited by Roy Adams and Noah Meltz. Metchuen, N.Y.: IMLR/Rutgers University and Scarecrow Press.

Golden-Biddle, Karen, and Karen Locke. 1993. "Appealing Work: An Investigation of How Ethnographic Texts Convince." *Organization Science* 4: 595-616.

Goldthorpe, John H. 1974. "Industrial Relations in Britain: A Critique of Reformism." *Politics and Society* 4: 419-52.

Goldthorpe, John H., et al.1968. *The Affluent Worker: Industrial Attitudes and Behaviour.* Cambridge: Cambridge University Press

Golembiewski, Robert, Keith Billingsley, and Samuel Yeager. 1976. "Measuring Change and Persistence in Human Affairs." *Journal of Applied Behavioural Science* 12: 133-57.

Gordon, Michael E., et al. 1980. "Commitment to the Union: Development of a Measure and an Examination of Its Correlates." *Journal of Applied Psychology* 65: 479-99.

Gospel, Howard. 1992. *Markets, Firms, and the Management of Labour in Modern Britain.* Cambridge: Cambridge University Press.

Gospel, Howard, and Craig Littler, eds. 1983. *Managerial Strategies and Industrial Relations.* London: Heinemann.

Gottesman, Michael H. 1991. "Whither Goest Labor Law: Law and Economics in the Workplace." *Yale Law Journal* 100: 2747.

Gouldner, Alvin. 1954a. *Patterns of Industrial Bureaucracy.* New York: Free Press.

——. 1954b. *Wildcat Strike.* New York: Harper.

Graham, Laurie. 1995. *On the Line at Subaru-Isuzu: The Japanese Model and the American Worker.* Ithaca, N.Y.: ILR Press.

Green, Francis. 1990. "Sex Discrimination in Job-Related Training." *British Journal of Industrial Relations* 29: 295-304.

Greenberg, Jerald. 1990. "Organizational Justice : Yesterday, Today, and Tomorrow." *Journal of Management* 16: 399-422.

Greenwood, Davydd, William F. Whyte, and Ira Harkavy. 1993. "Participatory Action Research as a Process and a Goal." *Human Relations* 46: 175-92.

Greenwood, Davydd, et al. 1991. *Estudio Antropologico de las Culturas de Fagor.* San Sebastián, Spain: Editorial Txertoa.

———. 1992. *Industrial Democracy in the Fagor Cooperative Group of Mondragón: Social Research for Social Action.* Assen/Maastrich, Netherlands: Van Gorcum.

Griffin, Mark, Paul Tesluk, and Rick Jacobs. 1995. "Bargaining Cycles and Work-Related Attitudes: Evidence of Threat-Rigidity Effects." *Academy of Management Journal* 38: 1709–25.

Gullahorn, John, and George Strauss. 1954. "The Field Worker in Union Research." *Human Organization* 13 (3): 28–32.

Gutman, Herbert. 1977. *Work , Culture, and Society in Industrializing America.* New York: Vintage.

Hackman, Richard, and Greg Oldham. 1976. "Motivation through the Design of Work: Test of a Theory." *Organizational Behavior and Human Performance* 16: 250–79.

Haire, Mason. 1955. "Role-Perceptions in Labor-Management Relations: An Experimental Approach." *Industrial and Labor Relations Review* 8: 144–57.

Hakim, Catherine. 1987. *Research Design.* London: Allen & Unwin.

———. 1992. "Explaining Trends in Occupational Segregation: The Measurement, Causes, and Consequences of the Sexual Division of Labor." *European Sociological Review* 8 (Sept.): 127–52.

Hammersley, Martyn. 1992. *What's Wrong with Ethnography?* London: Routledge.

Hammersley, Martyn, and Paul Atkinson. 1995. *Ethnography: Principles in Practice.* 2d ed. London: Routledge.

Hammond, Suzanne, and Raymond Harbridge. 1993. "The Impact of the Employment Contracts Act on Women at Work." *New Zealand Journal of Industrial Relations* 18: 15-30.

Hartley, Jean F. 1992. "The Psychology of Industrial Relations." In *International Review of Industrial and Organizational Psychology,* vol. 7, edited by Cary L. Cooper and Ivan T. Robertson. Chichester: Wiley.

———. 1994. "Case Studies in Organizational Research." In *Qualitative Methods in Organizational Research,* edited by Catherine Cassell and Gillian Symon. London: Sage.

———. 1995. "Challenge and Change in Employment Relations: Issues for Psychology, Trade Unions, and Managers." In *Changing Employment Relationships: An International Perspective,* edited by Julian Barling and Lois Tetrick. Washington, D.C.: American Psychological Association.

———. 1996. "The 'New' Service Sector: Employment Status, Ideology, and Trade Union Participation in the United Kingdom." In *Trade Unions: The Lost Perspective?* edited by Paul Pasture, J. Verbeckmoes, and H. de Witte. Aldershot: Avebury.

Hartley, Jean F., and John E. Kelly. 1986. "Psychology and IR: From Conflict to Cooperation?" *Journal of Occupational Psychology* 59: 161–76.

Hartley, Jean F., John E. Kelly, and Nigel Nicholson. 1983. *Steel Strike.* London: Batsford.

Hartley, Jean F., and Geoffrey Stephenson. 1992. *Employment Relations: The Psychology of Influence and Control at Work.* Oxford: Basil Blackwell.

Hartley, Jean F., et al. 1991. *Job Insecurity: Coping with Jobs at Risk.* London: Sage.

Hartnett, Donald L., and Lawrence L. Cummings. 1980. *Bargaining Behavior: An International Study.* Houston: Dame.

Hassard, John. 1993. *Sociology and Organization Theory: Positivism, Paradigms, and Postmodernity.* Cambridge: Cambridge University Press.

Hepple, Bob A., and William A. Brown. 1981. "Tasks for Labor Law Research." *Legal Studies* 1: 56.

Heyworth Committee. 1965. *Report of the Committee on Social Studies.* Cmnd 2660. London: HMSO.

Hibbs, Douglas A., Jr. 1976. "Industrial Conflict in Advanced Industrial Societies." *American Political Science Review* 70: 1033–58.

Higgs, Catherine, and Steven Ashworth. 1996. "Organizational Surveys—Tools for Assessment and Research." In *Organizational Surveys: Tools for Assessment and Change,* edited by Allen Kraut. San Francisco: Jossey Bass.

Hochschild, Arlie R. 1983. *The Managed Heart: Commercialization of Human Feeling.* Berkeley: University of California Press.

Hodson, Randy. 1995a. "The Worker as Active Subject: Enlivening the 'New' Sociology of Work." In *The New Modern Times: Factors Reshaping the World of Work,* edited by David Bills. Albany: State University of New York Press.

———. 1995b. "Worker Resistance: An Underdeveloped Concept in the Sociology of Work." *Economic and Industrial Democracy* 16 (Feb.): 79–110.

Hodson, Randy, et al. 1993. "Is Worker Solidarity Undermined by Autonomy and Participation? Patterns from the Ethnographic Literature." *American Sociological Review* 58: 398–416.

Hofstede, Gert. 1980. *Culture's Consequences.* Beverly Hills, Calif.: Sage.

Hofstede, Gert, and Michael Bond. 1988. "Confucius and Economic Growth: New Insights into Culture's Consequences." *Organizational Dynamics* 16: 4–21.

Holden, Len. 1991. "European Trends in Training and Development." *International Journal of Human Resource Management* 2: 113–32.

Horne, Julia. 1988. "The Camera Never Lies, Or Does It?: Interpreting Photographs." In *Locating Australia's Past. A Practical Guide to Writing Local History,* 2d ed., edited by the Local History Co-ordination Project. Kensington: New South Wales University Press.

House, Robert, Scott Shane, and David Herold. 1996. "Rumors of the Death of Dispositional Research Are Vastly Exaggerated." *Academy of Management Review* 21: 203–24.

Hughes, Everett C. 1952. "The Sociological Study of Work: An Editorial." *American Journal of Sociology* 57: 423–27.

Hunter, John E., and Hannah Hirsch. 1987. "Applications of Meta-analysis." In *International Review of Industrial and Organizational Psychology,* edited by Cary L. Cooper and Ivan T. Robertson. Chichester: Wiley.

Hunter, John E., Frank L. Schmidt, and Gregg B. Jackson. 1982. *Meta-analysis: Cumulating Research Findings across Studies.* Beverley Hills, Calif.: Sage.

Huselid, Mark A. 1995. "The Impact of Human Resource Management Practices on Turnover, Productivity, and Corporate Financial Performance." *Academy of Management Journal* 38: 635–72.

Hyman, Richard. 1975. *Industrial Relations: A Marxist Introduction.* London: Macmillan.

———. 1995. "Industrial Relations in Europe: Theory and Practice." *European Journal of Industrial Relations* 1(March): 17–41.

———. 1996. "Industrial Relations." In *The Social Science Encyclopaedia,* 2d ed., edited by Adam Kuper and Jessica Kuper. London: Routledge.

Hyman, Richard, Robert Price, and Michael A. Terry. 1988. *Reshaping the NUR: The Warwick Report.* London: National Union of Railwaymen.

Ichniowski, Casey, et al. 1996. "What Works at Work: An Overview and Assessment." *Industrial Relations* 35: 299–332.

Iffaldano, Michelle T., and Paul M. Muchinsky. 1985. "Job Satisfaction and Job Performance: A Meta-analysis." *Psychological Bulletin* 97: 251–73.

Industrial Democracy in Europe. 1981. *Industrial Democracy in Europe.* Oxford: Oxford University Press.

———. 1993. *Industrial Democracy in Europe Revisited.* Oxford: Oxford University Press.

Jacobs, Jerry. 1989. "Long-Term Trends in Occupational Segregation by Sex." *American Journal of Sociology* 95: 160-73.

Jacoby, Sanford M. 1990. "The New Institutionalism: What Can It Learn from the Old?" *Industrial Relations* 29: 316–40.

———. 1991. "Masters to Managers: An Introduction." In *Masters to Managers: Historical and Comparative Perspectives on American Employers,* edited by Sanford M. Jacoby. New York: Columbia University Press.

Jacofsky, Ellen F., and John L. Slocum. 1990. "Rejoinder to Payne's Comment on 'A Longitudinal Study of Climates.' " *Journal of Organizational Behavior* 11: 81–83.

Jarausch, Konard H., and Kenneth A. Hardy. 1991. *Quantitative Methods for Historians. A Guide to Research, Data, and Statistics.* Chapel Hill: University of North Carolina Press.

Jarrell, Stephen B., and T. D. Stanley. 1990. "A Meta-analysis of the Union-Nonunion Wage Gap." *Industrial and Labor Relations Review* 44: 54–67.

Jick, Todd. 1979. "Mixing Qualitative and Quantitative Methods: Triangulation in Action." *Administrative Science Quarterly* 24: 602–11.

Johnson, Gerry. 1987. *Strategic Change and the Management Process.* Oxford: Basil Blackwell.

Johnson, Jeffrey. 1990. *Selecting Ethnographic Informants.* Newbury Park, Calif.: Sage.

Johnson, Nancy Brown, Philip Bobko, and Linda S. Hartenian. 1992. "Union Influence on Local Union Leaders' Perceptions of Job Insecurity: An Empirical Test." *British Journal of Industrial Relations* 30: 45–60.

Johnstone, Richard, and Don McKenzie. 1995. "Empirical Research in Labor Law." In *Redefining Labor Law: New Perspectives on the Future of Teaching and Research,* edited by Richard Mitchell. Occasional Monograph Series no. 3. Melbourne: Centre for Employment and Labor Relations Law.

Jones, Michael. 1980. "CAC and Schedule 11: The Experience of Two Years." *Industrial Law Journal* 9: 28-44.

Kahn, Peggy, et al. 1983. *Picketing: Industrial Disputes, Tactics, and the Law.* London: Routledge.

Kahn-Freund, Otto. 1954. "The Legal Framework." In *The System of Industrial Relations in Great Britain: Its History, Law, and Institutions,* edited by Allan Flanders and Hugh Clegg. Oxford: Basil Blackwell.

———. 1965. *Labor Relations and the Law.* London: Stevens.

Kalleberg, Arne. 1994. "Studying Employers and Their Employees: Comparative Approaches." *Acta Sociologica* 37: 223–29.

Kalleberg, Arne, and Ivar Berg. 1987. *Work and Industry.* New York: Plenum.

Kanter, Rosabeth Moss. 1977. *Men and Women of the Corporation.* New York: HarperCollins.

Karskens, Grace. 1986. "Defiance, Defence, and Diligence: Three Views of Convicts in New South Wales Road Gangs." *Australian Journal of Historical Archaeology* 4: 17–28.

Katz, Jack. 1983. "A Theory of Qualitative Methodology: The Social System of Analytic Fieldwork." In *Contemporary Field Research: A Collection of Readings,* edited by Robert Emerson. Prospect Heights, Ill.: Waveland Press.

Kaufman, Bruce E. 1993. *The Origins and Evolution of the Field of Industrial Relations in the United States.* Ithaca, N.Y.: ILR Press.

Kealey, Gregory, and Gregory Patmore, eds. 1996. "Australia and Canada: Labour Compared." *Labour History* 71: 1–284.

Kelloway, E. Kevin. 1996. "Common Practices in Structural Equation Modeling." In *International Review of Industrial and Organizational Psychology,* vol. 2, edited by Cary L. Cooper and Ivan T. Robertson. New York: Wiley.

Kelloway, E. Kevin, and Julian Barling. 1993. "Members' Participation in Local Union Activities: Measurement, Prediction, and Replication." *Journal of Applied Psychology* 78: 262–79.

Kelloway, E. Kevin, and Laura Watts. 1994. "Preemployment Predictors of Union Attitudes: Replication and Extension." *Journal of Applied Psychology* 79: 631–34.

Kelly, Diana. 1990. "Defining the Workplace." In "Workplace Industrial Relations." ACIRRT Working Paper no. 4, University of Sydney.

Kennedy, Peter. 1992. *A Guide to Econometrics.* 3d ed. Oxford: Basil Blackwell.

Kerr, Clark.. 1983a. *The Future of Industrial Societies: Convergence or Continued Diversity?* Cambridge.: Harvard University Press

———. 1983b. ."A Perspective on Industrial Relations Research—Thirty-Six Years Later." In *Proceedings of the Thirty-Sixth Annual Winter Meeting of the Industrial Relations Research Association.* Madison, Wisc.: Industrial Relations Research Association.

Kerr, Clark, et al. 1960. *Industrialism and Modern Man.* Cambridge: Harvard University Press.

Kilbourne, Barbara, et al. 1994. "Returns to Skill, Compensating Differentials, and Gender Bias: Effects of Occupational Characteristics on the Wages of White Women and Men." *American Journal of Sociology* 100: 689–719.

Kimeldorf, Howard. 1991. "Bringing Unions Back in (or Why We Need a New Old Labor History)." *Labor History* 32: 91–103.

Kirk, Jerome, and Marc Miller. 1986. *Reliability and Validity in Qualitative Research.* Newbury Park, Calif.: Sage.

Kitay, Jim, and Russell Lansbury, eds. 1997. *Changing Employment Relations in Australia.* Melbourne: Oxford University Press

Klandermans, Bert. 1984. "Mobilisation and Participation in Trade Union Action: An Expectancy–Value Approach." *Journal of Occupational Psychology* 57: 107–20.

Klare, Karl E. 1990. "Critical Theory and Labor Relations Law." In *The Politics of Law: A Progressive Critique,* edited by David Kairys. New York: Pantheon.

Klein, Katherine, Fred Dansereau, and Rosalie Hall. 1994. "Levels Issues in Theory Development, Data Collection, and Analysis." *Academy of Management Review* 19: 195–229.

Klockars, Carl. 1974. *The Professional Fence.* London: Tavistock.

Knights, David, and Glen Morgan. 1991. "Corporate Strategy, Organizations, and Subjectivity: A Critique." *Organization Studies* 12: 251–73.

Knox, William. 1986. "Apprenticeship and De-skilling in Britain, 1850–1914." *International Review of Social History* 31: 166–84.

Kochan, Thomas A. 1976. "Theory, Policy Evaluation and Methodology in Collective Bargaining Research." In *Proceedings of the Twenty-Ninth Annual Winter Meeting of the Industrial Relations Research Association.* Madison, Wisc.: IRRA.

———. 1979. "How American Workers View Labor Unions." *Monthly Labor Review* 102: 23–31.

———. 1980. *Collective Bargaining and Industrial Relations.* Homewood, Ill.: Irwin.

———. 1993. "Teaching and Building Middle Range Industrial Relations Theory." In *Industrial Relations Theory: Its Nature, Scope, and Pedagogy,* edited by Roy J. Adams and Noah Meltz. Metuchen, N.J.: Scarecrow Press.

———. 1994. "Principles for a Post New Deal Employment Policy." In *Labor Economics and Industrial Relations,* edited by Clark Kerr and Paul D. Staudohar. Cambridge.: Harvard University Press.

———. 1996. "Launching a Renaissance in International Industrial Relations Research." *Relations Industrielles* 5: 247-67.

Kochan, Thomas A., Harry C. Katz, and Robert B. McKersie. 1994. *The Transformation of American Industrial Relations.* Ithaca, N.Y.: ILR Press. Reprint, New York: Basic Books, 1986.

Kochan, Thomas, and Michael Piore. 1990. "Proposal for Comparative Research on Industrial Relations and Human Resource Policy and Practice." MIT, unpublished manuscript.

Kolb, Deborah. 1983. *The Mediators.* Cambridge: MIT Press.

Krafcik, John. 1988. "A Methodology for Assembly Plant Performance Determination." International Motor Vehicle Program, MIT, unpublished manuscript.

Krause, Paul. 1992. *The Battle for Homestead, 1880–1892.* Pittsburgh: University of Pittsburgh Press.

Kraut, Allen. 1996. *Organizational Surveys: Tools for Assessment and Change.* San Francisco: Jossey Bass.

Kriegler, Roy. 1980. *Working for the Company: Work and Control in the Whyalla Shipyard.* Melbourne: Oxford University Press.

Kuhn, Thomas. 1970. *The Nature of Scientific Revolutions.* 2d ed. Chicago: University of Chicago Press.

Kuhnert, Karl, and Dan McCanley. 1996. "Applying Alternative Survey Methods." In *Organizational Surveys: Tools for Assessment and Change,* edited by Allen Kraut. San Francisco: Jossey Bass.

Kunda, Gideon. 1992. *Engineering Culture: Control and Commitment in a High-Tech Corporation.* Philadelphia: Temple University Press.

Kuruvilla, Sarosh, and Christopher Erickson. 1996. "Critical Junctures in the Transformation of Industrial Relations Systems: A Comparative Study of Nine Countries." In *Proceedings of the Fourth Bargaining Group Conference.* Toronto: Centre for Industrial Relations, University of Toronto.

LaLonde, Robert. 1986. "Evaluating the Econometric Evaluations of Training Programs with Experimental Data." *American Economic Review* 76: 604–20.

Lash, Scott. 1984. *The Militant Worker: Class and Radicalism in France and the U.S.* London: Heinemann.

Lawler, Edward E., Gerald Ledford, and Susan A. Mohrman. 1989. *Employee Involvement in America: A Study of Contemporary Practices.* Houston: American Productivity and Quality Center.

Lawler, Edward. E., Susan A. Mohrman, and Gerald Ledford. 1992. *Employee Involvement and TQM: Practice and Results in Fortune 5000 Companies.* San Francisco: Jossey-Bass.

Lawler, Edward J., Rebecca S. Ford, and Mary A. Blegen. 1988. "Coercive Capability in Conflict: A Test of Bilateral Deterrence Versus Conflict Spiral Theory." *Social Psychology Quarterly* 51: 93–107.

Lawrence, Paul, and Jay Lorsch. 1967. *Organization and Environment.* Cambridge.: Harvard University Press.

Leontieff, Wassily. 1982. "Academic Economics." *Science* 217: 104–7.

Levine, David, and Laura Tyson. 1990. "Participation, Productivity, and the Firm's Environment." In *Paying for Productivity,* edited by Alan Blinder. Washington, D.C.: Brookings Institution.

Lewis, Roy, Paul Davies, and Kenneth W. Wedderburn. 1979. *Industrial Relations Law and the Conservative Government.* London: Fabian Society.

Lincoln, James, and Arne Kalleberg. 1990. *Culture, Control, and Commitment: A Study of Work Organization and Work Attitudes in the United States and Japan.* Cambridge: Cambridge University Press.

Lipset, Seymour Martin. 1986. "Labor Unions in the Public Mind." In *Unions in Transition,* edited by Seymour Martin Lipset. San Francisco: ICS Press.

Lipset, Seymour Martin, Martin Trow, and James Coleman. 1956. *Union Democracy.* New York: Free Press.

Locke, Richard. 1992. "The Demise of National Unions in Italy: Lessons for Comparative Industrial Relations Theory." *Industrial and Labor Relations Review* 45: 229–49.

Locke, Richard, Thomas Kochan, and Michael Piore, eds. 1995. *Employment Relations in a Changing World Economy.* Cambridge: MIT Press.

Locke, Richard, and Kathleen Thelen. 1995. "Apples and Oranges Revisited: Contextualized Comparisons and the Study of Comparative Politics." *Politics and Society* 23: 337–67.

Lyddon, David, and Peter Smith. 1996. "Editorial: Industrial Relations and History." *Historical Studies in Industrial Relations* 1: 1–10.

Mabey, Chris, and Graeme Salaman. 1995. *Strategic Human Resource Management.* Cambridge: Blackwell Business.

MacDuffie, John Paul. 1995. "Human Resource Bundles and Manufacturing Performance: Organizational Logic and Flexible Production Systems in the World Auto Industry." *Industrial and Labor Relations Review* 48: 197–221.

MacDuffie, John Paul, and Fritz Pil. 1995. "The International Assembly Plant Study: Philosophical and Methodological Issues." In *Lean Production and Labor: Critical and Comparative Perspectives,* edited by Steve Babson. Detroit: Wayne State University Press.

Mach, Bogdan, Karl Mayer, and Michal Pohoski. 1994. "Job Changes in the Federal Republic of Germany and Poland: A Longitudinal Assessment of the Impact of Welfare-Capitalist and State-Socialist Labour Market Segmentation." *European Sociological Review* 10 (May): 1–28.

Macintyre, Stuart, and Richard Mitchell, eds. 1989. *Foundations of Arbitration: The Origins and Effects of State Compulsory Arbitration, 1890–1914.* Melbourne: Oxford University Press.

Maddala, G. S. 1983. *Limited-Dependent and Qualitative Variables in Econometrics.* Cambridge: Cambridge University Press.

———. 1988. *Introduction to Econometrics.* London: Collier Macmillan.

Manning, Alan. 1987. "An Integration of Trade Union Models in a Sequential Bargaining Framework." *Economic Journal* 97: 121–39.

Marginson, Paul, et al. 1988. *Beyond the Workplace: Managing Industrial Relations in the Multi-establishment Enterprise.* Oxford: Basil Blackwell.

Marini, Margaret Mooney. 1989. "Sex Differences in Earnings in the United States." In *Annual Review of Sociology* 15. Palo Alto, Calif.: Annual Review of Sociology.

Markey, Raymond. 1987. "Labour History and Industrial Relations in Australia." In *Contemporary Industrial Relations in Australia and New Zealand: Literature Surveys,* edited by Kevin Hince and A. Williams. Wellington: Association of Industrial Relations Academics of Australia and New Zealand.

Marshall, Catherine, and Gretchen B. Rossman. 1989. *Designing Qualitative Research.* Newbury Park, Calif.: Sage.

Martin, Roderick M. 1969. "Tribesmen into Trade Unionists: The African Experience and the Papua-New Guinea Prospect." *Journal of Industrial Relations* 11: 125–72.

Mathews, John. 1994. *Catching the Wave.* Sydney: Allen & Unwin.

Maurice, Mark, Francois Sellier, and Jean Jacques Silvestre. 1986. *The Social Foundations of Industrial Power: A Comparison of France and Germany.* Cambridge: MIT Press.

Maynard, Rebecca A. 1994. "Methods for Evaluating Employment and Training Programs: Lessons from the USA." In *The Market for Training,* edited by Robert McNabb and Keith Whitfield. Aldershot: Avebury.

McCarthy, William. 1994a. "The Involvement of Academics in British Industrial Relations." *British Journal of Industrial Relations* 32: 201–18.

———. 1994b. "Of Hats and Cattle: Or the Limits of Macro-Survey Research in Industrial Relations." *Industrial Relations Journal* 25: 315–22.

McDaniel, Darren. 1994. "On the Edge of Academia: A Study of the University of Mississippi's Physical Plant Department and the Working-Class Men of the Mobility in Organizations: The Effects of Hierarchy and Opportunity Structure." *European Sociological Review* 9 (Sept.): 173 –88.

McLennan, Gregor. 1981. *Marxism and the Methodologies of History.* London: Verso.

McLoughlin, Ian, and Scott Gourlay. 1992. "Transformed IR? Employee Attitudes in Non-Union Firms." *Human Resource Management Journal* 2: 8–28.

McNulty, Paul J. 1980. *The Origins and Development of Labor Economics.* Cambridge: MIT Press.

Mellish, Michael, and Linda Dickens. 1972. "Recognition Problems under the Industrial Relations Act." *Industrial Law Journal* 1: 229-41.

Meltz, Noah. 1993. "Industrial Relations Systems as a Framework for Organizing Contributions to Industrial Relations Theory." In *Industrial Relations Theory: Nature, Scope, and Pedagogy,* edited by Roy J. Adams and Noah Meltz. Metuchen, N.J.: Scarecrow Press.

Merritt, John. 1982. "Labour History." In *New History: Studying Australia Today,* edited by Graeme Osborne and William F. Mandle. Sydney: Allen & Unwin.

Messick, Dave M., and Diane Mackie. 1989. "Intergroup Relations." *Annual Review of Psychology* 40: 45–81.

Meyer, John P., and Natalie J. Allen. 1987. "A Longitudinal Analysis of the Early Development and Consequences of Organizational Commitment." *Canadian Journal of Behavioral Science* 19: 199–215.

Meyer, John P., D. Ramona Bobocel, and Natalie J. Allen. 1991. "Development of Organizational Commitment during the First Year of Employment: A Longitudinal Study of Pre- and Post-Entry Influences." *Journal of Management* 17: 717–33.

Meyerson, Eva. 1994. "Human Capital, Social Capital, and Compensation: The Relative Contribution of Social Contacts to Managers' Incomes." *Acta Sociologica* 37: 383–99.

Mill, John Stuart. 1974. "Of Four Methods of Experimental Inquiry." In *A System of Logic.* Reprint, Toronto: University of Toronto Press, 1843.

Millward, Neil. 1991. "Sampling Establishments for Social Survey Research." *The Statistician* 40: 145–52.

———. 1993. "Uses of the Workplace Industrial Relations Surveys by Labour Economists."

Discussion Paper no. 145, London School of Economics, Centre for Economic Performance.

———. 1994a. *The New Industrial Relations?* London: Policy Studies Institute.

———. 1994b. *The 1984–1990 Panel in the Workplace Industrial Relations Survey Series: Some Substantive Analysis and a Methodological Assessment.* London: Policy Studies Institute.

Millward, Neil, Paul Marginson, and Ron Callus. 1996. "Mapping, Monitoring, and Theory Development: Large-Scale, National Employer-Based Surveys." Working Paper no. 813, London School of Economics, Centre for Economic Performance.

Millward, Neil, and Stephen Woodland. 1995. *The British Workplace Industrial Relations Survey Series: A Bibliography of Research Based on WIRS.* London: Policy Studies Institute.

Millward, Neil, et al. 1992. *Workplace Industrial Relations in Transition: The ED/ESRC/PSI/ACAS Surveys.* Aldershot: Dartmouth Publishing.

Minesterio de Trabajo y Seguridad Social. 1994. *Revista de Economía y Sociología del Trabajo.* Madrid.

Montgomery, David. 1991. "The Limits of Union-Centred History: Responses to Howard Kimeldorf." *Labor History* 32: 110–16.

Morris, Timothy, and Stephen Wood. 1991. "Testing the Survey Method: Continuity and Change in British Industrial Relations." *Work, Employment and Society* 5: 259–72.

Morrow, Paula. 1997. "The Measurement of TQM Principles and Work-Related Outcomes." *Journal of Organizational Behavior* 18: 363-76.

Mossman, Mary J. 1986. "Feminism and Legal Method: The Difference It Makes." *Australian Journal of Law and Society* 3: 30-46.

Mowday, Richard, Lyman Porter, and Richard Steers. 1982. *Employee-Organization Linkages: The Psychology of Commitment, Absenteeism, and Turnover.* New York: Academic Press.

Mueller, Frank. 1994. "Teams between Hierarchy and Commitment: Change Strategies and the 'Internal Environment.' " *Journal of Management Studies* 31: 383–403.

Mueller, Frank, et al. 1994. "Employee Attachment and Noncoercive Conditions of Work." *Work and Society* 21:179-212.

Mulder, Mauk, and Henk Wilke. 1970. "Participation and Power Equalization." *Organizational Behavior and Human Performance* 5: 430–48.

Mulvey, Charles. 1986a. "Alternatives to Arbitration: Overview of the Debate." In *Alternatives to Arbitration,* edited by Richard Blandy and John Niland. Sydney: Allen & Unwin.

———. 1986b. "Wage Levels: Do Unions Make a Difference?" In *Wage Fixation in Australia,* edited by John Niland. Sydney: Allen & Unwin.

Nadler, David A. 1977. *Feedback and Organization Development: Using Data-Based Methods.* Reading, Mass.: Addison-Wesley.

Nichols, Theo, and Peter Armstrong. 1976. *Workers Divided.* Glasgow: Fontana.

Nichols, Theo, and Huw Beynon. 1977. *Living with Capitalism.* London: Routledge.

Nicholson, Nigel, and Anne Rees. 1994. "The Twenty Statements Test." In *Qualitative Methods in Organization Research,* edited by Catherine Cassell and Gillian Symon. London: Sage.

Nicholson, Nigel, Gillian Ursell, and Paul Blyton. 1981. *The Dynamics of White-Collar Unionism.* London: Academic Press.

Niland, John. 1989. "Transforming Industrial Relations in New South Wales: A Green Paper." New South Wales Government Printer.

Noon, Michael. 1990. "Strategy and Circumstance: The Success of the NUJ's New Technology Policy." *British Journal of Industrial Relations* 29: 259–76.

O'Creevy, Mark F. 1995. *Striking Off the Shackles: A Survey of Managers' Attitudes to Employee Involvement.* Corby, U.K.: Institute of Management.

Oliver, Nick, Rick Delbridge, and Jim Lowe. 1996. "Lean Production Practices: International Comparisons in the Auto Components Industry." *British Journal of Management* 7: S29–S44.

Olsen, Rod, Jane Romeyn, and Michael Alexander. 1995. "Making Use of the Australian Workplace Industrial Relations Survey (AWIRS 90): A Selected Annotated Bibliography." AWIRS 95 Working Paper Series Paper no. 3, Commonwealth Department of Industrial Relations, Canberra.

Olson, Craig A., Gregory G. Dell'Omo, and Paul Jarley. 1992. "A Comparison of Interest Arbitrator Decision-Making in Experimental and Field Settings." *Industrial and Labor Relations Review* 45: 711–23.

Orum, Anthony, Joe Feagin, and Gideon Sjoberg. 1991. "Introduction: The Nature of the Case Study." In *A Case for the Case Study,* edited by Joe Feagin, Anthony Orum, and Gideon Sjoberg. Chapel Hill: University of North Carolina Press.

Osterman, Paul. 1994. "How Common Is Workplace Transformation and Who Adopts It?" *Industrial and Labor Relations Review* 47: 173–87.

Ouellet, Lawrence. 1994. *Pedal to the Metal: The Work Lives of Truckers.* Philadelphia: Temple University Press.

Owens, Rosemary J. 1993. "Women, 'Atypical' Work Relationships, and the Law." *Melbourne University Law Review* 19: 399-430.

———. 1995. "The Traditional Labor Law Framework: A Critical Evaluation." In *Redefining Labor Law: New Perspectives on the Future of Teaching and Research,* edited by Richard Mitchell. Occasional Monograph Series no. 3. Melbourne: Centre for Employment and Labor Relations Law.

Paldam, Martin, and Peder Pedersen. 1982. "The Macroeconomic Strike Model: A Study of Seventeen Countries." *Industrial and Labor Relations Review* 35: 504–21.

Patmore, Gregory. 1988. "Reflections on Oral History: Its Uses in Studying the Conflict between the Australian Railways Union and the National Union of Railwaymen." *Oral History of Australia Journal* 10: 3–8.

———. 1994a. "American Hustling Methods—The Lithgow Small Arms Factory, 1912–22." *Labour History* 67: 42–56.

———. 1994b. "Australian Labor History." *International Labor and Working-Class History* 46: 161–71.

———. 1997. "Labour-Community Coalitions and State Enterprise: Retrenchment at the Lithgow Small Arms Factory, 1918–1932." *Journal of Industrial Relations* 39: 218-43.

Patrickson, Margaret, Val Bamber, and Greg Bamber, eds. 1995. *Organisational Change Strategies: Case Studies of Human Resource and Industrial Relations Issues.* Sydney: Longman.

Payne, Roy. 1990. "Madness in Our Method: A Comment on Jacofsky and Slocum's Paper 'A Longitudinal Study of Climates.' " *Journal of Organizational Behavior* 11: 77–80.

Payne, Roy, Peter Warr, and Jean F. Hartley. 1984. "Social Class and the Experience of Unemployment." *Sociology of Health and Illness* 6: 152–74.

Penn, Roger. 1990. *Class, Power, and Technology: Skilled Workers in Britain and America.* New York: St. Martin's.

Penn, Roger, Ann Martin, and Hilda Scattergood. 1991. "Gender Relations, Technology, and Employment Change in the Contemporary Textile Industry." *Sociology* 25: 569–87.

Penn, Roger, Hilda Scattergood, and John Sewel. 1992. "Technical Change and the Division of Labour in Rochdale and Aberdeen: Evidence from the Social Change and Economic Life Initiative." *British Journal of Sociology* 43: 657–80.

Peterson, Larry. 1992. "Producing Visual Traditions among Workers: The Uses of Photography at Pullman." *International Labor and Working-Class History* 42: 40–69.

Pettigrew, Andrew. 1990. "Longitudinal Field Research on Change: Theory and Practice." *Organization Science* 1: 267–92.

Pfeffer, Jeffrey. 1992. *Managing with Power*. Boston: Harvard Business School Press.

Pickett, Charles. 1988. "Interpreting Material Culture." In *Locating Australia's Past: A Practical Guide to Writing Local History*, edited by the Local History Co-ordination Project. Kensington: New South Wales University Press.

Piore, Michael J. 1983. "Qualitative Research Techniques in Economics." In *Qualitative Methodology*, edited by John Van Maanen. Beverly Hills, Calif.: Sage.

Piore, Michael J., and Charles Sabel. 1984. *The Second Industrial Divide*. New York: Basic Books.

Platt, Jennifer. 1988. "What Can Case Studies Do?". *Studies in Qualitative Methodology* 1: 1–23.

Poole, Michael. 1986. *Industrial Relations: Origins and Patterns of National Diversity*. London: Routledge.

Portelli, Alessandro. 1981. "The Peculiarities of Oral History." *History Workshop* 12: 96–107.

Premack, Stephen, and John Hunter. 1988. "Individual Unionization Decisions." *Psychological Bulletin* 103: 223–34.

Przeworski, Adam. 1987. "Methods of Cross-National Research." In *Comparative Policy Research: Learning from Experience*, edited by Meinolf Dierkes, Hans Weiler, and Ariane Antal. Aldershot: Gower.

Przeworksi, Adam, and Henry Tuene. 1970. *The Logic of Social Inquiry*. New York: Wiley.

Purcell, John. 1983. "The Management of Industrial Relations in the Modern Corporation: Agenda for Research." *British Journal of Industrial Relations* 21: 1–16.

——. 1996. "Human Resource Bundles of Best Practice: A Utopian Cul-de-Sac?" ESRC Seminar Series on the Contribution of HR Strategy to Business Performance, Cranfield School of Management.

Quinlan, Michael, and Margaret Gardner. 1994. "Researching Industrial Relations History: The Development of a Database on Australian Trade Unions, 1825–1900." *Labour History* 66: 90–113.

Ragin, Charles. 1987. *The Comparative Method*. Berkeley: University of California Press.

Ragin, Charles, and Howard Becker, eds. 1992. *What Is a Case?* Cambridge: Cambridge University Press

Ramsay, Harvie. 1980. "Cycles of Control: Worker Participation in Sociological and Historical Perspective." In *Work and Inequality: Ideology and Control in the Capitalist Labour Process*, edited by Paul Boreham and Geoff Dow. South Melbourne: Macmillan.

Räsänen, Keijo, and Richard Whipp. 1992. "National Business Recipes: A Sector Perspective." In *European Business Systems: Firms and Markets in their National Contexts*, edited by Richard Whitley. London: Sage.

Rees, Albert. 1977. "Policy Decisions and Research in Economics and Industrial Relations: An Exchange of Views." *Industrial and Labor Relations Review* 31: 3–4.

Reskin, Barbara, and Irene Padavic. 1994. *Women and Men at Work.* Thousand Oaks, Calif.: Pine Forge Press.

Reskin, Barbara, and Patricia A. Roos. 1990. *Job Queues, Gender Queues: Explaining Women's Inroads into Male Occupations.* Philadelphia: Temple University Press.

Reynolds, Michael. 1994. "Participatory Action Research to Redesign an Introductory Physics Course." Ph.D diss., Cornell University.

Richardson, Ray. 1977. "Trade Union Growth: A Review Article." *British Journal of Industrial Relations* 15: 279–82.

Roethlisberger, Fritz J., and William J. Dickson. 1939. *Management and the Worker.* Cambridge: Harvard University Press.

Rogers, Joel, and Wolfgang Streeck, ed. 1995. *Works Councils.* Chicago: University of Chicago Press.

Rollinson, Derek. 1993. *Understanding Employee Relations.* Wokingham, U.K.: Addison-Wesley.

Rosenfeld, Rachel. 1992. "Job Mobility and Career Processes." In *Annual Review of Sociology 18.* Palo Alto, Calif.: Annual Review of Sociology.

Rosenfeld, Rachel, and Arne Kalleberg. 1990. "A Cross-National Comparison of the Gender Gap in Income." *American Journal of Sociology* 96: 69–106.

Ross, Arthur M., and Paul Hartman. 1960. *Changing Patterns of Industrial Conflict.* New York: Wiley.

Rossi, Peter, and Harold Freeman. 1982. *Evaluation: A Systematic Approach.* 2d ed. Beverley Hills, Calif.: Sage.

Rothschild, Victor. 1971. *The Organisation and Management of Government R&D.* Cmnd 4814. London: HMSO.

———. 1982. *An Enquiry into Social Science Research.* Cmnd 8554. London: HMSO.

Rousseau, Denise. 1990. "New Hire Perceptions of Their Own and Their Employer's Obligations: A Study of Psychological Contracts." *Journal of Organizational Behavior* 11: 389–400.

———. 1995. *Understanding Written and Unwritten Agreements.* Thousand Oaks, Calif.: Sage.

Rousseau, Denise, and Judi Parks. 1993. "The Contracts of Individuals and Organizations." In *Research in Organizational Behavior,* edited by Lawrence L. Cummings and Barry M. Staw. Greenwich, Conn.: JAI Press.

Roy, Donald. 1954. "Efficiency and 'the Fix': Informal Intergroup Relations in a Piecework Machine Shop." *American Journal of Sociology* 60: 255–66.

Sako, Mari, and Susan Helper. 1995. "Supplier Relations and Performance in the Auto Industry: European–Japanese-U.S. Comparisons of the Voice/Exit Choice." Paper presented at the Annual Sponsors Meeting of the International Motor Vehicle Program, Toronto.

Salaman, Graeme. 1992. *Industrial Relations: Theory and Practice.* London: Prentice Hall.

Sayles, Leonard R., and George Strauss. 1953. *The Local Union.* New York: Harper.

Schein, Edwin H. 1980. *Organizational Psychology.* Englewood Cliffs, N.J.: Prentice Hall.

Schellenberg, Kathryn. 1996. "Taking It or Leaving It: Instability and Turnover in a High-Tech Firm." *Work and Occupations* 23: 190–213.

Schneider, Robert, and Leatta Hough. 1995. "Personality and Industrial/Organizational Psychology." In *International Review of Industrial and Organizational Psychology*, vol. 10, edited by Cary L. Cooper and Ivan T. Robertson. Chichester: Wiley.

Schuck, Paul H. 1989. "Why Don't Professors Do More Empirical Research?" *Journal of Legal Education* 39: 323-36.

Schutz, Alfred. 1967. *The Phenomenology of the Social World*. Evanston, Ill.: Northwestern University Press.

Schwartzman, Helen. 1993. *Ethnography in Organizations*. Newbury Park, Calif.: Sage.

Scott, John. 1990. *A Matter of Record: Documentary Sources in Social Research*. Cambridge: Polity Press.

Semmer, Norbert, Dieter Zapf, and Siegfried Greif. 1996. "Shared Job Strain: A New Approach for Assessing the Validity of Job Stress Measurements." *Journal of Occupational and Organizational Psychology* 69: 293–310.

Shalev, Michael. 1978. "Lies, Damned Lies, and Strike Statistics." In *Resurgence of Class Conflict in Western Europe since 1968*, edited by Colin Crouch and A. Pizzorno. London: Macmillan.

———. 1983. "Strikes and the Crisis: Industrial Conflict and Unemployment in Western Nations." *Economic and Industrial Democracy* 4:417-60.

Sheridan, Tom. 1994. "Australian Wharfies 1943–1967: Casual Attitudes, Militant Leadership, and Workplace Change." *Journal of Industrial Relations* 36: 258–84.

Shields, John. 1995. "Deskilling Revisited: Continuity and Change in Craft Work and Apprenticeship in Late Nineteenth Century New South Wales." *Labour History* 68: 1–29.

Shimmin, Sylvia, and Donald Wallis. 1994. "Fifty Years of Occupational Psychology in Britain." Leicester: *British Psychological Society*.

Shorter, Edward, and Charles Tilly. 1974. *Strikes in France, 1830–1968*. Cambridge: Cambridge University Press.

Shultz, George. 1968. "Priorities in Policy and Research for Industrial Relations." In *Proceedings of the Twenty-First Annual Winter Meeting of the Industrial Relations Research Association*. Madison, Wisc.: IRRA.

Sigman, Richard S., and Nash J. Monsour. 1995. "Selecting Samples from List Frames of Businesses." In *Business Survey Methods*, edited by Brenda G. Cox et al. New York: Wiley.

Sisson, Keith. 1987. *The Management of Collective Bargaining: An International Comparison*. Oxford: Oxford University Press.

———. 1993. "In Search of HRM." *British Journal of Industrial Relations* 31: 201–10.

Sjoberg, Gideon, et al. 1991. "The Case Study Approach in Social Research: Basic Methodological Issues." In *A Case for the Case Study*, edited by Joe Feagin, Anthony Orum, and Gideon Sjoberg. Chapel Hill: University of North Carolina Press.

Skinner, Christopher. 1996. "The Use of Sampling Weights in the Regression Analysis of WIRS Data." University of Southampton, typescript.

Smart, Carol. 1989. *Feminism and the Power of Law*. London: Routledge.

Smith, Chris, John Child, and Michael Rowlinson. 1990. *Reshaping Work: The Cadbury Experience*. Cambridge: Cambridge University Press.

Smith, Patricia C., L. M. Kendall, and Charles L. Hulin. 1969. *The Measurement of Satisfaction in Work and Retirement*. Chicago: Rand McNally.

Smith, Patricia C., et al. 1986. "Guidelines for Clean Data: Detection of Common Mistakes." *Journal of Applied Psychology* 71: 457–60.

Smith, Vicki. 1990. *Managing in the Corporate Interest.* Berkeley: University of California Press.

——. 1994. "Braverman's Legacy: The Labor Process Tradition at 20." *Work and Occupations* 21: 403–21.

Sorbom, Dag, and Karl G. Joreskog. 1981. "The Use of LISREL in Sociological Model Building." In *Factor Analysis and Measurement,* edited by David J. Jackson and Edgar F. Borgatta. London: Sage.

Sorensen, Annemette, and Heike Trappe. 1995. "The Persistence of German Inequality in Earnings in the German Democratic Republic." *American Sociological Review* 60: 398–406.

Sorge, Arndt, et al. 1983. *Microelectronics and Manpower in Manufacturing Applications of Computer Numerical Control in Great Britain and West Germany.* Farnborough, U.K.: Gower.

Sorrell, Geoff H. 1979. *Law in Labor Relations: An Australian Essay.* Sydney: Law Book Co.

Sparrow, Paul. 1996. "Generic Climate Maps: A Strategic Application of Climate Survey Data?" *Journal of Organizational Behavior* 17: 679-98.

Sprent, Peter. 1989. *Applied Nonparametric Statistical Methods.* London: Chapman and Hall.

Stahlberg, Dagmar, and Dieter Frey. 1988. "Attitudes 1: Structure, Measurement, and Functions." In *Introduction to Social Psychology,* edited by Miles Hewstone et al. Oxford: Basil Blackwell.

Starbuck, William H., and John M. Mezias. 1996. "Opening Pandora's Box: Studying the Accuracy of Managers' Perceptions." *Journal of Organizational Behavior* 17: 99–117.

Stern, Robert, and Daniel Cornfield (with Theresa Liska and Dee Anne Warmath). 1996. *The U.S. Labor Movement: References and Resources.* New York: G. K. Hall.

Stewart, Mark. 1983. "Relative Earnings and Individual Union Membership in the United Kingdom." *Economica* 50: 111–25.

Stoecker, Randy. 1991. "Evaluating and Rethinking the Case Study." *Sociological Review* 39: 88–112.

Stone, Katherine Van Wezel. 1981. "The Post-War Paradigm in American Labor Law." *Yale Law Journal* 90: 1509-80.

Strauss, George. 1991. "Commentary: State Policies and Workplace Relations." In *The Future of Industrial Relations,* edited by Harry C. Katz. Ithaca, N.Y.: Cornell University Press.

Strauss, George, and Peter Feuille. 1981. "Industrial Relations Research in the United States." In *Industrial Relations in International Perspective (Essays on Research and Policy),* edited by Peter B. Doeringer. New York: Holmes and Meier.

Sutton, Robert. 1994. "The Virtues of Closet Qualitative Research." Typescript.

Sverke, Magnus. 1995. "The Importance of Ideology in Trade Union Participation in Sweden: A Social-Psychological Model." In *Trade Unions: The Lost Perspective?* edited by Paul Pasture, J. Verbeckmoes, and H. de Witte. Aldershot: Avebury.

Szafran, Robert. 1996. "The Effect of Occupational Growth on Labor Force Task Characteristics." *Work and Occupations* 23: 54–86.

Szyszczak, Erika M. 1990. *Partial Unemployment: The Regulation of Part-Time Working in Britain.* London: Mansell.

Tebbit, Norman. 1988. *Upwardly Mobile.* London: Weidenfeld and Nicholson.

Tetrick, Lois, and Julian Barling. 1995. *Changing Employment Relations: Behavioral and Social Perspectives*. Washington, D.C.: American Psychological Association.

Thompson, Paul. 1975. *The Edwardians: The Remaking of British Society*. London: Weidenfeld and Nicholson.

———. 1988. *The Voice of the Past*. 2d ed. Oxford: Oxford University Press.

Thorsrud, Einar. 1971. "Democracy at Work: Norwegian Experience with Non-bureaucratic Forms of Organization." *Journal of Applied Behavioral Science* 13: 410–21.

Tolbert, Charles, Patrick Horan, and E. M. Beck. 1980. "The Structure of Economic Segmentation." *American Journal of Sociology* 85: 1095-116.

Tolliday, Steven, and Jonathan Zeitlin, eds. 1991. *The Power to Manage: Employers and Industrial Relations in Comparative Perspective*. London: Routledge.

Tomaskovic-Devey, Donald. 1993. *Gender and Racial Inequality at Work: The Sources and Consequences of Job Segregation*. Ithaca, N.Y.: ILR Press.

Tomaskovic-Devey, Donald, Geoffrey Leiter, and Shealy Thompson. 1994. "Organizational Survey Non-Response." *Administrative Science Quarterly* 39: 439–59.

Tomlins, Christopher L. 1985. *The State and the Unions: Labor Relations, Law, and the Organized Labor Movement in America, 1880–1960*. New York: Cambridge University Press.

Tomlins, Christopher L., and Andrew J. King, eds. 1992. *Labor Law in America: Historical and Critical Essays*. Baltimore: John Hopkins University Press.

Tracy, Joseph. 1987. "An Empirical Test of an Assymetric Information Model of Strikes." *Journal of Labor Economics* 5: 143–52.

Trubeck, David. M. 1984. "Where the Action Is: Critical Legal Studies and Empiricism." *Stanford Law Review* 36: 575-622.

Turner, Herbert A. 1962. *Trade Union Growth, Structure, and Policy*. London: Allen and Unwin.

Turner, Lowell. 1991. *Democracy at Work*. Ithaca, N.Y.: Cornell University Press.

Undy, Roger, and Roderick Martin. 1984. *Ballots and Trade Union Democracy*. Oxford: Basil Blackwell.

Vallas, Steven. 1993. *Power in the Workplace*. Albany: State University of New York Press.

Van Maanen, John. 1979. "Reclaiming Qualitative Methods for Organizational Research: A Preface." *Administrative Science Quarterly* 24: 520–26.

———. 1988. *Tales of the Field*. Chicago: University of Chicago Press.

———, ed. 1983. *Qualitative Methodology*. London: Sage.

Verma, Anil, Thomas A. Kochan, and Russell D. Lansbury, eds. 1995. *Employment Relations in the Growing Asian Economies*. London: Routledge.

Visser, Jelle. 1990. "In Search of Exclusive Unionism." *Bulletin of Comparative Labor Relations* 18: 1-278.

———. 1994. "Union Organization: Why Countries Differ." In *The Future of Industrial Relations*, edited by John R. Niland, Russell D. Lansbury, and Chrissie Verevis. London: Sage.

Von Beyme, Claus. 1980. *Challenge to Power: Trade Unions and Industrial Relations in Capitalist Countries*. London: Sage.

Wall, Toby, et al. 1986. "Outcomes of Autonomous Work Groups: A Long-Term Field Experiment." *Academy of Management Journal* 29: 280–304.

Walton, Richard E., and Robert B. McKersie. 1991. *A Behavioral Theory of Labor Negotiations*. Ithaca, N.Y.: ILR Press. Reprint, New York: McGraw Hill, 1965.

Watson, David, and Lee A. Clark. 1984. "Negative Affectivity: The Disposition to Experience Aversive Emotional States." *Psychological Bulletin* 96: 465–90.

Watson, Tony. 1994. *In Search of Management*. London: Routledge.

Webb, Sidney, and Beatrice Webb. 1895. *History of Trade Unionism*. London: Longman.

———. 1932. *Methods of Social Study*. London: Longman, Green.

———. 1987. *Industrial Democracy*. London: Longman. Reprint, London: Longman, Green, 1902.

Wedderburn, K. W.. 1986. *The Worker and the Law*. 3d ed. Harmondsworth: Penguin.

Weekes, Brian, et al. 1975. *Industrial Relations and the Limits of Law: The Industrial Effects of the Industrial Relations Act of 1971*. Oxford: Basil Blackwell.

Weick, Karl. 1995. *Sensemaking in Organizations*. Thousand Oaks, Calif.: Sage.

Weiler, Paul C. 1980. *Reconcilable Differences: New Directions in Canadian Labour Law Reform*. Angincourt, Ont.: Carsell.

———. 1990. *Governing the Workplace: The Future of Labor and Employment Law*. Cambridge: Harvard University Press.

Weinstein, Marc. 1995a. "Methodological Issues in Comparative Industrial Relations and Human Resource Management Survey Research." In *Proceedings of the Forty-Seventh Annual Meeting of the Industrial Relations Research Association*. Madison, Wisc.: Industrial Relations Research Association.

———. 1995b. "The Transformation of Post-Socialist Poland." Ph.D diss., Sloan School of Management, MIT.

Wharton, Amy. 1993. "The Affective Consequences of Service Work." *Work and Occupations* 20: 205-32.

Whipp, Richard. 1996. "Creative Deconstruction: Strategy and Organizations." In *Handbook of Organization Studies*, edited by Stewart Clegg, Cynthia Hardy, and Walter Nord. London: Sage.

Whitfield, Keith. 1994. "Adding It All Up: The Use of Quantitative Methods in Industrial Relations Research." In *Current Research in Industrial Relations*, edited by Ron Callus and Michelle Schumacher. Sydney: Association of Industrial Relations Academics in Australia and New Zealand.

Whitfield, Keith, Paul Marginson, and William Brown. 1994. "Workplace Industrial Relations under Different Regulatory Systems: A Survey-Based Comparison of Australia and Britain." *British Journal of Industrial Relations* 32: 319–38.

Whyte, William Foote. 1959. *Man and Organization: Three Problems in Human Relations in Industry*. Homewood, Ill.: Irwin.

———, ed. 1991. *Participatory Action Research*. Newbury Park, Calif.: Sage.

Whyte, William Foote, Davydd Greenwood, and Peter Lazes. 1989. "Participatory Action Research: Through Practice to Science in Social Research." *American Behavioral Scientist* 32: 513–51.

Whyte, William Foote, and Kathleen King Whyte. 1991. *Making Mondragón: The Growth and Dynamics of the Worker Cooperative Complex*. 2d ed. Ithaca, N.Y.: ILR Press.

Wilensky, Harold. 1956. *Intellectuals in Labor Unions*. Glencoe, Ill.: Free Press.

Wilkinson, Barry. 1983. *The Shopfloor Politics of New Technology*. Aldershot: Gower.

Williams, Glanville. 1982. *Learning the Law*. London: Stevens.

Williams, Karel, et al. 1994. *Cars: Analysis, History, Cases*. Providence, R.I.: Berghahn Books.

Wipper, Audrey, ed. 1994. *Work: The Sociology of Work in Canada*. Ottawa: Carleton University Press.

Womack, James, Daniel Jones, and Daniel Roos. 1990. *The Machine That Changed the World: The Triumph of Lean Production*. New York: Rawson.

Woods, H. D., et al. 1968. *Canadian Industrial Relations: The Report of the Task Force on Labour Relations.* Ontario: Privy Council.

Wright, Chris. 1995. *The Management of Labour. A History of Australian Employers.* Melbourne: Oxford University Press.

Yin, Robert. 1989. *Case Study Research Design and Methods.* Beverly Hills, Calif.: Sage.

———. 1994. *Case Study Research: Design and Methods.* 2d ed. Thousand Oaks, Calif.: Sage

Zappala, Gianni. 1993. "Methodological Issues in Labour Economics: Procedures for Procedural Rationality?" *Labour* 7: 209–29.

Zeitlin, Jonathan. 1987. "From Labour History to the History of Industrial Relations." *Economic History Review* 11: 159–84.

Zelditch, Morris. 1970. "Some Methodological Problems of Field Studies." In *Qualitative Methodology,* edited by William J. Filstead. Chicago: Markham.

Zimbalist, Andrew, ed. 1979. *Case Studies in the Labor Process.* New York: Monthly Review Press.

Zolberg, Aristede. 1986. "How Many Exceptionalisms?" In *Working Class Formation,* edited by Ira Katznelson. Princeton, N.J.: Princeton University Press.

Zuboff, Shoshana. 1988. *In the Age of the Smart Machine: The Future of Work and Power.* New York: Basic Books.

Contributors

Julian Barling is a professor of organizational behavior and psychology in the School of Business at Queen's University in Kingston, Ontario. He is the author of *Employment, Stress, and Family Functioning* and a coauthor of *The Union and Its Members: A Psychological Approach* and *Changing Employment Relations: Behavioral and Social Perspectives*. His current research interests include unions and their members, leadership, and work-related stress.

William Brown has been the Montague Burton Professor of Industrial Relations at the University of Cambridge since 1985. Before that, he was the director of the Social Science Research Council's Industrial Relations Research Unit at the University of Warwick. His research has focused on workplace bargaining, wage determination, payment systems, bargaining structure, income policies, and arbitration. He is currently studying the economic consequences of industrial relations legislation and the individualization of the employment contract in Britain.

Jan Bruins was a lecturer in psychology at the University of Essex in the United Kingdom. His research interests included the consequences of power and status differences between group members, determinants and consequences of power use in interpersonal and intergroup situations, and aspects of power and influence processes as they relate to procedural justice. He passed away shortly before this book went to press.

Ron Callus is director of the Australian Centre for Industrial Relations Research and Training (ACIRRT). Since ACIRRT was established in 1989, it has completed more than fifty projects, many involving the case study method. Before becoming the director of the center in 1991, Callus was director of the first Australian Workplace Industrial Relations Survey.

Daniel B. Cornfield is a professor of sociology at Vanderbilt University and editor of *Work and Occupations*. His research has addressed technological change in the workplace, labor movement decline and growth, the changing legislative agenda of the U.S. labor movement over the last century, corporate downsizing and restructuring, and business ethics in multinational high-tech manufacturing.

Rick Delbridge is a research fellow at Cardiff Business School. His research interests include workplace trade unionism and trade union responses to new management techniques. He is the author of *Life on the Line in Contemporary Manufacturing,* an account of periods of participant observation working on the shop floor in two manufacturing plants.

Raymond A. Friedman is a professor of management in the Owen Graduate School of Management at Vanderbilt University. He has written extensively on labor negotiations, including *Front Stage, Backstage: The Dramatic Structure of Labor Negotiations,* and has done joint labor-management training on "mutual gains" bargaining. He is currently studying network groups of minority and female employees and strategies for managing diversity.

Suzanne Hammond teaches industrial law at the University of New South Wales. Her main research interest include exploring legal regimes and their impact on women workers. She is currently undertaking a longitudinal study of the impact of deregulation on women workers in New Zealand.

Jean Hartley is the principal research fellow at the Local Government Centre in the Warwick Business School at the University of Warwick. She is a coauthor of three books: *Steel Strike, Job Insecurity: Coping with Jobs at Risk,* and *Employment Relations: The Psychology of Influence and Control at Work.* She is currently undertaking longitudinal research into the management of uncertainty and transformational change in the public sector.

Melinda D. Kane is a doctoral student in sociology at Vanderbilt University. Her primary research interests concern social inequality, including gender inequality, in the workplace and career mobility.

Jim Kitay is a senior lecturer in the Department of Industrial Relations at the University of Sydney. His main areas of teaching and research are industrial relations theory, industrial sociology, and workplace industrial relations.

Thomas A. Kochan is the George M. Bunker Professor of Management at the Sloan School of Management at the Massachusetts Institute of Technology. He has done research on a variety of topics related to industrial relations and human resource management in the public and private sectors. From 1993 to 1995, he was a member of the Clinton administration's Commission on the Future of Worker-Management Relations, which investigated methods to improve the productivity and global competitiveness of the American workplace. From 1992 to 1995, he served as president of the International Industrial Relations Association.

Paul Marginson is a professor of human resource management and employee relations at the University of Leeds and is an associate fellow in the Industrial Relations Research Unit (IRRU) at the University of Warwick. He was the lead researcher for the IRRU's 1985 and 1992 Company-Level Industrial Relations Surveys and was a member of the steering committee overseeing the 1997 Workplace Industrial Relations Survey. His own research focuses on industrial relations in multinational companies.

Darren C. McDaniel is a Ph.D. student in sociology at Vanderbilt University, where his main areas of interest are social psychology and the study of work and occupations. He is currently studying striving freelance musicians in Nashville and conducting ethnographic research on how churches organize their religious work. His primary areas of interests include social comparison theory, work and occupations, stratification, and the southern working class.

Neil Millward is a senior fellow and a program director at the Policy Studies Institute (PSI) in London. He was the lead researcher on the first two Workplace Industrial Relations Surveys while a principal research officer at the Department of Employment. He led the PSI research team for the 1997 Workplace Industrial Relations Survey, focusing on workplace change, and is engaged in other research using large-scale employer surveys.

Greg Patmore teaches industrial relations and labor history at the University of Sydney. He is the author of *Australian Labour History* and president of the Australian Society for the Study of Labour History. He is currently examining the history of industrial relations in the Lithgow Valley in Australia from 1892 to 1932 and comparing it with that of Sydney, Nova Scotia.

Paul Ronfeldt has taught industrial relations and labor law at the University of New South Wales, Sydney University, and Griffith University. His research interests include collective bargaining law, law and labor relations, and individual employment law. He is currently completing his Ph.D. at the University of Sydney, where he is examining the development of statutory termination law in Australia.

Jay S. Siegel is a member of the faculty at the John F. Kennedy School of Government at Harvard University, where he teaches labor policy and conflict resolution. A former chairman of the American Bar Association's Section of Labor and Employment Law, he was a labor-management lawyer for three decades and authored numerous journal articles on industrial relations. His current research focuses on U.S. alternative dispute resolution matters and Japanese workplace policy issues.

George Strauss is an emeritus professor in the Haas School of Business and emeritus director of the Institute of Industrial Relations at the University of California, Berkeley. He has served as president of the U.S. Industrial Relations Research Association and is a founder of the Organizational Behavior Teaching Association. His research interests include union government, worker participation, collective bargaining, and comparative industrial relations.

Richard Whipp is a professor of human resource management and the deputy director of Cardiff Business School. He has taught and researched at the Aston Management Centre and the Warwick Business School and has held visiting positions at the University of Uppsala, the Helsinki School of Economics, and the London School of Economics. He has published widely on the subjects of innovation, the management of strategic change, and the institutional analysis of sectors.

Keith Whitfield is a senior research fellow at Cardiff Business School and is coconvenor of the International Industrial Relations Association's Research Methods Study Group. His current research focuses on the analysis of new employer strategies for organizing employment and on the role of training in promoting high economic performance.

William Foote Whyte is an emeritus professor in the New York State School of Industrial and Labor Relations at Cornell University. He has served as president of the American Sociological Association and of the U.S. Industrial Relations Research Association. Although he is best known as the author of *Street Corner Society,* Whyte has conducted extensive research in recent years on worker participation in various countries.

Index